TIRED OF FRENCH OR ITALIAN FOOD?

Millions have discovered the zesty flavor of Spanish cooking—so why not you? AUTHENTIC SPANISH COOKING has over 400 exciting, easy-to-prepare recipes for such exotic dishes as

Clams Marinera
Basque Tournedo
Lamb and Veal Chops a la Ampurdesa
Chicken Paella
Mock Pheasants
Partridge in Champagne
Artichoke Hearts in Cheese Sauce
Duck Stuffed with Black Olives
Homemade Sausages with Truffles

ABOUT THE AUTHOR

Maruja Hatheway is a Chilean-born American citizen, and the wife of a retired Army Colonel. She is a graduate of the University of Chile, and the Cordon Bleu School of Cooking in Paris, France.

Mrs. Hatheway, who moved to Spain after her husband's retirement, writes a weekly column for *Guidepost* magazine, a publication for English-speaking people in Spain. She is also food editor of *Ronda* magazine, and with her husband, has recently formed the Gourmet Club of Madrid.

AUTHENTIC
SPANISH
COOKING

MARUJA HATHEWAY

PAPERBACK LIBRARY

New York

PAPERBACK LIBRARY EDITION
First Printing: April, 1969

DEDICATION

To my dear husband whose inspiring encouragement never failed me from my first uncertain steps as a beginner in the kitchen to the day of my graduation as a Cordon Bleu cook. I do also want to thank him for his valuable assistance in the documentation and preparation of this book.

ACKNOWLEDGMENTS

Special thanks to my friends Doña Pilar Primo de Rivera, Condesa del Castillo de la Mota, Director of Seccion Femenina of Spain, and Senor F. Javier Aguirre del Castillo, of the Ministerio de Informacion y Turismo, for the very interesting material they made available to me.

Thanks to the many Spanish restaurateurs and nice housewives for the many excellent recipes they gave me and the many quaint secrets of country cuisine I learned from them.

Maruja Hatheway
(Mrs. Maurice Hatheway, Jr.)

CONTENTS

INTRODUCTION

Spain is different! So say the tourist posters. And, I will add, marvelously different. Spanish cooking, too, is different, as different as a Flamenco dancer—full of color, vibrant, natural and always interesting. It has its roots deep in antiquity, and has been influenced by the many peoples that have passed through the land: Phoenicians, Greeks, Carthaginians, Romans, Goths, Arabs, Jews, and many others, each of whom has left its own distinctive touch on Spanish food and eating habits. Then, too, the cuisine has been affected by Spain's extensive contacts with the New World. But it has always retained its own zesty individuality; what has been adopted has been adapted.

Spanish cooking and Spanish food were highly esteemed by the Romans when they were masters of the world, just as were the graceful dancing girls from Cadiz and the brave Spanish soldiers. Particularly appreciated were the fish and seafood from the Peninsula and the Spanish touch in their preparation. A savory sauce called *garum,* then produced around Cadiz from fish by-products, pickled in wine vinegar with egg yolks, enjoyed a popularity in the ancient Mediterranean world comparable to that of Worcestershire sauce today—no doubt an unconscious recognition of the value of a vitamin supplement to the diet.

In modern days those who have discovered the attractive and sumptuous Spanish cuisine in such places as the Spanish Pavilion at the New York World's Fair, after trying *gazpacho* or *paella,* have become converts to its palate-tickling but restrained flavor combinations. They have also found out that it is not to be confused with Latin American cooking, most of whose dishes are completely unknown in Spain. Latin American cooking can stand on its own feet, but should not be called "Spanish." Another misconception is due to a French cooking term having crept into the English language. "Spanish" (*à l'espagnole*) in France means made with tomatoes, perhaps because the Spanish first introduced them into Europe. Tomatoes *are* used in Spanish cooking, but can hardly be called its distinguishing characteristic.

The Spanish say, "If you eat something blindfolded and can't tell what you're eating, you've been fooled." Their cooking is based on the idea of maintaining and bringing out the natural flavors of the food. It is the Spanish belief that herbs, spices and other seasonings should be used with a great deal of restraint—to highlight and add interest, not to mask. Hot, spicy dishes are as un-Spanish as an Eskimo igloo. The sauces that add so much to true Spanish dishes are normally prepared right along with them, as a part of the recipe rather than added as an afterthought at the time of serving. The beautiful and harmonious flavor so characteristic of their cookery comes from skillful blending of simple ingredients and careful, loving preparation.

If anything can be said to typify Spanish food, it is the nearly universal use of olive oil to the exclusion of lard, margarine or butter. This is because good, refined olive oil does not alter the taste of food cooked with it. However, olive oil is the cheapest oil in Spain, and this fact greatly influences the partiality toward it. Other neutral cooking and salad oils produce fine results. In all of the recipes given in this book you can use your favorite cooking oil with the assurance of good results. To every rule there is, of course, an exception—in *paella* a small amount of real olive oil does lend a special secret savor to it that you won't get with anything else.

Wine is much used as an essential ingredient, and it does several things for food. First, it is a flavor enhancer—used discreetly it brings in its own special bouquet and makes many an otherwise flat dish sing. Further, it acts as a tenderizer; when it is used to marinate it breaks down tough, fibrous parts of meat, particularly if used with a small amount of wine vinegar. It also stabilizes the taste of water used in cooking—again, often in combination with a little wine vinegar. Both American wine and wine vinegar can be used in the recipes with full success.

Spain has a long seacoast fronting on two very different types of water—the Mediterranean and the Atlantic—both of which abound in all kinds of fish and seafood. These play a key role in the diet and, as you might expect, the Spanish are experts in using and preparing this bounty from the sea. Here is where one finds the greatest variety in methods of cooking, combinations of flavors, and presentation. Still, the ingredients are fairly simple—even in the sumptuous *paella* or the dramatic *bacalao al pil pil*—and the recipes are designed to conserve the natural flavors. Not only are the Spanish methods of preparation and cooking of seafood different from other cuisines, they differ from one region of the country to another.

What is true of fish and seafood is true of other types of cooking; there are many variations from region to region. The Spanish say, "In the South they fry, in the Center they roast, and in the North they stew." This is an oversimplification. There are at least 15 different regions in Spain, each with its own specialities. While some of the regional variations are due to local preferences, tradition or prejudices, many of the dishes reflect the cooks' efforts to make the best use of what they find in their own markets, and to produce delicious meals economically. For, like her sisters in every other country, the Spanish housewife is very budget-minded. And she knows her business!

You will find that many Spanish dishes, even some of the best ones with a real gourmet touch, are true budget-stretchers. Not only that, but some of them will provide exciting and imaginative ways to use leftovers. For the Spanish cook is always keenly interested in using leftovers—*aprovechamientos,* as they say. Many of the recipes in this book are not to be found, normally, in restaurants, particularly the de luxe tourist type, but are rather examples of everyday household cooking—dishes whose secrets are often passed on from mother to daughter. For in Spain, as everywhere else, restaurants and hotels tend to internationalize and institutionalize their cooking, while the real culinary traditions with all their color remain household, family, affairs. So in this book there are recipes in the grand manner, as well as the "little" recipes of the village housewife who triumphantly prepares them to the applause of her family and friends.

To say that Spanish cooking depends on careful preparation does not necessarily mean that we have to use tedious, complicated methods. You will find that these recipes make much use of simplified procedures and time-saving appliances. In fact, you may wonder if such procedures are not "un-Spanish." Rest assured, they are not. The Spanish have no prejudice against innovations; prepared foods, beaters, blenders etc. are available and much used. Often the mortar and pestle once used for blending wind up as a kitchen decoration. And while in certain places you can still see graceful Spanish girls filling their water jugs at a quaint fountain, you can be sure that they are all eagerly awaiting the time when they can have running water in their homes. And the same woman that brings her water to the house this way may well use a pressure cooker. The Spanish themselves have always been innovators in food. Among the many things they introduced into Europe are potatoes, strawberries, turkeys, tomatoes and chocolate. And particularly in the last few years, with domestic help scarce and expensive, and the working wife becoming a commonplace, simplification is the order of the day. In a typically Spanish gesture all these improved techniques are sought for and eagerly embraced as friendly allies in meeting the challenge of preparing good *Spanish* meals with less time to do it.

The recipes in this book are all completely authentic, and have been specially selected to give a true sample of Spanish cooking in all its splendor and variety. They have also been thoroughly tested to make sure that the reader who follows the recipe carefully will come out triumphant on the first try. You will find that their preparation doesn't require any utensils or apparatus not normally found in an American kitchen. Spanish cooks produce even their great masterpieces with simple working tools. For instance, in Spain a great many dishes are made in earthenware pots; either normal casseroles or flameproof glass can be used (and are used in Spain) with complete success. The ingredients for the recipes are all things you will find in your normal shopping—you don't have to look for them in specialty shops or try to get hard-to-find imported items. The foods you can buy in your favorite store are the same type and quality as those in Spain. If fresh materials are not available for some recipe you want to try, don't hesitate to use frozen, or even canned ones. You will still get results you will be proud of, and on the first try. And now, as the Spanish say, *Buen provecho, amigos* (Good appetite, friends).

COOKING HINTS

Fresh bread will not crumble if cut with a hot knife.

Do not let the fat smoke, as it will form indigestible acids.

Use as little water as possible in cooking vegetables. This will preserve vitamins and minerals.

Bake apples, potatoes, sweet potatoes and squash as often as possible. All too often in peeling and pouring away the water in which the vegetables have been cooked, we lose most of the minerals and vitamins.

To rid vegetables of insects, soak in strong salt water solution 1 hour before preparing.

Water should not be poured on burning fat; it will spread the blaze. Salt or bicarbonate of soda will extinguish the blaze.

Mustard and baking powder settle in cans and should be stirred before using.

Sugar, either white or brown, which has hardened in its package, will soften if placed in the refrigerator.

To extract onion juice, cut a small piece from the bottom, then twist the onion on a grater.

Grease the dish in which chocolate is to be melted to insure that it may be easily removed.

Grease the cup before measuring molasses or syrup for the same reason.

Before scalding milk, rinse the pan with cold water to prevent sticking.

A few drops of oil in the water in which you are cooking spaghetti will keep it from boiling over.

When using grated rind of lemons or oranges for flavoring do not grate too deep; the white part makes food taste bitter.

Use sharp kitchen shears to cut parsley and other herbs. You will preserve the fresh flavor which is lost by chopping them. Parsley keeps fresh for a long time if you place it in the refrigerator in a closed jar.

To fasten your meat grinder more securely to the table, fold an old towel around the edge of the table before tightening the screw.

When whipping or beating ingredients in a bowl, place it on a damp folded cloth on the table to keep it steady.

To remove skins from almonds after shelling, let them stand in boiling water until skin peels off. They may be toasted in a lightly greased pan in the oven.

To loosen the cake from the center of an angel cake tube, move a steel knitting needle around the center.

To treat new skillets or pans, grease well and place in a 450° oven for 30 minutes. Scour well with steel wool.

Dip kitchen shears in flour before cutting marshmallows.

To whiten and fluff rice, add 1 teaspoon lemon juice to each quart of water while cooking.

To dissolve lumps from starch or gravy, use a wire eggbeater.

To flour chicken, rabbit, or meats of any kind, place flour and meat in a paper bag and shake well.

To mix liquid and flour for sauces and gravies, place the required amount of flour in a jar, add the liquid, cover and shake well until blended.

To season when doubling a recipe, watch out! Do not double seasoning. Add a little more—then taste.

Herb bags—make up some of these and keep on hand, stored in a covered jar: In 4-inch squares of heavy cheese cloth place: 1/2 teaspoon each of dried basil, marjoram, savory, thyme, parsley, celery etc. Gather corners together and tie.

To keep crust from burning on a fruit pie fasten a piece of 4-inch damp cloth around the edge of the pie while baking. Remove while pie still hot.

In cooking any dish made up largely of eggs, always use a low temperature.

If you burn the vegetables, the stew, or any other dish you are cooking, immediately put the pot in deep cold water and keep it there for 3 or 4 minutes. Carefully remove with a spoon all the unburned part and continue cooking it in another pot. No traces of burned flavor will remain in the portion you have saved.

Salt curdles milk, so when preparing dishes that call for milk add the salt at the last moment.

If you cry when peeling onions, storing them in the refrigerator will save you many tears.

To make hamburgers for a crowd, pat down on a table the hamburger mix, as thick as you want them. Cut the hamburgers with a tin can or cup. Gather the scraps and pat them down again. Cut. The last one will be a meat ball that you flat down with your hands to the right shape.

To make meat balls for a buffet supper, when you are entertaining a large crowd, roll the meat mix into long, very thin sausages. Cut them into pieces as small as you wish, and roll them in your hand. They come out even and they look beautiful in your chafing dish.

FIRST ONE UP IS A——

One of my readers was telling me how distressed she had been when making an 8-egg cake, and the seventh egg she added to the other eggs already in the bowl was rotten. Of course the whole thing was spoiled.

Here is a very easy way to test eggs before you start using them: Place all the eggs in a large bowl of cold water. The very fresh ones will stay in the bottom of the bowl, leaning sideways. The 3- to 4-day old eggs will stand up leaning at an angle. The 10-day old eggs, or older, will stand up pointing down; the spoiled eggs will float to the surface.

FIESTAS

A holiday in Spain is called "fiesta," and just as we associate certain foods with certain holidays, so do the Spanish. Christmas with its fruitcake and plum pudding has its counterpart in *Navidad* with its *Roscon,* a sweet type of bread baked in a ring, and *turrón,* a nougat-like candy made with almonds. No holiday could be complete without these interesting accompaniments—New Year's Eve *(Noche Vieja)* when everybody must eat 12 grapes, one on each strike of midnight, and drink champagne; New Year's Day *(Año Nuevo)* with *pavo* (turkey) and a wide variety of traditional food, which varies from region to region.

But "fiesta" also means a party, and we like to think of them as gay occasions with colorful costumes, dancing and singing in the streets—and of course eating and drinking. This type of celebration is found in the local fiestas rather than in the nationwide holidays. Every Spanish town or village, large or small, has its own local fiesta, sometimes more than one, to celebrate its patron saint's day, or to commemorate some historical happening. These fiestas always have two phases— the solemn, religious and official ceremonies in which everyone takes part, then the merrymaking with processions, folkdancing and music *(folklore* in Spanish). At this time the traditional regional costumes are worn. There is feasting, with emphasis on eating some traditional dish associated with the fiesta, and in general as the Spanish say *(tiran la casa por la ventana)*—"they throw the house out the window."

There is hardly a day in the whole year when some locality is not celebrating its annual fiesta. Some of these have become world-famous, such as *San Fermín* in Pamplona (July 7-20) popularized by Hemingway, where they loose bulls in the streets for amateur bullfighters. The typical dish here is "Ajo Arriero" (Muleteer's Garlic Stew). But there are many equally interesting fiestas in small villages, known only locally. One such is celebrated in the little village of Zamarramala (800 inhabitants) near Segovia on February 4 when the women rule the town, electing their own mayoress to celebrate the day in the 12th century when, the men being away, the women repulsed an attack by the Moors. Here the special food is a typical sausage, *longaniza*, specially prepared for this day, washed down with a red wine of the region.

GARLIC STEW MULETEERS' STYLE
(*Ajo al Arriero*)

4 large potatoes	2 red peppers (or pimientos)
1 cup oil	3/4 cup tomato sauce
4 garlic cloves, minced	parsley, chopped
1 lb. onions, chopped	white pepper to taste
2 lbs. salted codfish, soaked in water overnight	salt to taste

Wash (do not pare) and boil the potatoes in salted water until tender but firm. Cut potatoes into small cubes. Put 6 tablespoons oil in the frying pan, sauté onion and one of the garlic cloves. Add potatoes and peppers, cut into small squares. Add the tomato sauce.

In an earthenware casserole pour the rest of the oil. Add 3 minced garlic cloves and the flaked codfish. Put over low fire, shaking the casserole continuously to make the sauce, about 10 minutes. Add the tomato-potato mixture, chopped parsley and white pepper. Serve this fish stew in individual earthenware casseroles. Serves 6 to 8.

TYPICAL DISHES: "FIESTAS DEL ROCIO EN ALMONTE"
COUNTY STEW
(*Caldereta del Condado*)

2 lbs. lamb or veal	2 tomatoes
1 onion	8 tablespoons oil
1 green pepper	1 sprig parsley
1 garlic head, whole	salt to taste

Cut meat in regular sized pieces. Put in a pan and cover with cold water. Bring it to a boil. Simmer. Add the vegetables, cut in large pieces, parsley, the whole head of garlic, oil and salt. Simmer about 1-1/2 hours or until meat is tender. At the end of this time add a *majado* (paste) that you make as follows. Serves 4.

1 piece of soft bread crumbs, the size of an egg
1/4 teaspoon cloves
1 teaspoon paprika

1/2 cup water
1/4 teaspoon cumin seeds

Mix all the above ingredients to make a very smooth paste. Stir it in the stew pot.

CALDERETA

For this dish proportions depend on the number of people you are going to serve.

In an earthenware casserole, place part of a mix you have made with chopped onions, garlic, parsley and diced ham. Add 1 or 2 bay leaves and a few peppercorns. Cover the onion mix with small pieces of lamb, and then the lamb with onion mix. Repeat this operation until you use all the onion mix and meat. Add a glass of dry white wine, a cup of water and oil, and simmer slowly about 1-1/2 hours, or until the meat is tender. At the end dissolve 1 tablespoon or more of toasted flour in a little bit of water and add to pot.

CADIZ: MANTECADOS

1 lb. flour
1/2 teaspoon cinnamon
4-1/2 oz. blanched, toasted almonds ground very fine

1 lb. confectioners' sugar, sifted
1/2 lb. refined lard

On a tray in a low oven (350°) toast the flour. Stir it once in a while with a wooden spoon until it acquires a beautiful golden color. Let it cool and add the almonds. Place lard in a bowl and beat until foamy; add sugar, cinnamon and flour-almond mix. Spread this mix evenly on a smooth surface (marble, glass, formica) and cut rounds with a small glass. Place them side by side on a cooky sheet. Dry in a warm oven. Wrap in paper. Makes about 40 cookies.

BANO DE LA ENCINA, PATRON SAINT'S DAY
BANUELO MEAT LOAF
(Rollo de Bañuelo)

2 lbs. beef	1 cup water
4 oz. bacon cut in strips	2 eggs
(reserve one)	4 oz. ham, minced
1 bay leaf	1 cup grated bread crumbs
1 hard-boiled egg, sliced	pepper, oil, flour; salt to taste
1 cup dry white wine	

Chop the beef very finely, season with salt and pepper and add the 2 raw eggs. Add the bread crumbs and mix well. Dust the counter with flour, spread half of the meat mix on it, patting it down with your hands. Place on top the sliced egg, bacon strips in short pieces and minced ham. Place the other half of the meat on top, pressing the edges with your finger. Roll loaf in flour, and sauté it in oil in a large frying pan until golden in color all over. Add to the pan wine and water, the bacon you have reserved, the bay leaf and a few peppercorns. Simmer 1-1/2 hours. Let it cool and cut in thin slices. Serve hot or cold with or without tomato sauce. Serves 4.

RINGS
(Roscos)

3 eggs	2 tablespoons sugar
1/4 cup oil	flour, enough to make a soft
grated rind of 1 lemon	dough

At high speed beat eggs with sugar and oil. When you have reached the maximum volume add the lemon rind and enough flour to make a soft dough (amount varies with the kind of flour you use). Oil your hands to avoid stickiness, and knead dough. Make thin ribbons, and then rings. Fry in deep hot oil. Paint over with beaten egg whites and dip them in powdered sugar. Makes about 2 dozen.

CADIZ: TYPICAL DISH OF THE "ISLAND SAINTS" DAY
SOLE OR FLOUNDER PLATTER STYLE
(Lenguado al Plato)

2-1/4 lbs. sole or flounder
1/2 cup oil
1 cup stock
1/2 cup dry white wine

1 onion, chopped very finely
bread crumbs, grated fine
salt and pepper to taste

Clean the fish, remove skin, and place whole into an oval earthenware oven dish. Spread the onion on top. Mix stock with wine and pour over fish. Sprinkle with bread crumbs, season with salt and pepper and sprinkle the oil on top. Cook in a preheated oven (425°) 15 or 20 minutes. Serves 4.

SHORT COOKIES
(Mantecado de Harina)

Here is a traditional Christmas cooky that is different and easy to make. It will be popular with your family and friends, and it keeps very well. Refined lard is used but you could substitute vegetable shortening. However, refined lard is completely digestible and the flavor is definitely better.

6-1/2 oz. lard
1 lb. 2 oz. flour

7 oz. confectioners' sugar
1 teaspoon cinnamon

Place the flour on a tray in the oven, stirring constantly until golden brown. Whip lard with sugar until very fluffy, add cinnamon and then flour little by little until it forms a very soft dough. Spread dough on a smooth surface, patting down with your hands until it is 3/8" thick. Cut the *mantecados* with a cooky cutter. Let them dry, or dry them in a warm oven with the door open, dust with sugar and wrap each one in tissue paper. Makes about 40.

CAKES WITH CREAM FILLING
(Bizcochos Rellenos)

1/2 cup sugar	1/4 teaspoon vinegar
3 eggs	*Filling:*
3/4 cup flour	1/2 cup sugar
Syrup:	1/4 cup water
1/2 cup sugar	6 egg yolks
1/4 cup water	

Beat the 3 eggs well with the sugar until thick. Fold in flour. Line baking pan with paper. Press dough through pastry bag (plain big hole tube) forming long strips on pan. Sprinkle with a little sugar. Bake in a 325° oven for 20-25 minutes. Let cool. Separate paper from the cake by moistening paper with a wet brush. Cut sheet in squares. Form sandwiches, spreading filling between two squares. Dip in syrup. Dry 2 minutes in the oven. Makes about 12.

Filling: Put sugar and water in a pan. Boil slowly until syrup forms a thread. Pour slowly over beaten egg yolks until well incorporated. Let it cool.

Syrup: Put 1/2 cup sugar in pan with 1/4 cup water and the vinegar. Boil until syrup forms a thread. Beat syrup with a wooden spoon until it whites. Using as icing for the little cakes.

ALL SAINTS' DAY PUMPKIN
(Calabaza de Todos Los Santos)

In the Basque countries, Spanish and French, the pumpkin is also associated with the supernatural feeling of the Halloween season. This dish is traditionally found on November the first in many peasant homes.

1 large pumpkin	1 tablespoon grated onion
1 lb. rice, uncooked	2 tablespoons butter
2 cloves garlic	salt and pepper to taste
1 large green pepper	
2 lbs. medium shrimps, sautéed in butter	

Clean and devein shrimps; chop green pepper and garlic. Sauté in 1 tablespoon butter and add onion. Cut the top from pumpkin, remove all the seeds. (Save the top to use as a lid.) Place rice in pumpkin, put the rest of the ingredients on top of the rice, and sprinkle with salt and pepper. Attach the lid with toothpicks. Place pumpkin on baking tray and bake in a 325° oven for 2-1/2 hours. To serve, remove the lid and scoop out the pumpkin-rice-shrimp mix. Serves 6 to 8.

CHRISTMAS IN SPAIN

Christmas, celebrated with the same joy all over the world, has kept more of its true religious meaning in Spain. The official opening of the holy season takes place around the 19th of December with the *Pregón de Navidad* ("Christmas Call") given by the mayor of the city or another outstanding personality. The season lasts to the sixth of January—"Kings Day" in Spain—symbolizing the arrival of the Wise Men to the manger of Bethlehem to deliver their gifts of gold, frankincense and myrrh to the holy child. Though we are starting to see many Christmas trees in the main cities of Spain, the manger is still the true symbol of Christmas in the Spanish home, and even in the most humble ones a light blazes dimly in the lovely homemade nativity scenes illuminating the mystery of the birth of the Christ child. In these nativity scenes the three Wise Men and their servants are placed at first at a distance from the manger itself and each day are placed a little closer to simulate the steps of their 12-day journey to deliver their present to the holy infant. The sixth of January is also the night when the children of Spain get their Christmas presents, brought to them, as the legend tells them, by the Kings.

Christmas eve is a family affair in Spain; mother, father, children, grandparents, uncles, aunts, and cousins get together in one home to celebrate the birth of the holy child with the singing of *villancicos*—Spanish carols of simple melody and naive poetry. At midnight, the whole family attends the *Misa del Gallo* (mass of the cock) that takes place at midnight amidst the happy pealing of the church bells, the noise of the firecrackers and *sambombas,* (noise boxes) and the clacking of the castanets of the gypsy girls who are deeply religious and always among the crowds. After church service the family goes home and sits around a beautifully arranged table with traditional food and Christmas sweets that have been made weeks ahead of time by the women in the family.

21

Turron, yemas, polvorones and colored marzipan are used as decoration and dessert. Punch, wine and liquors are drunk that night by the adults while the children enjoy hot spiced chocolate and *horchata*, a beverage made with ground almonds, sugar and water. Roasted pig, turkey or baked fish are the traditional main dishes.

WINE TURRON
(Turron de Vino)

1 glass white wine	2 tablespoons toasted
1 lb. sugar in cubes	slivered almonds
4 egg whites	

Make a heavy syrup with the wine and sugar. Beat egg whites until stiff. Pour the wine syrup into the whites little by little, beating well after each addition. Continue beating until firm. Serve cool in well-chilled small wine glasses sprinkled with the almonds. Serves 6.

STUFFED BREAM
(Besugo Relleno)

1 3-lb. bream	2 onions
3 oz. bacon	3 tablespoons olive oil
1/2 lb. lean ham	salt and pepper to taste
1 sprig parsley	
1/2 cup grated bread crumbs	

Clean the fish, split the abdomen and carefully remove the backbone. (The fishman will prepare the fish for you if you ask him.) For the stuffing prepare:
Chop the bacon, the ham, 1 onion and the parsley and add the bread crumbs; season, knead together, stuff the bream and sew it up. Slice the second onion and lay on the bottom of an oven dish. Put the bream on top, sprinkle with a tablespoon of oil and put in moderate oven (325°) for 30 minutes or until tender. Before serving, put the bream on a heated serving dish, remove the thread and cover with its own sauce. Serves 4.

GYPSY CAKE
(*Tarta Gitana*)

3 cups sifted flour
1/2 teaspoon salt
1 cup sugar
1 teaspoon cinnamon
1 cup brown sugar

1/2 cup lard
1/4 cup chopped almonds
1 cup chopped dates
1 cup sour milk
1 teaspoon soda

Grease an 8x12 inch baking pan. Sift dry ingredients and brown sugar. Cut lard into mixture until completely blended. Take out 1/2 cup of this mixture for topping. Add dates and nutmeats. Dissolve soda in sour milk and add to cake mixture. Mix well. Spread in greased pan. Sprinkle topping on cake. Bake in a moderate oven (350°F.) for 35 or 40 minutes. Serves 8.

ONION SCALLOPS
(*Escalopes de Cebolla*)

6 large mild onions
4 tablespoons butter
1/2 cup soft bread crumbs
1/4 lb. grated Gruyère or
   other mild white cheese

1/2 teaspoon paprika
salt and pepper to taste

Skin and slice onions. Sauté in butter until transparent. Season with salt and pepper and place in shallow baking dish. Sprinkle bread crumbs, cheese and paprika on top. Bake in a 375° F. oven until crumbs are brown. Serves 4.

ALFAJORES

1 lb. almonds
1 lb. sugar

water

Peel almonds, removing all the skin, and grind until very fine. Make a syrup with the sugar and just enough water to cover it. Bring it to a boil and simmer until thick. Add the almonds, stirring all the time. When the mix starts to separate from the pan remove from fire and pour over a marble surface dusted with powdered sugar. Roll out paste very thin with a rolling pin and cut into small circles using a small glass. Stick two circles together with the Filling. Makes about 2 dozen.

Filling of Manjar Blanco

2-1/2 cups sugar	1/2 cup ground walnuts
3-1/2 cups milk	1 teaspoon vanilla

Mix sugar and milk and simmer very slowly for about 1 hour or until thick. Add walnuts and vanilla. Let it cool very well before using.

ROAST PORK CASTILIAN STYLE
(*Cochinillo Asado*)

Preheat oven to 350°F.

Score the skin and fat of a fresh ham, piglet or baby lamb, weighing 12 to 14 pounds. Place in a shallow roasting pan (in Spain in an oval earthenware one) and rub the skin with 4 tablespoons of butter or shortening.

Mix:

3 bay leaves, crumbled	2 tablespoons chopped
3 cloves garlic, minced	parsley
1/2 teaspoon dry thyme	3 tablespoons minced onion

Sprinkle mixture over meat.
Sprinkle meat with:

juice of 1 lemon	2 tablespoons sweet paprika
1/3 cup of white wine	2 teaspoons salt

Roast the meat for 1-1/2 hours. Remove fat that has accumulated in pan.
Add to pan:

1/3 cup white wine	1 cup water

Continue to roast for 3-1/2 to 4-1/2 hours longer, or a total of 25 minutes per pound, basting every 1/2 hour with the liquid in the pan. Serves 12.

12TH NIGHT CAKE
(*Roscón de Reyes*)

13-1/2 oz. flour
5 oz. sugar
3-1/2 oz. butter
4-1/2 oz. almonds, ground
   finely
2 oz. whole almonds, peeled
2 eggs

1 egg white
1 package dry yeast
1/4 cup warm water (not
   hot)
1 large lima bean or 1 small
   glass animal figure

In a large bowl beat the butter until foamy. Add the eggs, beating well after each addition. Add the sugar and beat, the flour and beat, the almonds and the yeast dissolved in the water. Put the mix on a floured board and work the dough just enough to blend the ingredients well. Place it in a well-greased ring mold (12 inches in diameter) and let it rise for 1 hour. Paint the top with egg white, introduce here and there the whole almonds and very deep the lima bean or the glass figure. Sprinkle with 2 tablespoons sugar and let it rise 30 more minutes. Bake in a preheated oven (400°F.) 30 to 35 minutes.

The superstition is that the person that gets the piece of cake with the lima bean or the glass figure will be lucky during that whole year.

Santa Teresa (Saint Theresa of Avila) is one of the great figures of Spanish literary and religious history. She founded a religious order of great vigor that is still prominent throughout the whole Catholic world. In addition to her other activities, she promoted good cooking in her convents. When one of her high-born novices complained of having to learn to cook, Saint Theresa told her, *"Entre los pucheros anda el señor"* ("The Lord walks among the cooking pots"). Many Spanish specialties still bear her name, 400 years after she lived. One of these, always associated with Holy Week and Easter, is *Torrijas de Santa Teresa.*

FRIED TOAST ST. TERESA
(*Torrijas de Santa Teresa*)

1/2 lb. stale French bread,
  cut into 1/2-inch slices
3 cups milk
1-1/2 oz. sugar

2 cups oil
1 cup granulated sugar
  mixed with
1 teaspoon cinnamon

Mix the 3 cups of milk with the 1-1/2 ounces of sugar. Soak the slices of bread for about 20 minutes. Drain well. Dip into the very well beaten eggs until completely coated. Drain off excess egg. Fry in the very hot oil until golden on both sides. Drain off excess oil and dip in the sugar mixed with the cinnamon. Fry a few slices of bread at a time, skimming from time to time the foam that forms while you are frying. Serves 4.

FRIED TOAST WITH WINE
(*Torrijas de Vino*)

Follow the recipe for *Torrijas de Santa Teresa* but use half white wine and half cream for soaking the bread.

CARNIVAL SOUP
(*Sopas de Carnaval*)

These slices are traditionally eaten for dessert at Carnaval (Mardis Gras). Despite the name of the recipe, the only connection it has with soup is that children sometimes place the slices in a soup bowl, pour milk on top and eat it with a spoon.

1 loaf of French bread
  (stale)
2 cups honey
1/4 teaspoon anise seeds

rind of 1 lemon
1/8 teaspoon cinnamon
2 dozen peeled, roasted
  almonds

Cut the bread into 1/4 inch slices and put them on a platter. Mix honey, lemon rind, cinnamon and anise and bring it to a boil. Remove from fire and add almonds. Spread mix on the sliced bread. Let cool before serving. Serves 8.

SPANISH WINES AND BEVERAGES

From the earliest time of which we have any record, Spain
has been one of the largest wine-producing countries of the
Mediterranean. It is probable that wine was introduced into
the country by the Phoenicians between 1000 and 600 B. C.
In antiquity, as today, these wines have always been famous
for their excellent quality and wide variety. The soil and
climatic conditions of the different regions of Spain produce
grapes of such varying characteristics that it is difficult to
establish a too rigid classification, because wines are the combined results of soil, climate and vine. Spanish wines are
mainly known by their geographical names according to the
region where they are produced. The finest ones are further
distinguished by the producer's name which is also printed on
the bottle label.

Though all Spanish wines are good, some regions have
become especially famous for their wines, such as Rioja in the
Old Castille Region; Toledo and Valdepeñas in the New
Castille; Ampurdan, Priorato and Tarragona from the vast
vineyard country of Cataluña; in Andalucía, near Córdoba,
Montillas and Moriles wines are the pride of the region;
Burgos produces clarets and rosés of superior quality,
medium-bodied, rich and fruity with a soft fragrance. Also in
Andalucía the world famous *jerez* (sherry) is produced which
is unique in flavor and bouquet, ranging from dry to sweet;
and in San Lucar de Barrameda, at the mouth of the Guadal-
quivir river, the famous *manzanilla* wine is produced. Malaga
produces, among others, its famous dessert wine called *vino
de Málaga;* Galicia, the well known *Riveiro;* and the province
of Barcelona the most famous Spanish champagnes.

Virtually all wines fit into five classes: red table wines, white
table wines, appetizer wines, sweet dessert wines and sparkling
wines followed by two designations: common wines, and
wines for blending.

COMMON WINES *(Vinos Comunes)*: are those that are

consumed during the same year that they are produced. By law these wines cannot be sold for more than twice the original wholesale price and they range today from 6 to 10 pesetas per liter. These wines are very popular and widely consumed in homes, restaurants and the local tavern (called the "poor man's club", in the villages) where men meet regularly after work or holidays to talk and to drink a *chato*, a glass of wine. If you travel around Spain, try these regional wines which are usually of excellent quality; the local people are proud of them and happy to serve them to you.

WINES FOR BLENDING (*Vinos de Mezcla*): are usually heavy-bodied, of high alcoholic content, rich in color, and neutral in flavor. They are used to improve lesser wines from other vineyards. Every year Spain exports large quantities of this type of wine to other wine producing countries.

TABLE WINES (*Vinos de Mesa*): To this group belong those wines that for their excellent characteristics have been aged, or blended and aged, improving by these processes their flavor and bouquet. They are usually bottled and labeled and sold two or more years after they are produced.

RED WINES (*Vinos Tintos*). Ranging in color from light ruby to the darkest of garnets, they derive their color and flavor from the pulp and the skin of the grapes that are left with the juice during fermentation. The dark ones are full-bodied and rich in flavor and aroma, while the claret types are dry, medium-bodied, with a fruity taste and aroma. All these wines are served at slightly below room temperature and are usually served to accompany red meats and main course dishes.

WHITE WINES (*Vinos Blancos*): Fermented without the skin or with a very small part of the skin, their bouquet and flavor are delicate and their colors range from pale straw to golden yellow. A few of them are amber-toned. Their flavors vary from extremely dry and rather tart to sweet and full-bodied, fragrant and fruity. They should be served well chilled. White wine flavor blends best with seafood, fowl or white meats.

ROSE WINES (*Vinos Rosados*): These pink wines are normally produced by leaving the grapeskin with the must (grape juice) for only a fraction of the fermentation period. Sometimes a part of red must is added to the white must during fermentation. These wines have a delicate sweetness, are light-bodied and aromatic and can be served with any food. Like white wine, rosés should be served well chilled.

APPETIZER WINES (*Vinos de Aperitivos*). *Jerez, Montilla,*

Moriles, etc. are favored for before meal use, and they range from dry to sweet. *Jerez* (sherry), the most widely known around the world, is characterized by a special inimitable flavor obtained after the addition of a pure special grape brandy to the partly fermented grape juice and aging is at an even temperature. Its alcoholic content volume is 17% to 20%.

SPARKLING WINES *(Vinos Espumosos)*: Their natural effervescence comes from adding sugar to the must and a second fermentation conducted in closed containers. Spanish champagne, the most festive of all these wines, is mainly made in San Sadurni de Noya, Barcelona, from specially selected wines, and it goes through a very complicated process of aging and second fermentation conducted either in bottles with strong corks fastened with wire, to prevent the escape of carbon dioxide, or in large airtight bulk containers. These wines may be light yellow, pink, or red, and they can range in flavor from very dry *(muy seco)* to sweet *(dulce)*. The most popular types are champagne and sparkling burgundy *(tinto espumoso)*. Champagne should always be served very well chilled, and can be served before dinner with or without appetizers; with almost any dinner entree, and with desserts. Red sparkling wine is full-bodied and moderately dry and it goes best with red meats and game. It also should be served chilled.

DESSERT WINES *(Vinos de Postre o Genersos)*: In these wines most of the sugar has been retained by adding grape brandy to arrest the fermentation of the must. In muscatel types, such as *vino de Málaga,* the fermentation is arrested very early. These wines are full-bodied, very sweet, tasty, aromatic, and golden or amber. They are usually served with the dessert or as a refreshment during the afternoon or the evening.

The following is a list of the principal Spanish wines with their origin and type. Some of their names are protected by international trademark law.

TABLE OF WINES, COMMON AND FINE

NAME	ORIGIN	CLASS
Rioja	Logroño & Alava	Dry
Rivero	Galicia	Dry
Rueda	Valladolid	Dry
Valdepeñas	Ciudad Real	Dry
Del Panadés	Barcelona	Dry
Conca de Barbar	Tarragona	Dry and Sweet
Valencia	Valencia	Dry and Sweet
Utiel	Valencia	Dry
Cheste	Valencia	Dry
Alicante	Alicante	Dry and Sweet
Cariñena	Zaragoza	Sweet
La Mancha	Ciudad Real, Toledo, Cuenca & Albacete	
Del Condado	Huelva	Dry
Noblejas	Toledo	Dry
Manzanares	Ciudad Real	Dry
Toro	Zamora	Dry
Navarra	Navarra	Dry
Martorell	Barcelona	Dry
Extremadura	Badajoz & Cáceres	Dry
Huelva	Huelva	Dry
Barcelona	Barcelona	Dry and Sweet

APPETIZER WINES AND DESSERT WINES

Jerez	Cádiz	Dry and Sweet
Málaga	Málaga	Sweet
Manzanilla	Cádiz	Dry
Moscatel (muscatel)	Different localities	Sweet
Malvasia de Sitges	Barcelona	Sweet
Tarragona	Tarragona	Sweet
Priorato	Tarragona	Sweet
Moriles	Córdoba	Dry
Montilla	Córdoba	Dry
Tostado de Riveiro	Galicia	Semi-dry
Valencia	Valencia	Sweet
Rancios (aged)	Different localities	Dry and Sweet

The Grape Crop

In Spanish wines the year of the grape crop is not particularly significant. The weather and other growing conditions are remarkably constant in Spain, so that one year's wine shows little if any variation from another's. Each wine, however, has its peak period so many years after production, and this varies with the type. The vintners, particularly those who export, control this factor very strictly so that the purchaser of a Spanish wine is assured that the bottle he purchases is at its best. An outstanding characteristic of these wines is their ability to "travel." There are many wines in the world that are splendid and fully satisfying when tasted in the area where they are produced, but become flat and uninteresting when moved any distance. The ability of a wine to "travel" increases basically with its alcoholic content. Spanish wines all have an alcoholic content high enough to stand a rigorous sea journey and arrive still blooming, with all their subtle bouquet and exquisite taste.

Spanish brandies are notably aromatic, full-bodied, and high proof. Every wine region produces them; the best known and most exported are those from the Jerez region where they are distilled from the same wine stocks that are blended to make Sherry. These easily rank among the finest in the world.

A great many liqueurs and cordials are produced in Spain. Some of them are known only locally in their home region; others are world-famous, such as Chartreuse produced by the Carthusian monks at Tarragona. Another that has become well known and much exported is *Anis*, a liqueur distilled from anise seed, somewhat similar to anisette. It has a flavor somewhat similar to licorice, and is strong and aromatic. It is produced in several degrees of sweetness, from dry (*seco*) to sweet (*dulce*). The Spanish often drink it half and half with brandy, when it is called a *sol y sombra* (sun and shade).

In the northern provinces a substantial part of an abundant apple crop is used to make "*sidra*," a hard cider. A process has been introduced to carbonate it so as to produce a sparkling cider. This has a very agreeable taste and makes a festive party drink. It lends itself to punches; in Asturias it is used at the table instead of wine.

The Spanish, living in a country of hot, sometimes semi-tropical summers, have developed a whole gamut of cooling beverages. Drinking water is stored in semiporous earthenware jugs (*botijos*) that keep the contents ice-cold by evaporation of a small amount of seepage through the walls of the container. *Sangria* is the typical summer drink in all parts of Spain; it is a refreshing mild combination of wine, sugar, lemon peel, and soda, thoroughly iced—it is often varied with the addition of fresh fruit, such as peaches, apricots, oranges, or strawberries. *Agua, azucarillos y aguardiente,* a traditional beverage at summer fairs and festivals, especially in Madrid, is a simple concoction of a small amount of brandy, *azucarillos* (made of egg white and sugar syrup), water and ice.

I also include several recipes to illustrate the boundless variety of non-alcoholic beverages. Perhaps the greatest and most delicious of all these is *horchata,* made either from *chufa* nuts or almonds. To the best of my knowledge the chufa is available only from the Valencia region in Spain. If you can get some of them, try them in the recipe. If not, use almonds—you will find almond *horchata* delicious and very refreshing on a hot summer day.

ALMOND HORCHATA
(Horchata de Almendras)

8-1/2 oz. toasted almonds, peeled and ground
8-1/2 oz. sugar

4 cups water
2 cups cream
a large piece lemon peel

Place the water and sugar in a saucepan, add the lemon peel and bring it to a boil. Add almonds and continue boiling 5 more minutes. Remove from fire and let it cool. When cold, strain, and add the cream. Serve with ice cubes in tall glasses.

HORCHATA FRAPPE
(Horchata Granizada)

2-1/2 cups water
7 oz. sugar
1/2 lb. fresh crushed
  pineapple

1/2 lemon, the juice
4 oz. toasted peeled
  almonds, ground

Mix water and sugar and boil 10 minutes. Cool. Pass the pineapple through a sieve with the lemon juice; add the almonds. Put the pineapple mix and the syrup in an icecream freezer. Freeze until solid but soft. Serve in tall glasses with straws.

CHUFA OR ALMOND QUICK HORCHATA
(Horchata Rápida de Chufas o Almendras)

7 oz. chufas
5 cups water

1/2 lb. sugar

Wash chufas in several waters, then soak for 12 hours in the 5 cups of water. Crush in a mortar or in a blender. Mix again with the water, add the sugar and strain through a sieve. Ice well. For almond horchata substitute almonds for chufas. For quick horchata the soaking period can be omitted.

SANGRIA 1

1 bottle red wine
1/2 bottle soda
peel of 1 lemon, cut in 1
  continuous spiral

sugar to taste

Mix all the ingredients and chill in the refrigerator for 1 hour. Pour from large pitcher filled with ice.

SANGRIA 2

1 bottle red wine   1 tablespoon sugar
peel of 1 lemon   splash of soda

Put the sugar and lemon peel in the bottom of a large pitcher.
Fill pitcher with ice cubes, pour red wine in, stir with a
wooden spoon. Splash with soda on top. Serve immediately.

AZUCARILLOS

8 egg whites   1 tablespoon anise, lemon,
4 tablespoons sugar   or almond flavoring

Beat the egg whites until stiff with the sugar and flavoring.
Grease well a large oven tray and drop the egg white mixture
by tablespoons, giving them an oval shape. Cook quickly in a
hot oven until set. Remove to a tray. They should be completely white. Makes about 36. Serve in tall glasses in the
following manner: Place 2 ice cubes in the glass, 1 *azucarillo*,
1 jigger *aguardiente* (white brandy) and fill the glass with
water. (Leftover *azuacarillos* may be stored in glass jars or tin
cannisters.)

ROSE PETAL PUNCH
(Ponche de Petalos de Rosa)

7 oz. rose petals   juice of 2 lemons
2 cups water   2 cups sherry
4 cups medium sugar syrup   4 egg whites beaten with a
   (made with 2 cups sugar   pinch of salt
   and 2 cups water)

Make an infusion with rose petals and water and mix it with
the syrup. When cold add the lemon juice and freeze. When
the mixture is still soft, add the sherry and the egg whites.
Serve in champagne glasses decorated with rose petals. Serves
12.
The rose petals: Make a heavy syrup, remove from fire and
while still warm dip the rose petals in it. Dust petals lightly
with powdered sugar and let them dry.

CHAMPAGNE COCKTAIL
(Coctel de Champaña)

5 champagne glasses
1/2 cup sliced strawberries
powdered sugar

juice of 1 orange
1 bottle of champagne

Pour the orange juice in a saucer, wet in it the edge of the glasses then dip them in powdered sugar. Put the glasses in the freezer. When ready to serve, put a few strawberry slices in each glass and fill the glasses with the ice-cold champagne. Serves 6 to 8.

TAPAS AND *ENTREMESES:*

THE SPANISH HORS D'OEUVRES

People who visit Spain always carry away fond memories of the Spanish appetizers, *tapas,* that they had in the local taverns called *tascas.* In the gay, relaxed atmosphere of these friendly, club-like places the habitués play cards or dominoes, or engage in animated but amicable discussions while sipping a small glass of wine (a *chato*) and munching on some succulent little tidbits, *especialidades de la casa.* It is an exciting environment, but not boisterous, for the Spaniard goes there to enjoy himself with his wife and friends, not to get drunk—he treats the *tasca* as a club. Sometimes a Gypsy guitarist will wander in and serenade the place with typical *coplas.* Other times the evening will be enlivened by a visit from the *tunas,* university students in the tradition of wandering minstrels, dressed in medieval costumes, who electrify the air with the sweet music of their stringed instruments and their fine voices. These boys can sing anything, traditional songs or the latest numbers. Everyone joins in with the *tunas,* and at the end when they pass around their tambourine for tips, everybody loves to be generous with them.

Behind the bar you can see a tier of quaint wine casks holding the house wines *(vinos de la casa),* the pride of the owner, and on a long, marble-topped counter by the bar is an attractive and colorful display of the *tapas.* These exist in a seemingly endless variety and, as might be expected, each region has its own specialties. They are always small and savory, and normally simply prepared. The Spanish divide them into two classes—*naturales,* served as is, such as olives, ham, oysters, all kinds of sausage, cheese, etc., and *de cocina,* or cooked ones. Often a *tapa de cocina* will be a small portion of some dish normally used as an entree; *paella* served in small earthenware casseroles, *bacalao al pil pil,* and tripe *a la Madrileña* are much used this way. A small grilled lamb chop is very popular, so is the *pincho moruno,* a miniature shish kabob introduced into Spain by the Arabs. In any bar or *tasca* your drink, even if it is no more than a small five-cent glass of beer (a *caña*) is always accompanied by a little snack, perhaps a pickled mussel, a few olives, or a pickled anchovy (*boqueron*), compliments of the house.

Often the first course of a lunch or dinner, as a change from soup or fish, will consist of *entremeses*. These are almost the same thing as *tapas*, but emphasize *naturales,* especially cold cuts, salads and seafood. They are served in small oval dishes that give the table a festive and colorful touch. Sometimes the *entremeses* are offered as a version of the smörgasbord with the Spanish touch. To this, cold roast beef, fowl, game, seafood, and some hot specialities of the Spanish cuisine are added. In this case, the cold courses are eaten first, followed by the hot ones. In Cádiz or Jerez (the home of sherry), these are usually washed down with a glass of dry, golden sherry; as they say there, "All of the sun of Andalusia in one glass." Whether served this way or washed down with some other beverage, you will find that *tapas* and *entremeses* make elegant and appreciated food for cocktail parties and buffets, where they are always conversation pieces.

LIST OF NATURAL *TAPAS*

Olives, black and green, plain or stuffed with onions, pimientos, anchovies or almonds
Radishes
Lettuce hearts with sauce vinaigrette or mayonnaise
Artichoke hearts with sauce vinaigrette or mayonnaise
Canned pimientos with vinaigrette
Oysters on the half shell with lemon juice
Mussels on the half shell with lemon juice
Codfish, shredded
Pickled anchovies (*boquerones*)
Salted shrimps, natural
Pickled sardines, in tomato juice or olive oil
Pickled tunafish
Tunafish in olive oil
Squids in their own ink
Ham, smoked, boiled; diced
Moorish Salad, (black olives, goat cheese, onion and vinaigrette sauce)
Pickled mushrooms

Pickled cucumbers
Salted almonds and other nuts
Croutons (*picatostes*)

TAPAS DE COCINA

CHICKEN LIVERS ON TOAST

12 chicken livers
1/2 teaspoon paprika
1 teaspoon salt
2 tablespoons flour (save
  1 teaspoon)
2 tablespoons butter

2 tablespoons chopped
  onions
1/2 cup chicken stock
1/2 teaspoon Worces-
  tershire sauce
2 teaspoons sherry

Cut livers in four pieces, season with salt and paprika. Roll in flour. Melt butter in saucepan and sauté the onion. Add the livers and sauté until golden brown. Stir in 1 teaspoon flour and cook 2 more minutes, then add stock slowly. Add Worcestershire sauce, correct seasoning. Cook 2 more minutes. Add sherry just before serving. Serve on toast. Serves 4.

BRAINS SPRINGTIME STYLE
(Sesos a la Primavera)

1 pair brains
salt
1 tablespoon lemon juice

1 garlic clove
1 sprig of parsley

Wash brains (can be calves' or lambs' brains), soak in water 1 hour and remove arteries and membranes. Cover with cold water, mixed with the rest of the ingredients and simmer for 30 minutes or until tender. Let them cool. Cut in thin slices, place on lettuce leaves. Garnish with asparagus tips and mayonnaise. Place around small ripe quartered tomatoes and radishes. Serves 3.

MOORISH PIMIENTOS
(Pimientos Moros)

1 7-oz. can pimientos, or
  roasted fresh red peppers
1 6-oz. can tunafish, packed
  in oil
2 tablespoons butter

2 anchovy fillets
2 tablespoons lemon juice
1 tablespoon parsley,
  chopped   ✓

Cut pimientos in strips. Make a paste with tunafish, butter
and anchovies. Fill the pimiento strips with the paste. Roll
and hold with toothpicks. Cool well. Cut between toothpicks;
place in a dish. Sprinkle with lemon juice and parsley. Serves
3.

OLIVE SANDWICHES
(Bocadillos de Aceitunas)

1 unsliced loaf of bread
2/3 cup ripe olives,
  chopped
1 tablespoon minced onion
6 hard-cooked eggs

1/2 cup minced cooked
  ham
butter or margarine for
  spreading
mayonnaise

Trim the crust from a loaf of bread and cut lengthwise into 6
equal slices. Spread with butter. Blend olives, chopped eggs,
onion and ham with sufficient mayonnaise to give it spreading
consistency. Spread on buttered side of bread and roll each
slice as for a jelly roll. Wrap tightly in a moist towel, twisting
the ends. Chill. To serve, unwrap and slice. Makes about 2
dozen.

ANCHOVY CANAPES
(Canapes de Anchoas)

1 can anchovy fillets
equal quantity of butter

lemon juice
pepper to taste

Mash the anchovies with butter to make a paste. Add a few
drops of lemon juice and pepper to taste. Serve on toasted
bread or unsalted crackers.

MUSHROOMS IN GARLIC SAUCE
(Champiñones al Ajillo)

Slice the mushrooms and place in an earthenware casserole with a piece of dry red hot pepper. Sprinkle with chopped garlic and salt. Pour boiling olive oil over the mushrooms and continue cooking over the fire 5 more minutes. Serve immediately.

MUSHROOMS AU GRATIN
(Champiñones al Gratin)

1 lb. mushrooms	1 tablespoon oil
2 tablespoons fine bread crumbs	1 cup white wine
1/4 cup chopped parsley	1 teaspoon butter
1/2 teaspoon salt	stock, if necessary
1/4 teaspoon red hot pepper	

Wash well the mushrooms under running water. Remove and chop the stems. Mix with the parsley and bread crumbs. Lay mushrooms, heads down, in a buttered dish and cover with the mixed ingredients. Sprinkle with salt and pepper, and the oil. Pour in the wine and bake in 350 F. oven about 20 minutes. If the sauce evaporates too quickly, add some stock. Serves 6.

MUSHROOMS WITH TOMATO SAUCE
(Champiñones en Salsa de Tomate)

mushrooms cups	salt, red pepper, paprika to taste
grated cheese, three times the weight of the mushrooms	olive oil
bread crumbs, 1 third the weight of the cheese	tomato puree

Put mushrooms in a pan and dot with tomato puree. Season and sprinkle with the rest of the ingredients. Bake 40 minutes in a 300° F. oven.

MOORISH BROCHETTE
(Pinchos Morunos)

1 lb. veal, beef, lamb, liver,
   or kidney
1 clove garlic, minced
1/4 cup vinegar

2 tablespoons olive oil
salt to taste
hot red pepper to taste
1/4 lb. bacon, diced

Cut meat into 1-inch pieces. Marinate for at least 1 hour in a sauce made with the rest of the ingredients. Put on small skewers (about 6 inches long) alternating with bacon. Grill 10 minutes. Serves 4.

IMPERIAL EGGPLANT BOATS
(Barquitas de berenjenas a la Imperial)

3 small eggplants
1/4 cup oil
3 oz. pickled tunafish
3 oz. anchovy fillets
1-1/2 oz. butter

1-1/2 oz. cooked string
   beans, cut French style
1 beet, cooked
salt and pepper to taste
1 hard-boiled egg, chopped

Peel eggplants, cut in half lengthwise, and make some cuts inside. Fry in oil and let them cool. When cold, spoon out the inside to make the boat. Mix the part of the eggplant you have spooned out with tunafish and anchovies, mash in a mortar with pestle (or whirl in a blender) to make a smooth puree. Add butter and seasoning; mix well. Fill the eggplant boats with this mixture. Place on a platter and decorate top with the string beans, chopped hard-boiled egg and thin slices of beet. Serve cold. Serves 6.

EGGPLANT BOATS PROVENCAL
(Barquitas de Berenjena a la Provenzal)

3 small eggplants
2 hard-boiled eggs
2 anchovies
1-1/2 oz. finely chopped
  onion

1 teaspoon mustard
1 tablespoon chopped
  parsley
salt and pepper to taste

You can also use small zucchinis for this dish.
Peel eggplants and cut lengthwise. Place in an oven dish, sprinkle with salt, half of the oil and cook in a 375° oven 25 minutes. Remove from oven, let them cool and spoon out the inside of the eggplant. Make a paste of eggs and anchovies in a mortar (or whirl in a blender); add onion, season to taste with salt and pepper and fill the eggplant with the mix. In a small bowl mix the rest of the oil with vinegar, and mustard, and pour over the eggplants. Serves 6.

MEAT TURNOVERS
(Empanadas Fritas)

3/4 cup lard or shortening
3 cups sifted flour

1 tablespoon salt
3/4 cup hot water

Cut shortening into flour. Dissolve salt in water, add to the flour mixture. Knead the pastry until soft. On a pastry board sprinkled with flour, roll out the dough as thin as possible. Cut circles (3-1/2" to 4" in diameter) out of the pastry. Put some filling on each (about 1 tablespoon). Pinch the edges or crimp them with a fork. Fry in deep hot oil (380°). Drain on paper towels. Yields 40 empanadas.

continued on next page

Filling:

2 tablespoons oil
1/2 lb. ground pork
1 small onion, chopped
1/2 green pepper, chopped

1/2 red pepper, chopped
60 medium pitless olives
2 tablespoons raisins
1 teaspoon paprika

Sauté onion with pork. Add the rest of the ingredients and mix well. Season to taste with salt and pepper. You can add 1 chopped hard-boiled egg to the filling if you wish.

LIVER PATE
(Pastel de Higado)

1 lb. fresh lean pork
1/2 lb. chicken livers
1/2 lb. calf liver
1 small onion, chopped
2 tablespoons chopped
   parsley
2 teaspoons freshly ground
   pepper

1/2 teaspoon powdered
   ginger
1/4 teaspoon cinnamon
2-1/4 teaspoons salt
2 tablespoons brandy

Put pork and liver several times through the finest blade of the meat grinder. Add the rest of the ingredients and mix thoroughly. Line a loaf pan with strips of bacon, pack the meat mixture in and bake in a 350° F. oven for 1-1/2 hours. Cool pâté under pressure (another loaf pan filled with rice or beans). This will pack the meat down to firm consistency. Serve cold.

KIDNEYS IN SHERRY
(Riñones al Jerez)

5 oz. sliced kidneys
1 oz. meat juice
2 tablespoons olive oil

salt and pepper to taste
3 tablespoons sherry

Prepare meat juice by squeezing thin slices of meat through a press.
Sauté kidneys in oil over a hot fire for less than a minute and

drain. Then place in a pan with the meat juice and sherry. Cook for 3 or 4 minutes. Season to taste with salt and pepper. For this dish the best kidneys are those of a young lamb. Serves 1.

STUFFED CLAMS
(Almejas Rellenas)

12 large clams	1 tablespoon flour
1/4 cup water	1-1/2 oz. butter
2 tablespoons tomato puree	2 tablespoons Parmesan
1 onion, finely chopped	cheese, grated
4 small pickles, chopped	1 tablespoon chopped
1 small can mushrooms,	parsley
chopped	1 lemon
1 glass dry white wine	salt and pepper to taste

Place clams in a pot with the water. Cover and cook about 5 minutes or until shells open.

Melt butter, add onion and sauté until golden. Add flour, mix well, then add tomato puree dissolved in the wine. Add pickles and mushrooms. Season to taste with salt and pepper. Simmer all together about 20 minutes. Place 1 teaspoon of this mix on each clam. Sprinkle with cheese and parsley, dot with butter and place in hot oven 10 minutes. Place on a platter and garnish with sprigs of parsley and lemon slices. Serves 3.

CLAMS OR MUSSELS VIRGIN-OF-THE-SEA STYLE
(Almejas o Mejillones a la Virgen del Mar)

24 large clams or mussels	2 tablespoons vinegar
1 oz. capers	1/4 teaspoon pepper
2 tomatoes, fresh or canned	1/4 teaspoon mustard
1 hard-boiled egg	salt to taste
2 tablespoons oil	chopped parsley for garnish
2 anchovies	

Clean and wash the clams, place in a pan with 1/4 cup water and boil for 5 minutes or until shells open. Remove clams from shell and place in an oval dish. Put tomatoes, capers, oil, hard-boiled eggs and anchovies in a mortar and mash with pestle (or whirl in a blender) to make a puree.

Season to taste with salt, vinegar, pepper and mustard. Pass this puree through a sieve, if necessary, and pour over the clams. Sprinkle with chopped parsley. Serve cold. Serves 4 to 6.

NATURAL CLAMS
(Almejas al Natural)

1 tablespoon olive oil	2 bay leaves
1 lemon	24 fresh clams or mussels
1 chopped onion	

Scrub the clams, rinse thoroughly.
Heat oil, add onion and bay leaves and place the clams on top. Do not add water, as the clams provide their own juice. As soon as they are open they are ready. Remove bay leaves, pour pan juices over all, and serve with lemon slices. Serves 4.

BAKED OYSTERS WITH ALMONDS
(Ostras al Horno con Almendras)

1 dozen oysters on the half shell	1/3 cup butter
	1/2 garlic clove, crushed
2 oz. ground blanched almonds	2 tablespoons brandy
	cayenne pepper to taste

Cream together almonds and butter. Blend in garlic, brandy, and cayenne. Pour off some of the liquor from oysters and cover each one of them with 1 teaspoon of the almond mix. Bake in a 450° oven for about 5 minutes. Serves 2.

MUSHROOM SALAD
(Ensalada de Champiñones)

Wash and dry, but do not peel, firm white mushrooms caps. Slice them thinly. Pour the following dressing over them: 1 part red wine vinegar and 3 parts olive oil, salt and pepper to taste. Sprinkle them with chopped chives and parsley before serving.

PICKLED ANCHOVIES
(Boquerones en Vinagre)

1 lb. *boquerones* or any small fish
1 cup vinegar
1 bay leaf
1/2 teaspoon salt
2 tablespoons parsley, finely chopped
2 cloves garlic, finely chopped
2 tablespoons olive oil
1 teaspoon lemon juice

Clean the fish well under running water. Snap off heads and backbone with one motion. Cut them in two along the middle; place in a bowl and cover with vinegar. Add the bay leaf and let stand overnight or for at least 12 hours. Remove from vinegar and rinse lightly under fresh water to remove excess vinegar. Place on a platter, sprinkle with garlic, olive oil, parsley, salt and lemon juice, being careful that each fish gets well coated. Serves 6.

PICKLED MUSHROOMS
(Champiñones en Escabeche)

1/2 lb. mushrooms
1 bay leaf
6 peppercorns
1 clove garlic
1 teaspoon salt
1-1/2 cups vinegar

Wipe mushrooms well with a cloth. Heat vinegar until warm. Put mushrooms in a glass jar, and add spices, garlic and vinegar. Cover the jar. Set aside for 2 days. Serves 2.

GRILLED LAMB CHOPS
(Chuletas de Cordero a la Parrilla)

6 lamb chops
1 garlic clove, minced
1 teaspoon red pepper
salt to taste

Mix well all the ingredients and let stand for at least 30 minutes. Place chops on hot grill and turn to grill both sides.

GRILLED FILLET CANAPES
(Montados de Lomitos)

Cut steak fillets in rounds a half inch thick. Dip in olive oil, season with salt and pepper, and grill. Serve them on rounds of toasted or fried bread.

KIDNEYS EN BROCHETTE
(Riñones en Agujas)

6 to 9 kidneys	3 oz. bread crumbs
3 oz. ham	2 oz. parsley, chopped
3 oz. bacon	4 tablespoons oil

Soak the kidneys in 1 qt. water with 3 tablespoons vinegar, 1 hour. Remove fat; slice into 1-inch pieces. Scald with boiling water, rinse with several cold waters. Dry with a towel. Cut the ham and the bacon into pieces. Fill skewers, alternating bacon, kidney, and ham. Mix oil or butter with the bread crumbs and parsley. (Use oil if you plan to grill the skewers; butter, if you plan to bake them.) Season with salt and pepper and coat the skewers with the mixture. Grill or bake in hot oven for 12 minutes. Serve 1 skewer to each person.

FRIED SWEETBREADS
(Mollejas Fritas)

Soak sweetbreads in cold water for 1 hour. Boil 1/4 hour in boiled salted water. Drain and rinse in cold water. Take off skin, cut away membrane and slice. Sprinkle with a few drops of lemon juice and more salt if needed. Dip in beaten egg and flour and fry in deep oil.

FRIED FRESH ANCHOVIES
(Boquerones Fritos)

Remove the head and intestines from the fish. Dip in beaten egg, then in flour seasoned with salt and pepper. Take 4 or 5 fishes by the tail in a fan-shaped bundle and fry in very hot oil. Any small fish can be prepared in the same fashion.

SQUIDS ROMAN STYLE
(Calamares a la Romana)

2 lbs. squids	flour
1 lemon	oil
1 egg	salt and pepper to taste

Clean the squids, remove heads from body and cut sacs into rings. Add lemon juice and let them stand 30 minutes. Dry the squids with a towel, season with salt and pepper and fry in hot olive oil. Serves 6 to 8.

GRILLED SHRIMPS
(Gambas a la Plancha)

Wash shrimps (about 1/2 lb. per person). Do not remove the shells. Sprinkle with salt, lemon juice, and oil. Place on a hot grill, sprinkling from time to time with 1/2 cup water that has been mixed with 1 tablespoon lemon juice and a little salt. The shrimps are done when their shells turn orange red. This will take about 4 minutes on one side and 3 on the other. Serve immediately.

SHRIMPS IN GARLIC SAUCE
(Gambas al Ajillo)

peeled shrimps	oil, or butter
garlic, finely chopped	
pieces of dry chili pepper to taste	

Place the shrimps in individual earthenware casseroles. Sprinkle with garlic and pieces of chili pepper. Pour over hot olive oil or butter, sprinkle with a little salt and cook for a few minutes over the fire. Serve sizzling hot in the same casserole.

FRIED SHRIMPS
(Gambas Fritas)

Shell raw shrimps, sprinkle with lemon juice, salt and a few drops of oil. Roll them in beaten egg and flour and fry in deep hot oil. Serve immediately.

SHRIMP SALAD
(Ensalada de Gambas)

Boil shrimps in just enough water to cover, chill and shell them and arrange them around a platter. Fill the center with potato salad dressed with sauce tartare: 1 cup mayonnaise, 2 tablespoons capers, 1 tablespoon chopped green olives, 1/4 cup pickled cucumbers, chopped. Mix all these ingredients. Pour some on the shrimps and mix the rest with the potato salad.

COLD SOUPS

THE ORIGIN OF *GAZPACHO*

When the Roman soldiers gave Christ upon the Cross a sponge wet with water and vinegar, they were offering him the "canteen" of the Roman Army (a sponge) and the normal soldier's field drink, *posca*—water and vinegar. Each soldier was issued a sponge—placed moist inside his helmet, it helped overcome the heat and absorbed the shock of blows on the head. It also held the liquid with which he refreshed himself when thirsty. The vinegar added to the water to make *posca* was considered a purifier. Soldiers used this beverage during years of campaigning and continued to use it after retirement. Spain was largely colonized by retired Roman soldiers (Merida, Zaragoza, Leon, Sevilla, Tarragona, etc.).

The first known recipe for gazpacho was simply made with water, vinegar, garlic, bread and onion. Another dish, *gazpachillo,* was eggs poached in water and vinegar. In the modern Spanish cuisine there are at least 40 different recipes for gazpacho. The imagination of the cook has led to many experiments that have resulted in successful combinations. Tomato, for example, one of the modern recipe's basic ingredients, was added after the discovery of America.

Today this refreshing soup is internationally known and has jumped from the country folk's kitchen to the most aristocratic tables of the world.

GAZPACHO ANDALUZ #1

1/2 lb. ripe tomatoes
2 slices of bread soaked in
  water
1 onion
2 cloves garlic

1 medium cucumber
1/2 cup wine vinegar
1/4 cup olive oil
2 cups water
salt and pepper to taste

In addition prepare separately: Chopped green pepper, chopped tomatoes, chopped cucumbers, chopped onions, and cubes of toasted bread.

Preparation: Mash in a mortar (or run through a blender at high speed) the first five ingredients and strain. Add the oil and vinegar to the liquid and mix well. Let it rest in a cold place or refrigerator for 1 hour. Add the water, mix and serve very cold, adding seasoning just before serving. Serve in separate dishes the chopped vegetables and bread croutons to sprinkle on soup as desired. Each person serves himself to his own taste. Serves 4.

GAZPACHO IMPERIAL

1 lb. ripe tomatoes
1/2 cucumber
1 clove garlic
1 tablespoon vinegar
2 cups cold water

1 tablespoon oil
1/4 cup soft bread crumbs
1 cup cream
salt to taste

Place the above ingredients except the cream and salt in a blender and run them for 2 minutes at high speed. Chill well. When ready to serve, add the seasoning and cream. Serves 4.

GAZPACHO ANDALUZ #2

3 tomatoes
1 cucumber
2 tablespoons onion
1 garlic clove
1 sweet green pepper

2 tablespoons vinegar
salt and pepper to taste
slices of bread
2 tablespoons olive oil
1 qt. cold water

Pound tomatoes, cucumber, garlic, and sweet pepper all

together in a mortar or whirl in a blender. Slowly heat the olive oil, sauté the onion and add tomato mix. Add the vinegar and season to taste with salt and pepper. Add water; sieve, and serve iced if possible. Serves 6.

WHITE GAZPACHO WITH GRAPES
(Gazpacho Blanco con Uvas)

5 oz. almonds, blanched	1 oz. oil
3 cloves garlic	2 oz. wine vinegar
1 teaspoon salt	salt and pepper to taste
3 oz. soft bread crumbs,	1/2 lb. grapes, peeled
moistened in water	1 qt. cold water

Place all these ingredients in a blender (except grapes) and blend well. Chill it well in the refrigerator.
Serve with peeled grapes and small twisted bread sticks. Serves 4 to 6.

MALAGA GAZPACHO
(Gazpacho Malagueño)

2 cups water	1/2 cup soft bread crumbs,
2 cloves garlic	soaked in water
1 teaspoon salt	2 tablespoons olive oil
1 green pepper cut in pieces	1 tablespoon vinegar
1/2 lb. tomatoes, peeled	

Whirl in a blender all ingredients, except the vinegar. Chill well. Just before serving add the vinegar. Serve with bread cubes. Serves 4.

COLD ROSE CONSOMME
(Consomme Rosa Fria)

1 lb. very lean beef cut in
pieces
2 lbs. tomatoes
1-1/2 qts. chicken
consommé

salt and paprika to taste
2 egg whites

Place all these ingredients in a pot and simmer about 1-1/2 hours. Strain, using a very fine strainer and chill well.
If there is a formation of fat on the top skim it off. (The meat can be used for cold plates or spaghetti sauce.) Serves 4.

ALMOND SOUP
(Gazpacho Blanco)

2-1/2 ozs. blanched
almonds
3-1/2 ozs. bread crumbs
soaked in water and
squeezed out

1 clove garlic
4 tablespoons oil
1-1/2 qts. water
salt to taste

Whirl in a blender all the above ingredients. Chill well and serve with croutons. Serves 6.

Spanish Method: In a mortar place almonds, salt and a little water and press with pestle to make a paste. Add bread crumbs and continue working, adding also the oil by drops. When all the oil is used up add the vinegar. Now place the water in a jar with a tight lid, add almond paste and shake well until the mix is completely blended.

COLD SHRIMP SOUP
(Sopa de Gambas, Fria)

1 lb. shrimps or prawns,
  cooked
3 tablespoons soft bread
  crumbs
1-1/2 qts. fish stock
1 cup milk
1 egg yolk
pinch nutmeg and fennel
salt and pepper to taste

juice of 1/2 lemon
1/2 small cucumber, peeled
  and diced
Stock:
water
1 small onion
small piece of lemon peel
1/2 lb. white fish

Make stock by simmering for about 20 minutes the shrimp
shells, fish, onion and lemon peel. Strain and add the bread
crumbs. Place cooked shrimp in a blender with lemon juice,
nutmeg, egg yolk, and milk. Add 1/2 cup of the stock and
whirl in the blender. The mixture should be creamy. A little at
a time add the rest of the stock. Return soup to a pot and heat
it for about 5 minutes. Do *not* let it boil. Then press it
through a fine sieve. Chill well. To serve, sprinkle on top the
cucumber and chopped fresh fennel, if you have some, and
garnish each bowl of soup with a thin slice of lemon. Serves 6.

COLD CUCUMBER SOUP
(Sopa Fria de Pepinos)

2 cups chicken consommé
2 tablespoons sherry
1 small cucumber, diced

pinch of nutmeg
salt to taste

Chill the chicken consommé and all skim fat from surface.
Add the sherry, cucumber and seasonings and keep in the
refrigerator for at least 1 hour before serving. Serve in soup
bowls. Serves 2.

MOORISH ALMOND SOUP
(Sopa Mora de Almendras)

2 cups milk
2 oz. blanched ground
   almonds

1 egg
salt to taste

Mix milk and almonds; let stand 1 hour. Add salt and put through a sieve. Separate the egg, beating the yolk and white separately. Stir the yolk in the soup. Add the egg white just before serving. Serves 2.

CREAM OF CLAMS
(Crema de Almejas)

1 qt. cream
1 cup cognac
1 cup port
1 cup white wine
1 cup water

5 egg yolks
2 lbs. clams
2 carrots
1 onion
salt and pepper to taste

Put the clams in a pot with the onion and carrots, chopped fine. Add the white wine and 1 cup of water. Bring to a boil and continue simmering until the clams open. Strain the broth and pour in a tureen. Add the well beaten egg yolks and mix well. Add cognac and port. Add the cream, mixing well. Place in the refrigerator 1 hour before serving. Serve with chopped chives, if you wish. Serves 8.

Note: The clams are delicious served as a separate course in any fashion that calls for cooked clams.

COLD POTATO SOUP
(Sopa de patatas fria)

1 qt. chicken consommé
1/2 leek, chopped fine
1 tablespoon butter
3 medium potatoes, boiled

1/2 qt. milk
pinch of nutmeg
salt to taste

Sauté leek in butter until transparent and soft. Add to the consommé and bring it to a boil. Mash the potatoes and add to the soup. Let it cool. Pass soup through a fine sieve and add the milk. Correct seasoning and add the nutmeg. Place in the refrigerator to chill. Serve sprinkled with chopped green onions or chives. Serves 6.

With a blender: Sauté leek in butter until transparent and soft and add it to consommé. Bring it to a boil. Add the rest of the ingredients and whirl in a blender until very smooth. Chill and serve as indicated above.

PINK SOUP
(Sopa Rosada)

Same as above, but add one ripe tomato to sautéed onions.

GOLDEN SOUP
(Sopa Dorada)

Same as cold potato soup, but add 1/2 teaspoon saffron to consommé before boiling it.

CONSOME MADRILENO

1 qt. chicken broth	1 teaspoon gelatin
2 lbs. ripe tomatoes	1/2 cup water

Simmer the tomatoes with broth about 1 hour. Remove from fire and let it set. Strain. Add the gelatin dissolved in the water; return consommé to fire and bring to a boil. Let it cool and place in the refrigerator until set. Serve with lemon wedges. Serves 4 to 6.

WHITE GARLIC SOUP
(Ajo Blanco)

1 egg	3 slices white bread, soaked
2 cloves garlic	in water
1 teaspoon salt	3 tablespoons vinegar
5 tablespoons oil	1-1/2 qts. water

Put garlic and salt in a mortar and pound it well until you

have a paste. Squeeze crumbs and add to mortar, mixing well into the garlic paste. Add the egg and mix well. Drop by drop, add the oil until all of it has been used. Add vinegar, 1 tablespoon at a time, and 1 cup of water. Put this into a tureen, add the rest of the water and mix well. Chill very well before serving. When ready to serve, add toasted croutons. Serves 6.

Blender Method: Put the ingredients in the order given into the blender, using only 1 cup of water. Whirl at high speed about 3 minutes. Pour this mix into a tureen; add the rest of the water and mix well. Chill well before serving.

HOT SOUPS

COCIDOS

Spain has a universal dish—it is called by a variety of names and exists in numerous variations, changing name and type in every region. Its base is always meat, sausages, beans or chick peas and vegetables. In Madrid it is made with chick peas *(garbanzos)* and called *cocido;* in Galicia it is known as *pote,* in other places has such names as *potage* and *olla* (pot). In addition, every housewife has her own version of the recipe and the ingredients change from season to season according to what is available in the market. Normally this dish is served as two courses; first it provides a good rich soup that always hits the spot, particularly in winter time. Then the meat and vegetables are served as a second course, sometimes accompanied with a sauce such as *pebre* or with mustard.

This dish in any of its variations is particularly good for a busy day—it is simple to make, requires little attention while it is cooking and it is a whole meal. Further, it is a budget stretcher, as it uses the cheapest cuts of meat and you can take advantage of vegetables and meats that are in season and easily adapt these recipes to use leftovers.

In any of the recipes that follow you can use beef, veal, lamb, stewing chicken or any other meat. But a word of warning—if you use tender meat, such as veal or lamb, then the meat and chick peas or beans can be put to cook together at the same time. If, on the other hand, you use a tougher meat, then the meat must be started one hour earlier.

1 lb. lamb shoulder or stew meat in one piece	3 qts. water
1 small blood sausage	1 lb. potatoes
1 cup chick peas	2 carrots
1/4 lb. chorizo (Spanish sausage)	1/4 lb. bacon
	1 small head of cabbage
	salt and pepper to taste

Soak chick peas overnight. In a deep kettle put the meat, chick peas, Spanish sausage, bacon and bone. Add water, bring it to a boil and simmer slowly for about 2 hours until meat is tender. At this time correct seasoning. Add potatoes, blood sausage, and carrots and boil slowly until they are done. In a separate kettle cook cabbage in water with salt to taste, about 30 minutes. Drain and keep hot. Now drain the meat stock and make a soup, adding 2 oz. vermicelli. If you don't have enough liquid for the soup add some of the cabbage stock. Serve the soup as a first course. Place sliced meat, sausages, vegetables and chick peas on a large platter and bring it to the table. Each person gets a piece of everything. Serves 6

Pebre, the sauce for *Cocido*

1 small onion, chopped	1/4 cup olive oil
1 tablespoon chopped parsley	1/4 cup wine vinegar
1/2 cup water	salt and pepper to taste

Mix all these ingredients and use it, if you desire, as a topping for the meat and vegetables.

SPANISH COCIDO
(Cocido Español)

1 lb. beef	3 carrots
2 bones	1 leek
1/2 lb. chicken	small bunch parsley
1 cup chick peas, soaked overnight	1/4 teaspoon saffron
	salt and pepper to taste
2 qts. water	

Cut the meat into small pieces, crack the bones, and put into a kettle. Add the chicken at the same time. Cover with water and put on the fire. When it starts boiling, skim it off and add the chick peas. Let it simmer 1 hour. Add sliced carrots, leek, and parsley and continue cooking another hour. Add more water if necessary; you must have always about 3 pints of water in the pot. At the end of this time season to taste with salt and pepper and add the saffron. Cook slowly 30 more minutes. Serve as indicated above. Serves 6.

WHITE BEAN COCIDO
(Cocido de Judías Blancas)

1 lb. white beans	1 piece ham bone
3 oz. bacon	1 teaspoon salt
3 oz. Spanish sausage (chorizo)	1 small onion
	1 carrot
1 blood sausage	1 lb. potatoes

Soak beans overnight, rinse under cold water and put in a large pot. Add bacon, ham bone, Spanish sausage and enough water to cover all the ingredients well. Bring to a boil, reduce fire and simmer for 1 hour. Add onion, salt, carrot and blood sausage; continue cooking another hour. If bacon and sausages are cooked, remove to a side dish, keeping them hot. Add peeled whole potatoes and cook until done. In a separate pot cook 1 lb. green beans, cabbage or chards.

Remove vegetables from broth and add to it some of the cabbage stock. Make a soup with toasted bread or vermicelli and serve it as first course. Serve the beans and vegetables garnished with the bacon and sausages. Serves 8.

GYPSY POT
(Olla Gitana)

2 qts. water	1 medium onion
1/2 lb. string beans	2 tablespoons oil
1 parsnip	1 tablespoon flour
1 eggplant	2 medium tomatoes
1 squash	salt

Cook string beans and parsnip in water. Add salt to taste. When these vegetables are done add the chopped eggplant, squash and potatoes. Chop onion fine and fry until golden brown in the oil. Chop the tomatoes and sauté with the onion for 2 minutes. Blend in the flour. Add this mixture to the ingredients in the pot. Continue cooking for 1 more hour. The liquid in the pot should be thick. Serve in a tureen. Serves 6.

OLLA SACROMONTE

Keep all bits of bone, cooked meat, chicken, carcasses and roast trimmings, vegetable parings, outer leaves of lettuce, unshapely or overripe tomatoes, celery tops, parsley or anything good for the soup pot. Reserve liquid from canned vegetables and store in the refrigerator until ready to use. There are no set proportions to be used in this pot, but a good rule is to use twice as much water or stock as meat, bone and fat, adding the vegetables as desired.

An earthenware soup pot with a tightly fitted lid is preferable. It gives a special flavor to the soup and you can take it to the table.

To draw the juices, soak meat for 1 hour in the water that is going to be used to make the soup. Soups made from cooked meats and leftovers require less cooking time than soups made from fresh ingredients. One to two hours simmering time is enough to extract the juices and blend the leftover flavors. This pot eliminates all waste, can be varied in many ways, is rich in vitamins and thoroughly delicious.

CATALAN STEW
(Cocido Catalán)

3 qts. water
3/4 lb. breast of veal
5 oz. bacon
6 oz. blood sausages
1/2 lb. chick peas
1/2 lb. potatoes
1 soup bone
1/4 chicken
1 turnip
1 carrot
1 stalk celery
3 oz. vermicelli
salt and pepper to taste

The Meat Ball:
5 oz. lamb or veal, ground
1 egg
1/2 cup soft bread crumbs
milk
flour
salt and pepper to taste

Place the water in a deep pan. When it starts to boil, add veal, bacon, bone and chicken, and chick peas that have been soaked in water over night. Add turnip, carrot and celery. Season and simmer for about 3 hours or until meats are tender. In the last 30 minutes add sausage and the meat ball. Continue cooking 15 more minutes.

Make the meat ball by mixing the ground meat and bread crumbs soaked in milk and egg. Knead with your hands and mold, using the dry flour.

Separate the broth. Strain and boil with vermicelli to make the soup that is served as a first course.

Boil the potatoes in a separate pot.

Arrange meats, sausage, meat ball and bacon on a platter. In another platter place the chick peas, carrots, and potatoes. If you wish, you can add cabbage leaves to this stew. It is very tasty. If you want more color, add a pinch of saffron and small ripe tomato. Serves 6.

GALICIAN STEW
(Pote Gallego)

This is one of those dishes that improve with long, slow cooking.

1/2 lb. white beans	1/2 lb. salted pork
1/2 lb. chorizo (Spanish sausage)	1/2 lb. ham
	1 small ham bone
1 lb. potatoes	1 gallon water
2 lbs. mixed green vegetables, chopped	salt and pepper to taste

Place beans in cold water and when it starts to boil add sausage, pork, ham, bone and potatoes cut in fourths. Add green vegetables and let simmer 4 or 5 hours. When you are almost ready to serve it, brown 1 tablespoon flour in 2 tablespoons olive oil and add to the pot. Correct seasoning and add 1/2 teaspoon paprika. Cook 10 minutes longer.

Serve the stew in a tureen. The sausage, ham and pork are served in a separate dish. Serves 4.

CLAM SOUP FROM MALAGA
(Sopa de Almejas a la Malagueña)

1 lb. medium size clams	1 pinch each, thyme and fennel
1/2 lb. tomatoes, peeled	
1 onion, finely minced	2 oz. oil
1 clove garlic, finely minced	1 qt. water
1 bay leaf	salt and pepper to taste

Wash the clams and put in the boiling water. Add herbs and cook 5 minutes. Remove top shell from each clam. Sauté onion in oil until tender; add garlic, add tomatoes and cook until tender. Season to taste. Pass through a sieve, pouring over the stock. Simmer 5 more minutes. Add the clams. Serve with lemon wedges. Serves 4.

WALNUT SOUP
(Sopa de Nueces)

3 cups chicken broth
1 tablespoon butter
2 tablespoons flour
salt and pepper to taste
2 egg yolks

4 tablespoons cream
1 cup walnuts, broken, peeled
1 teaspoon lemon juice

Heat the chicken broth, without boiling. Blend the butter and flour together and cook 1 minute over the fire without browning it. Add to broth, stirring until well incorporated. Bring it to a boil. Remove from fire and add egg yolks blended with a little broth, and the seasoning. Mix the nuts with the cream and lemon juice and blend well into the soup. Serves 4.

To remove skin from walnuts, soak them in a cup of hot water. This will loosen the skin.

SOUP CADIZ STYLE
(Sopa Gaditana)

3 tablespoons olive oil
5 oz. ham, cut in small squares
1 egg yolk
2 hard-boiled eggs

1-1/2 oz. sherry
2 cloves garlic
1 teaspoon chopped parsley
1-1/2 qts. beef broth
4 slices of bread, diced

Fry the bread. Sauté ham and place in a tureen with the parsley, sautéed garlic and hard-boiled egg cut in strips. Blend the egg yolk and the sherry and add to the rest of the ingredients. When ready to serve, add the piping hot beef broth. Serves 6.

GARLIC SOUP, BASQUE STYLE
(Sopa de Ajo a la Vascongada)

This is one of the most popular soups of the Basque provinces. There it is prepared with an exquisite type of bread called *pistola* (pistol), which is spongy in texture and makes this soup very tasty. White toasted bread can be substituted for *pistola*.

5 cups water	4 cloves garlic
4 slices toasted white bread, cut in squares	2 tablespoons tomato paste
2 tablespoons olive oil	2 eggs
	salt and pepper to taste

Place water and bread in a pot, season to taste and bring it to a boil. Put oil in a frying pan and when it starts to smoke, add the garlic and fry until dark brown. Remove garlic. Add tomato paste and sauté 2 minutes. Add this mixture to the water and bread mixture and boil together for 10 more minutes. Beat the eggs and add to soup when ready to serve. Serves 4.

SOPA VERONICA

2 lbs. tomatoes, peeled and chopped	5 oz. cream
3 oz. tomato puree	2 oz. butter
3 oz. cream of wheat	salt to taste
	2 qts. water

Melt butter in a pan and sauté the tomatoes. Add the water and cook 20 minutes. Add tomato puree. Let it cool. Pass through a sieve. Put soup back in the pan and bring it to boil. Season. Now add cream of wheat, sprinkling it thinly over the boiling soup, stirring all the time. Simmer 10 more minutes. Add the cream when ready to serve. Serves 8.

CREAM SOUP
(Sopa de Crema)

1 tablespoon butter
1/4 cup flour
2 cups beef stock
1 egg yolk

1 tablespoon water
1-1/2 oz. sherry
salt and pepper to taste

Melt butter in a pot; add flour and mix well, cooking it for about 2 minutes. Add hot stock, stirring as you add it to avoid the formation of lumps, until the flour is well blended with the stock. Boil 5 more minutes. Blend egg yolk in water and add to the soup. Keep it warm. When ready to serve add sherry. Serves 4.

FISHERMAN SOUP
(Sopa de Pescadores)

1/4 cup olive oil
2 onions, finely chopped
4 cloves garlic, mashed
1 lb. halibut or other fish, cut in pieces
1 lb. clams or any other seafood

1 bottle dry white wine
1 bottle water
2 lbs. tomatoes, peeled and seeded
salt and pepper to taste

Sauté onion and garlic in the oil until transparent. Add fish and clams and sauté all together, mixing well, 5 more minutes. Add wine and water and then the tomatoes. Season to taste and cook 15 more minutes. Serve on slices of fried bread. Serves 6.

POTATO, HAM AND EGG SOUP
(Sopa de Patatas con Jamón y Huevo)

1-1/2 qts. stock
2 eggs
3 medium potatoes, diced

3 oz. ham
salt and pepper to taste

Bring the stock to a boil. Add potatoes and mix well. Boil the eggs, remove the yolks. Chop the egg whites and ham and mix with mashed egg yolks. Add to the soup. Stir well and serve. Serves 6.

BULLFIGHTER'S SOUP
(Sopa del Torero)

1 lb. leftover roast beef
3 onions, sliced very thin
2 tablespoons oil
2 tablespoons butter
1/2 teaspoon paprika
1 teaspoon chopped parsley
2 qts. beef broth

4 tablespoons meat juice
  (from roast beef)
Pinch oregano
1 lb. cooked potatoes, diced
1 tablespoon lemon juice
1 hard-boiled egg, sliced
1/2 teaspoon cumin seeds

Cut meat into thin strips. Save all the juice. Put oil and butter in a pan, heat, and sauté the onion. Add paprika and spices. Add potatoes and continue cooking until potatoes start to get some coloring. Add broth and simmer about 10 minutes or until done. When ready to serve add meat and meat juice. To serve: Put the egg in the bottom of a tureen, mix well with the lemon juice, pour soup on top. Serves 6.

CHEESE SOUP
(Sopa de Queso)

2 tablespoons oil
1/2 sliced onion
1/2 sliced tomato
1/4 teaspoon paprika
1/4 teaspoon cinnamon
1 bay leaf
3 cups boiling water

2 oz. noodles
1 egg
1 tablespoon butter or
  margarine, softened
1 cup grated Edam cheese
salt to taste

Using a heavy pot, sauté the onion, tomato and bay leaf in the oil. Add paprika and cinnamon. Add water and salt, cover and simmer 1-1/2 hours. Strain, reserving 1 ladle of the clear soup. Put the rest of the soup back in the pan; add noodles and simmer 15 minutes or until noodles are tender. Beat the egg with the butter and add cheese. Add the cold reserved clear soup, and blend well. Pour this mixture in a tureen, then add hot noodle soup. Serves 4.

ARTICHOKE SOUP
(Sopa de Alcachofas)

1 qt. hot vegetable stock
6 artichokes
1 cup cream
2 tablespoons butter

2 tablespoons cornstarch
2 tablespoons white wine
1 egg
salt and pepper to taste

Cook artichokes and make a puree with the bottoms and soft part of the leaves. Melt butter, add cornstarch and stock, stirring well as you add it. Add wine. Season with salt and pepper. Add artichoke puree, blending it well. When ready to serve, beat the egg, blend well with the cream and add to the soup. Serve with croutons, if desired. Serves 4 to 6.

GREEN SOUP
(Sopa Verde)

2 lbs. mashed potatoes
4 large cabbage leaves, finely sliced
4 qts. stock

1 clove garlic
1 medium onion, finely chopped
salt and pepper to taste

Simmer cabbage in the stock until tender. Add garlic, onion and seasoning; continue simmering until onion is soft. Slowly blend in the mashed potatoes. Correct seasoning and simmer until creamy, about 20 minutes. Serves 10 to 12.

TOASTED ALMOND SOUP
(Sopa de Almendras Tostadas)

5 oz. blanched almonds, toasted
1 qt. beef or ham stock
3 tablespoons bread crumbs
1 clove garlic, crushed
1 tablespoon parsley, chopped

1/4 teaspoon saffron, crushed
4 eggs
4 tablespoons croutons

Grind almonds and put in a pot with the stock, bread crumbs and a mix made with garlic, parsley and saffron. Cook 5

minutes and pour into an earthenware casserole. Add 1 egg
and 1 tablespoon croutons for each portion. Sprinkle with salt
and put the casserole in a hot oven (475°F.) 5 minutes, or until eggs are set to your taste. Serves 4.

ROYAL SOUP
(Sopa Real)

Consommé (1 cup per per-   ham cut into thin strips, to
    son)   taste
egg yolk (1 per person)

Blend egg yolks with a little cold consommé and add to the
rest of hot consommé. Sauté ham in 1 teaspoon butter and add
to consommé. Correct seasoning and serve in soup bowls.

CHRISTMAS ALMOND SOUP
(Sopa de Almendras Navideña)

5 oz. almonds   4 slices white bread
1 qt. milk   pinch of salt
5 oz. sugar

Peel the almonds and place with the sugar in a blender (or
mortar) and crush well. Dissolve this mix in the milk and simmer for 15 minutes. Remove from fire. Cut the crust from the
bread, cut into small squares and add to the milk. Cover for a
few minutes. Serve it hot. You might add more milk if you
desire. Serves 4.

CREAM SOUP GOOD WOMAN STYLE
(Crema Buena Señora)

1 cucumber   2 tablespoons butter
1 qt. consommé   2 egg yolks
1 lettuce heart   1/2 cup cream or milk
1/8 teaspoon tarragon   salt and pepper to taste

Chop the lettuce heart very fine. Peel and cut cucumber into
very thin sticks. Place butter in a pan and when it melts sauté
the lettuce and cucumber 5 minutes. Season with salt, pepper
and tarragon, add the consommé and simmer 15 minutes.

Remove from fire to cool it for two minutes. Beat egg yolks slightly, mix with the cream or milk and add to the soup, blending well. When ready to serve return soup to fire and heat over low fire until hot but without boiling it. Serves 4.

CREAM SOUP ANDALUSIAN STYLE
(Crema a la Andaluza)

2 qts. vegetable stock
2 pimientos, chopped
3 tablespoons butter
1 clove garlic, minced
1 sugar cube, burned*
salt and pepper to taste
6 tablespoons onion, chopped

4 tomatoes, chopped
2 tablespoons rice
1 tablespoon lemon juice
2 tablespoons cream or top milk

Sauté garlic and pimientos in butter. Remove to a side dish. In the same butter sauté onion until golden in color and transparent and tender. Add tomatoes, rice and vegetable stock and cook until rice is tender, about 20 minutes. Strain soup and sieve the vegetables (or pass them through a blender) to make a puree. Add puree to the soup, add lemon juice and sugar cube and blend well. Bring to a boil and when ready to serve add the cream. Serves 8.

*Hold the sugar cube with a tweezer over a gas or alcohol flame. It will ignite immediately. Twist it around to burn it evenly.

OLD-FASHIONED GARLIC SOUP
(Sopa de Ajo a la Antigua)

2 tablespoons olive oil
4 cloves garlic
1 teaspoon paprika
1 qt. beef broth

salt to taste
4 slices bread
4 eggs

Put the oil in a frying pan, add the garlic and sauté until dark but not burned. Add paprika and broth. Place 4 slices of bread in an earthenware casserole and break an egg on each. Pour soup over bread. Place the casserole over the fire until eggs are done to taste. Serves 4.

GREEN MEADOW SOUP
(Sopa de la Pradera)

1 qt. good beef stock	1/2 cup cooked peas
4 teaspoons tapioca	1/2 cup asparagus tips
1/2 cup spinach puree	

When stock is boiling, add the tapioca, stirring all the time. Boil 5 minutes. Add spinach puree, peas and asparagus, stirring well. Correct the seasoning. In a bowl beat 1 egg yolk with 1 teaspoon milk and 1 teaspoon chopped parsley. Add to the soup when ready to serve. This last detail is optional. Serves 4.

In Spain the meat used for stock making is cut in very small pieces, the bones are crushed and meat and bones are placed in cold water that gets heated gradually. The advantage of this method is that the albumen contained in the meat dissolves completely.

GARLIC SOUP QUEEN STYLE
(Sopa de Ajo a la Reina)

3 tablespoons olive oil	3 eggs, separated
6 cloves garlic	6 slices stale bread
1-1/2 qts. stock	
a pinch of pepper, mace and	
nutmeg	

Gently sauté the garlic in 2 tablespoons olive oil. When golden, add the stock and seasoning. Boil a few minutes and strain. In a bowl beat the egg yolks with the 1 tablespoon olive oil. Stir some of the soup into the yolks, then pour the yolk mixture into the soup. Keep the soup hot but don't let it boil.

Toast slices of bread in the oven; spread over them the unbeaten egg whites and let them set. Place these slices of bread into soup plates and pour soup over them. Serves 6.

PRINCELY EGGS
(*Huevos Principescos*)

When Carlos IV was the Prince of Asturias, he had a lovely petite palace built for his wife, María Amelia of Saxony, known as *La Casita del Principe* (The Prince's Little House) near the Palace of El Pardo. The young couple often went there to have some privacy and to get away from the strict etiquette of the Court of Carlos II. For the first dinner in the lovely dining room of the little mansion, whose walls were covered with rich embroidered silk and illuminated by crystal chandeliers, the chef wanted to create something very special, so he developed a delicate egg dish that he named *Huevos Principescos* (Princely Eggs)—a dish very much appreciated by the princely couple. From then on this dish was served very often at the royal table at *La Casita del Principe.*

This recipe has been reconstructed from an old manuscript where only sketchy indications were given:

The Dough:
2 cups flour
2 egg yolks
2 egg whites, beaten firm
1/2 teaspoon salt
1/4 cup milk (more or less)
1/4 cup butter

The Filling:
6 fresh eggs, poached
2 cups bechamel sauce
1/2 lb. small shrimps, cleaned and sautéed in butter, seasoned to taste with salt and pepper

Mix all the dough ingredients except the butter, adding enough milk to make the dough. (The amount of milk needed depends on the egg's size used). Roll out the dough very thin. Divide the butter in two parts. Spread half of the butter on dough, dusting over abundantly with flour. Fold dough in fourths and roll it out thin. Repeat the operation with the other half of the butter. Roll out the dough thin and cut pastry rounds with a 3-inch cutter. Fit rounds into small ungreased muffin pan, prick with a fork and bake in hot oven (425°F.) 10 to 12 minutes. Place 1 poached egg in every cup; cover with bechamel sauce. Arrange the prepared shrimps in a crown form on top. Serves 6.

Bechamel Sauce:
1-1/2 cups chicken stock
1 sliced onion
1 sliced carrot
1/2 teaspoon salt
1/8 teaspoon pepper
6 peppercorns
1/4 cup butter
1/4 cup flour
1 cup scalded milk, or half
  cream and half milk
1 sprig of parsley

Cook stock 20 minutes with onion, carrot, parsley and peppercorns. Strain. There should be 1 cup. Melt butter, add flour and gradually hot stock and milk. Season to taste with salt and pepper.

EGGS COUNTRY STYLE
(Huevos Campesina)

Fry eggs and place with fried sausage over Brussels sprouts.

EGGS CAONTIN
(Huevos Caontin)

Make a potato puree. Spread it into a buttered casserole. Make indentation with a spoon and place 1 egg into each hollow. Cover casserole and cook over low fire 5 minutes or until eggs are set. You can also place the casserole in a low oven (325°F.) for about the same time.

EGGS FRONTIER
(Huevos a la Frontera)

6 eggs, separated   1 oz. butter

Beat egg whites. In another bowl beat the yolks. Blend together. Butter several soufflé molds and fill with eggs. Place molds on a tray with hot water and cook in a 425°F. preheated oven 10 minutes or until set. Unmold.

3 eggs   10 oz. prepared tomato
10 oz. cooked peas   sauce
1/4 cup flour   2 oz. foie gras
3 oz. butter   salt and pepper
2 cups milk

Make a bechamel with the flour, milk and half of the butter. (Use remaining butter to butter the molds; if any is left add it to the tomato sauce.) Season with salt and pepper. Add foie-gras, beating all the time, and then beat in the eggs one by one. Remove from fire. Pour into buttered molds and put in oven on a tray with hot water for about 10 minutes or until set. Unmold on a platter. To serve, alternate egg molds with bechamel molds. Cover with tomato sauce and garnish with peas. Serves 6.

ROMAN EGGS
(Huevos a la Romana)

6 hard-boiled eggs   6 oz. tomato sauce
1-1/2 oz. butter, divided in   2 cups milk
  two   2 tablespoons grated cheese
1-1/2 oz. flour

Cut eggs lengthwise in halves. Remove the yolks. Make a bechamel with the flour, milk and half of the butter. (See pg. 74). Reserve half of the sauce. To the sauce in the pan add the well-mashed egg yolks, mix well and stuff the egg whites with it. Place eggs on buttered baking dish. Mix the other half of the bechamel with the tomato sauce. Correct seasoning and pour over the eggs. Dot with the rest of the butter, sprinkle over with the cheese and put in a 475°F. oven for five minutes. Serves 6.

EGGS PRINCESS STYLE
(Huevos Princesa)

6 eggs
6 round rolls
1 oz. butter
3 oz. Spanish sausage, or
  any other spicy sausage
  cut into 6 slices

1 cup oil
1 cup milk

Scoop out the center of each roll and soak briefly in milk. They shouldn't get too soft. Place a piece of sausage inside each hole, a dot of butter and break one egg inside the hole. Heat oil in frying pan and when hot sauté the rolls and spoon hot oil on top of eggs until they get done. Season with salt and serve with prepared tomato sauce. Serves 6.

EGGS IN NESTS
(Huevos al Nido)

6 eggs
1 cup milk
1 cup oil for frying

1 loaf of bread
salt and pepper to taste

Cut the bread in 2-inch slices. Scoop out the center of each slice and soak quickly in milk. Heat oil in frying pan and when it starts to smoke, fry the bread, at the same time breaking 1 egg inside each "nest." The bread should be fried by the time the egg is cooked. Season egg and serve immediately. Serves 6.

EGGS BOHEMIAN
(Huevos Bohemios)

6 tartlet shells
6 eggs, poached

2 oz. foie gras
2 tablespoons grated cheese

Spread the tartlets with the foie gras. Poach eggs and place each egg inside a tartlet. Sprinkle with cheese and bake 5 minutes in a 425°F. oven. Serve immediately. Serves 6.

EGGS IN JACKETS
(Huevos con Casaca)

6 eggs, poached	1 cup oil
2 oz. grated bread crumbs	1 cup thick white sauce
1 beaten egg	

Poach the eggs, remove from pan and cool. Make a thick white sauce. On a platter place one spoonful of sauce. Place one egg on top and cover it with sauce. Repeat this operation until all eggs are done. Cut around the egg to eliminate uneven edges. Dip in beaten egg, roll in bread crumbs and fry in deep hot oil. They are usually served with fried ham or sausages. Serves 6.

EGGS WITH ONION RINGS
(Huevos con Anillos de Cebolla)

To fry the eggs put 1 cup of oil into a medium size frying pan. Break the eggs one by one into a side dish. When the oil is hot slip egg from dish to frying pan.

1/2 cup milk	1/4 cup flour
1/2 cup oil	salt to taste
1 onion, cut into rings	

Soak onion rings in milk mixed with 1/2 cup oil. Dip in flour and fry in deep oil until golden brown. Remove from fire and place on paper towels to absorb the excess oil. Sprinkle with salt and serve with the fried eggs.

EGGS MANCHA STYLE
(Huevos a la Manchega)

1/4 cup oil
1 clove garlic
1-1/2 cups ham, diced
1 small onion, sliced fine
2 pimientos, roasted
1 lb. tomatoes, diced and
  seeded

1 teaspoon sugar
1 teaspoon salt
1 tablespoon cooked or
  canned peas

Put oil into frying pan. When hot add garlic, ham and onion, and cook over low fire 5 minutes. Add pimientos cut into strips and tomatoes. Add seasoning and let simmer 5 more minutes. Then add the peas. Serve with fried eggs.

EGGS WITH BANANAS
(Huevos con Plátanos)

Peel medium ripe bananas. Soak in milk, dip in flour and fry in hot deep oil. Serve with fried eggs done to your taste.

EGGS CARDINAL
(Huevos Cardenal)

6 large round tomatoes
6 eggs
1 tablespoon chopped
  parsley

2 cloves garlic, minced
salt and pepper
3 tablespoons hot butter

Cut off a lid from each tomato and spoon out 3/4 of the pulp. Place into a 425°F. oven 15 minutes. Break one egg inside each tomato, season with salt and pepper, sprinkle with garlic and parsley, and drizzle with melted butter. Return to hot oven for 3 more minutes. Serve sprinkled with buttered toasted bread crumbs. Serves 6.

EGGS RONCAL STYLE
(Huevos del Roncal)

1 tablespoon lard
6 slices red sausage (chorizo)

2 eggs
1 slice of fried bread, ground

In earthenware (or Pyrex) casserole put lard. Break eggs over it. Cover with thin slices of sausage. Sprinkle the bread crumbs on top. Put in a 425°F. oven until eggs are set. Serves 1.

EGGS CATALAN STYLE
(Huevos a la Catalana)

6 eggs, poached
6 pieces toasted bread
1 small can foie gras
2-1/2 tablespoons butter

1/3 cup flour
1/2 cup chicken broth
2 tablespoons tomato sauce

Poach the eggs to your taste. Spread foie gras on toast and place one egg on each toast. Cover eggs with bechamel, made with butter, flour and chicken broth, to which you add the tomato sauce. Serve them with fried sausages. Serves 3.

EGGS FLAMENCO STYLE (1)
(Huevos a la Flamenca)

6 ozs. ham, cut into pieces
6 oz. string beans, cut
   French style and cooked
6 oz. *chorizo* (red sausage)
1/4 cup oil
6 eggs

1 lb. tomatoes, peeled and
   chopped
1 clove garlic, minced
1 medium onion, chopped
1/2 cup cooked peas

Heat the oil in a frying pan. Add onion and garlic and sauté until golden. Add ham, sauté it for 2 minutes; add tomatoes and cook for 10 minutes. Season with salt and pepper. Add string beans, the peas, and sausage, finely sliced. Divide sauce into 3 individual casseroles. Break eggs over sauce and put in the oven (425°F.) until eggs are set. Serves 3.

EGGS FLAMENCO STYLE (2)
(Huevos a la Flamenca)

8 eggs

5 oz. can tomato paste
diluted with equal amount
of water

1 small onion, chopped fine

3 tablespoons olive oil

1/2 lb. boiled ham cut in
squares

salt and pepper to taste

Heat olive oil in frying pan. Add onion and sauté until tender.
Add tomato paste and cook slowly for 5 minutes. Divide
tomato sauce among 4 individual casseroles followed by the
ham that has been also divided into four portions. Break 2
eggs in each casserole. Bake 10 minutes in 400°F. oven or until the eggs are done. Serves 4.

GYPSY EGGS
(Huevos Gitanos)

6 eggs

1/3 cup oil

2 cloves garlic

12 almonds, slivered

1/2 slice bread

1/2 teaspoon saffron

1/2 teaspoon cumin seeds

a pinch of cinnamon

salt and pepper to taste

Heat the oil in a frying pan. Sauté garlic, almonds and bread
until golden in color. Remove from heat. Place saffron and
cumin in a mortar and mash well; add almonds, cinnamon
and a few drops of oil from pan. When you have a smooth
paste add the rest of the oil and enough water to make a medium thick sauce. Season to taste. Boil sauce 1 minute and
put into a fireproof casserole. Break eggs over sauce and bake
a few minutes in a hot oven (425°F.) until egg whites are set.
The yolks should be soft. Serve with buttered toast. This egg
dish can be also cooked on top of the stove. Serves 3.

EGG DOLLS FOR CHILDREN'S PARTIES
(Muñecos de Huevo, Para Fiestas de Niños)

1 hard-boiled egg for each   anchovies
     child   tomatoes
olives

Cut a tip from each egg (about 1/3 of the egg) and put aside
to be used as hats. Place the eggs flat side down on a dish.
This part will be the body. The heads are olives, fastened with
toothpicks to the eggs at the top. Slice anchovies into thin
strips and pin them onto the olives as pigtails. Top with the
"hats." Slice the tomatoes and fasten them with toothpicks into position as umbrellas for the dolls. Serve with a festive-
looking potato salad.

EGGS LAS PALMAS STYLE
(Huevos a Las Palmas)

4 eggs   2 teaspoons mustard
2 tablespoons finely chopped   1/2 teaspoon salt
     onion   1/2 teaspoon paprika
3 tablespoons butter   1/2 cup milk
2 cups canned tomatoes   2 teaspoons Worcestershire
3 tablespoons flour   sauce

Brown onion in butter. Add drained tomatoes, flour, mustard,
paprika and salt. Beat eggs, add the milk, continue beating
and add to the skillet. Add Worcestershire sauce, and stir until done to your taste. Serve on toast. Serves 4 to 6.

SPRINGTIME EGGS
(Huevos Primavera)

6 eggs   1 oz. grated cheese
1 lb. string beans   3 tablespoons oil
6 small tomatoes   sprig of parsley
1 oz. ham, chopped   1 teaspoon salt
1/2 cup stock   butter
1 onion
1 tablespoon grated bread
     crumbs

Cut string beans French style and cook in salted water, uncovered to preserve their color. Wash the tomatoes and scoop out the pulp. Sauté onion in oil, add the chopped pulp from tomatoes and the chopped ham. Continue cooking until vegetables are done and add bread crumbs. Let the mixture cool and stuff the tomatoes with it. Put the stuffed tomatoes in a buttered dish, dot each tomato with a small piece of butter and put in the oven for 20 minutes, at 425°F. Butter a large oven dish, place the tomatoes around the string beans which are placed in the center. In between each tomato break one egg at a time. Season with salt, pour in the stock, sprinkle with cheese and cook in the oven for a few minutes until the eggs are set. Serves 6.

DOS AND DON'TS ABOUT OMELETS

Never use an sticky pan to make an omelette. If you like omelets and make them often, have a special pan for this purpose. An omelet pan must be cured, or treated, and there are many ways to do it. The Spanish way is as follows:

For a new or rusty pan: Rinse the pan well with cold water. Pour milk into pan and bring it to a boil. This seals the porous surface. Allow milk to cool and discard it. Scrub with an "estropajo" (a sponge of natural fibres)—a plastic sponge makes a wonderful substitute—until all milk particles are removed. Dry the pan, holding it above a burner, then sprinkle salt inside the pan and shake well over heat until salt gets hot. Discard salt and wipe the pan with paper. Pour a little oil inside the pan and spread it all over the pan surface, rubbing well with a paper.

A 7-inch pan is ideal for making 2- or 3-egg omelets.

The eggs should be lightly beaten, just long enough to blend yolks and whites.

Simple steps to make an omelet:

1. Beat the eggs and add the seasoning.

2. Add butter or oil to pan, and when it sizzles or begins to smoke, add eggs.

3. When omelet is almost set, take the pan by the handle and shake vigorously to loosen omelet from bottom.

4. Add filling, fold over with the back of a fork, holding the pan at an angle to brown the sides of the omelette.

5. To serve: Slide omelet from pan to plate.

Fillings for omelets:

Asparagus: Add cooked and sautéed asparagus tips.

Cauliflower: Cooked and sautéed in butter, or sliced and creamed.

Chicken: Chopped and creamed.

Cheese: Sprinkle 2 tablespoons of cheese on omelet before folding it.

Chicken livers: Cooked in any fashion and minced (see recipes).

Kidneys: Cooked in any fashion and minced (see recipes).

Seafood: Crabs, shrimps, mussels, sautéed in butter and minced.

Tomato: Slice it featherwise. Sauté in butter, drain excess juice.

Omelets are wonderful money-savers because any bits of left-overs can be used for filling; sautéed alone or combined with chopped onion, green pepper etc.

An omelet for dessert is always spectacular, whether flambéed or not, and many times you will find that it is a lifesaver when you do not have the time or have forgotten to make a dessert. Here also any bits of jam, marmalades, or canned fruits can be used as fillings. To make a sweet omelet, add from 1/4 to 1/2 teaspoon sugar for 1 egg and use a pinch of salt.

SPANISH POTATO OMELET
(*Tortilla Española*)

The Spanish potato omelet is undoubtedly the most Spanish of all omelets. To assure a perfect result, the potatoes and onion should be cooked very slowly and be completely done before anything else is added. The Spanish cooks say that the *"tortilla española es muy agradecida,"* which really means that the Spanish omelet is very flexible, lending itself to many marvelous combinations. You can add to it anything you want; ham, sausages, peas, asparagus, tomato, or many things combined, and you will find the results always rewarding. When finished this omelet must be round in shape, golden brown on both sides and juicy in the middle. It can be eaten hot or cold, cut into small squares to be served at cocktail parties and it is also wonderful to take on picnics, as it always retains shape, flavor and moisture.

CLASSIC SPANISH OMELET (1)
(*La Clásica Tortilla Española*)

4 eggs, beaten

4 large potatoes, peeled and chopped fine

1 medium onion, peeled and minced

1-1/2 cups olive oil

salt and pepper to taste

Use an 8-inch heavy skillet. Warm the oil, add the potatoes and onion and cook over low heat, very slowly. Do not allow vegetables to brown; they should simmer in the oil until very soft. Press with a fork as they cook so they puree a bit. Sprinkle with salt. Drain excess oil. Beat the eggs until foamy, add one third at a time to the pan, lifting up as the egg firms to allow uncooked egg to run under. Repeat until all egg has been added. Cook until lightly browned on bottom, lifting up with a spatula to prevent sticking. Invert a plate over pan, turn over so the browned part of the omelet is on top. Scrape out any bits sticking to the pan. If necessary add a little more oil. The pan must be coated with oil. Slide omelet back in again, with the browned side up and cook until the underside is golden. Makes 4 servings.

SPANISH POTATO OMELET (2)
(Tortilla Española)

3 medium potatoes, cut in   1 medium onion, sliced fine
    thin slices   4 eggs
1/4 cup chopped ham

Warm a big frying pan on the fire, then add a large quantity
of olive oil. When it begins to smoke, take it off the fire and
cool a little. Add the chopped ham. Add the onion and simmer until soft. Add the potatoes and cook until soft.
Thoroughly drain off the excess oil. Put back into the pan,
sprinkle with salt and add the well-beaten eggs. Cook as indicated above.

SPANISH OMELET (3)
(Tortilla Española)

Here is a foolproof recipe for *tortilla española*. If you follow
these instructions carefully you will not be disappointed with
the result.

This omelet is juicy inside, and nicely browned on both sides.

1 lb. potatoes, very thinly   1-1/2 cups oil
    sliced   4 large eggs
1 medium onion, sliced thin   salt and pepper to taste

Heat a 10-inch frying pan, pour in the oil and when it begins
to smoke remove from fire and add the onions. Stir well.
When onion starts to take color, add the potatoes and return
pan to the fire. Cook the potatoes very slowly until very soft,
stirring often and pressing with the fork as you stir them.
Remove potatoes from oil, and add to the beaten eggs. Mix
well. Season to taste with salt and pepper. Drain all but 1
tablespoon of oil from pan. Pour back into pan the potato
mix. Form the omelet and brown well. To brown the other
side, invert plate over top of pan and turn over. Add another
tablespoon oil to pan, slide omelet back in again and brown
the other side. Serves 4.

SPANISH OMELET (4)
(Tortilla Española)

6 eggs
1/2 teaspoon salt
1/4 teaspoon pepper
1 lb. potatoes, sliced thin

2 tablespoons butter
1 teaspoon chopped parsley
1 cup cream
1-1/2 cups oil

Cook potatoes in the oil until soft. Drain off oil. Beat the eggs with the parsley and cream; season to taste. Heat the butter in a frying pan and when it sizzles, add the egg mixed with the drained potatoes. Reduce heat and when the omelet is set, turn it over. Serves 4 to 6.

CHEESE OMELET
(Tortilla de Queso)

2 tablespoons butter
6 eggs
1/2 teaspoon salt

a pinch of nutmeg
3/4 cup whipping cream
2 oz. grated cheese

Beat the cream lightly. Beat the eggs and fold the cream into the eggs. Put in the cheese and seasoning and pour in frying pan, where you have melted the butter. Reduce heat and when the omelet is set, fold in half or in thirds and serve immediately. Serves 3.

BASQUE OMELET
(Pipérada)

A pipérada is not quite an omelet nor quite scrambled eggs, but something in between:

2 tablespoons olive oil
1 small green pepper
1 small onion
4 eggs

1 small clove garlic
1 large ripe tomato
2 tablespoons chopped ham
1 tablespoon butter

In the oil sauté the finely chopped onion, green pepper and garlic. Add tomato, peeled and seeded and finely chopped.

Add the ham and simmer for about 20 minutes. When the vegetables are soft, stir in the butter, let it melt and add the slightly beaten eggs. Season to taste with salt and pepper, stir just once or twice, wait for the eggs to set and serve directly from pan. Serves 2.

OMELET WITH HERBS
(Tortilla de Yerbas)

6 eggs
3 tablespoons water
salt and pepper to taste
1 teaspoon chopped parsley

1 teaspoon chopped chives
2 teaspoons chopped chervil
1 tablespoon butter

Add water to eggs and season with salt and pepper. Stir in the herbs. Put the butter in an omelet pan just hot enough to make it sizzle. Pour in the eggs and stir with a fork. Shake the pan so the omelet does not stick to bottom. As soon as it is set, fold over. It should be cooked through but soft. Serves 3.

CHICKEN LIVER OMELET
(Tortilla de Higados de Pollo)

4 eggs
1/2 lb. chicken livers,
    chopped fine
2 tablespoons beef broth
1/4 cup wine

1 teaspoon tarragon
2 oz. pine nuts
2 oz. chopped mushrooms
3 oz. butter
1/8 cup flour

Cook chicken livers in broth mixed with the wine and tarragon. Make a roux with 1 tablespoon butter and the flour and add to livers. Mix well. In 1 tablespoon butter sauté mushrooms, season with salt and pepper. Beat eggs and make the omelet over low heat. Add the liver mixture to the mushrooms. When the omelet is cooked outside but still runny inside, add half of the liver-mushroom mixture, pouring it on the omelet. Fold it over and cook 1 minute more. Turn it out on a platter and garnish with the rest of the liver-mushroom mixture and chopped parsley. Serves 3.

OMELET PASTEL
(Pastel de Tortillas)

Make several 8-inch omelets:

1 potato omelet, 1 spinach omelet, 1 artichoke omelet and 1 peas-ham omelet	2 cups bechamel sauce 2-1/2 oz. Parmesan cheese

Place the potato omelet on a buttered round oven dish. Spread some bechamel sauce on omelet. Stack the other omelets, on top of the first, using the bechamel in between as filling. Cover the "pastel" with the rest of the bechamel and sprinkle with the cheese. Place in a 425°F. oven for about 10 minutes or until cheese melts. Serves 4.

For buffet suppers make several 10-inch Omelet Pastels. You can combine any flavor you wish. These are delicious and a conversation piece.

CHEESE OMELET MANCHEGO STYLE
(Tortilla de Queso a la Manchega)

1-1/2 cup Manchego cheese 1 cup milk 3 eggs	3 tablespoons butter 1/2 teaspoon salt pinch of pepper

Dice the cheese finely and combine with milk. Let it stand overnight. Drain, reserving milk. Beat eggs until fluffy. Over very low heat melt butter and add cheese with 1/4 cup of the milk. Stir until cheese is completely melted. Remove from heat, add salt and pepper and the beaten eggs. Continue cooking slowly until the mixture is creamy, but not dry, about 5 minutes. Serve over toast. Serves 4.

OMELET MERCEDES
(Tortilla Mercedes)

8 eggs
1/4 cup spinach puree
4 tomatoes
salt and pepper to taste
1 clove garlic
2 teaspoons parsley, minced

1/2 lb. mushrooms
2 shallots, chopped
3 oz. red sausage, sliced
1 egg yolk
1/4 cup beef stock

Make 2 omelets, the first one with 4 eggs, the spinach and sautéed shallots. This omelet should be green. The second one should be the same size and it is made with the chopped tomatoes, parsley and seasoning.

In another pan sauté chopped mushrooms with the sausage and chopped parsley. Add stock and reduce. Beat the egg yolk and add to mixture. Place the spinach omelet on a platter, use mushroom-sausage mix as filling, and cover with the tomato omelet. Serves 4.

NATURAL OMELET
(Tortilla Natural)

4 eggs
2 tablespoons water

salt to taste
1 tablespoon butter

Beat the eggs with water and salt. In an omelet pan, melt the butter and pour in the eggs. Mix well with a fork until eggs begin to set. Turn it over and brown the other side. Serves 2.

MIXED OMELET (Tortilla Compuesta): Make it the same way as the Natural Omelet but add cheese, any cooked vegetable, chopped, or chopped meat, ham or fish.

KIDNEY OMELET (Tortilla de Riñones): Just before folding place in the center kidneys that have been sautéed in butter and cooked with sherry or dry white wine. (See kidney recipes). Fold, and when edges are set shake the pan well so the kidney juice penetrates the eggs.

89

EGGPLANT OMELET (*Tortilla de Berenjenas*): Dice egg-plant, sauté in oil, season. Add the beaten eggs. When one side is done, cover pan with a plate and turn it over. Slide omelet back into the pan to brown the other side.

SQUASH OMELET (*Tortilla de Calabacines*): Just like eggplant omelet.

FILLED OMELET
(*Tortilla Rellena*)

Make 2 natural omelets, removing them from pan when only the bottom side is brown. Place the first one in a well-oiled round casserole, add any desired filling, cover with the second omelet, raw side down, and seal the edges with raw egg whites. Add to casserole 1/4 cup water, and simmer 3 minutes. Make a sauce combining: 1/4 cup ground almonds, 2 tablespoons bread crumbs, 1 teaspoon chopped parsley, 2 tablespoons oil and enough milk to make a paste. Season to taste and spread over the omelet. Cook 3 more minutes before serving. Serves 4 to 6.

RUM OMELET
(*Tortilla al Ron*)

2 eggs	1/2 teaspoon sugar
1 tablespoon milk	1 tablespoon rum
pinch of salt	butter

Beat eggs with milk and rum. Add salt and sugar. Melt butter, and when it starts to sizzle, add the egg mix. Work the eggs with a fork until they are almost set, let it brown a bit and turn it over with the back of the fork. Roll it a bit so it browns well. Remove omelet to a flameproof platter; dust abundantly with powdered sugar. Heat 1/2 cup rum over warm water, pour it over the omelet and ignite. Serve the omelet while still flaming. Serves 1.

RUM OMELET SOUFFLE
(Tortilla Soufflé al Ron)

8 eggs, separated
1-1/2 oz. rum
1/2 cup sugar
1 tablespoon butter

1/2 teaspoon vanilla
1 cup brandy, warmed over
   hot water

Beat the egg yolks with the sugar. In another bowl beat the
whites until stiff and fold into the yolks. Add rum and vanilla
and pour into a buttered soufflé dish. Bake twenty minutes in
a 425°F. oven. Remove from oven, pour warmed brandy over
and ignite. Serve immediately. Serves 4 to 6.

APPLE OMELET
(Tortilla de Manzanas)

4 medium apples
1/4 cup flour
pinch of salt
3 eggs

1/2 cup sugar
1 cup milk
1 cup rum
2 tablespoons butter

Peel and core the apples and cut into very thin slices. Cover
with half of the sugar, pour over the rum and let them rest for
1 hour.
Mix remaining sugar and flour, and add the milk little by little, stirring all the time to make a creamy mixture. Add the
beaten eggs and apples to flour mixture. Melt butter in an
omelet pan until it sizzles. Make omelet in the usual way, fold
it over, sprinkle with powdered sugar and serve immediately.
Serves 2.

ASTURIAN DESSERT OMELET
(Postre Tortilla Asturiana)

7 eggs
6 tablespoons flour
1 grated lemon rind

3/4 cup sugar
4 cups milk

Separate eggs. Beat yolks with the sugar, flour and lemon rind. Add 2 cups warm milk. Cook this mixture over low fire until you get a thick custard. Remove from fire. Cool. Beat the egg whites until stiff and fold into the custard. Grease the inside of two shallow pans and pour the mixture into them. Put pan in a 375°F. oven for 15 minutes, until set. Invert the omelet onto a platter, spread the middle with cream, or jelly and place the second omelet on top. Sprinkle with powdered sugar and burn a design on top with a hot poker. Serves 10.

BASQUE OMELET
(Tortilla Vasca)

6 eggs	2 tablespoons butter
1 cup croutons	1 teaspoon pimiento juice
1 teaspoon onion juice	4 oz. Parmesan cheese
salt and pepper to taste	1 tablespoon cream
4 tomatoes	1 cup ham, chopped

Beat the eggs until foamy, add cheese, ham and croutons. Season with salt and pepper, mix well. Add the rest of the ingredients. Oil well the bottom of a 10-inch frying pan. Heat, pour mix in the pan, form the omelet and brown well. Cover the pan with a big lid, turn the pan upside down, leaving the omelet on the lid, then slide it back, uncooked side down, into the hot pan. Both sides should be an appetizing golden brown. Serves 4.

OMELET WITH ASPARAGUS SAUCE
(Tortilla con Salsa de Espárragos)

5 eggs	1/2 teaspoon flour
1/2 cup milk	salt to taste

Beat egg yolks with the flour. In another bowl beat the egg whites and when almost stiff fold in the yolks. Pour into a well-buttered frying pan. The omelet should be golden on both sides. Place omelet on a platter and cover with Asparagus Sauce:

| 1 tablespoon butter | 1 tablespoon flour |
| 1 cup asparagus tips, canned | 1/2 cup coffee cream |

Melt butter, add flour and mix well. Add hot cream, little by little, stirring all the time. Cook 10 minutes in all. Add asparagus tips. Serves 3.

CHEESE AND CROUTONS OMELET
(Tortilla de Queso y Picatostes)

1/2 cup hot croutons	1 tablespoon hot butter
5 eggs	
2 tablespoons grated	
Gruyère cheese	

Beat eggs and pour into hot butter in the omelet pan. Put on the croutons and sprinkle with the cheese. Fold the omelet over quickly and slide onto a hot dish. Serves 3.

RIOJA OMELET
(Tortilla Riojana)

6 eggs	1/2 lb. *chorizo* (red
2 oz. ham, chopped	Spanish sausage), sliced
salt and pepper to taste	thin
2 tablespoons oil	2 red pimientos

Fry the ham and sausage together. Cut the pimientos into square pieces; add to the frying pan. Beat the eggs, pour into the frying pan with all the ingredients. Season to taste. Make a round omelet. Do not fold it. Serves 4.

SOUFFLES WITHOUT TOIL OR TEARS

There is no mystery about soufflé making, no reason for the beginning cook to be afraid to try her hand at it. A soufflé is only a creamy sauce, thick or runny, to which the egg yolks are added and well beaten in. Then any desired ingredient is added, and left to cool slightly. Then the stiffly beaten egg whites are folded in. The soufflé dish should be prepared ahead of time. For entrée soufflés, the dish is buttered and sprinkled with fine bread crumbs. For dessert soufflés, the dish is buttered and sprinkled with sugar. A soufflé made with a thick sauce can wait to be cooked; a soufflé made with a runny sauce, (usually dessert soufflés) must be cooked right away. A rule of thumb is: When the sauce is heavy and sticks to the spoon and separates from the sides of the pan, you can wait to cook the soufflé. When the sauce is thin, and just coats the spoon, cook your soufflé immediately. When you cook soufflé made with a thick sauce, you can turn it around, you can open the door while it is cooking, even bang it, and nothing will happen to your soufflé. When you cook a delicate soufflé, made with a light sauce, cook it immediately, do not open the door; it will fall.

The success of a soufflé depends very much on the way the egg whites are beaten. The conservative cook always beats the egg whites with a wire whisk—the balloon type is considered best, as it incorporates more air into the egg whites. Bowl and beater must be immaculately clean; any grease particles or yolk bits will prevent egg whites from rising. If you use an electric beater, beat the egg whites at moderate speed, adding a pinch of cream of tartar to them. In Spain many professional cooks have a copper bowl to beat egg whites for soufflés. They say that by using it the egg whites fluff more. Even when these cooks prepare soufflés for a large number of people, as in a banquet, the egg whites are beaten by hand. It is a glory to see, in the kitchen of some leading restaurants, four or five young *pinches de cocina* (kitchen helpers) in their fresh white uniforms, beating the egg whites for the soufflés in sparkling copper bowls. Normally in these restaurants mechanical beaters are used for beating anything else, but the soufflé is the exception.

Oven Temperature: Here the opinions are divided. Some chefs recommend a low temperature, about 325°, and a longer cooking period; others prefer 475° and a shorter cooking period. A soufflé cooked slowly is firmer and cuts clean; a soufflé cooked at high temperature is creamy inside with a golden crust on top. If the soufflé dish is set in a pan with about one inch of boiling water and cooked at low temperature, it can not fail. I always recommend this system to young brides who are not yet expert cooks.

BASIC DESSERT SOUFFLE

1/4 cup butter
1/4 cup flour
1 cup milk
5 tablespoons sugar

4 eggs, separated
2 teaspoons vanilla
pinch of salt

Melt butter over low heat. Add flour and cook 1 minute, without browning it. Add milk and 4 tablespoons of sugar, stirring well. When sauce coats the spoon, remove from fire. One by one beat in the egg yolks, blending well. Add vanilla. Let it cool. Beat egg whites until soft peaks are formed. Add the remaining tablespoon sugar. Continue beating until stiff. Fold into custard mixture, using a large serving fork to lift the whole from bottom up. Do not worry if white strips of egg whites are shown. Pour into a 1-1/2 quart soufflé casserole, which you have prepared ahead of time by buttering and sprinkling with sugar, and bake 40 minutes in a 375° preheated oven. To test, insert from side to center a clean thin wire. If it comes out clean the soufflé is ready. Serve immediately. Makes 4 to 6 servings.

Instead of vanilla any other flavor can be added.

For fruit soufflés, use 1/2 cup of fruit pulp, reducing the milk to 1/2 cup.

Orange Soufflé: Instead of vanilla, use 1/3 cup orange juice and 2 tablespoons orange rind.

Lemon Soufflé: Instead of orange juice and rind, use lemon.

Mocha Soufflé: Use 3/4 cup very strong coffee and 1/4 cup cream in place of the milk, adding to it 2 squares chocolate, melted over hot water.

BASIC ENTREE SOUFFLE
(Suflé Básico Para Primer Plato)

1/4 cup butter or margarine	salt and pepper to taste
1/4 cup flour	10 oz. any desired chopped cooked vegetable, fish or meat, well drained
1 cup milk	
4 eggs, separated	pinch of nutmeg

In a heavy pan, over low heat, melt butter, add flour and cook for 1 minute without browning it. Gradually stir in the milk and bring it to a boil. When sauce sticks to spoon it is ready. Remove from heat and beat in the egg yolks one by one until well blended. Stir in your chosen ingredient and let it cool slightly. Beat egg whites until stiff peaks form. Stir about 2 tablespoons egg whites into yolks mixture. With the aid of a large serving fork, lifting the mixture from bottom up, fold in the rest of the egg whites. It does not matter if a few streaks of egg white remain. Carefully pour mix into a 1-1/2 quart prepared soufflé dish. Bake at 375° preheated oven, 35 to 40 minutes. Serves 4.

Serve with a cheese sauce, if desired.

HAKE SOUFFLE
(Sufle de Merluza)

2 lbs. poached hake, flaked	1 cup milk
2 tablespoons butter	3 eggs
1 onion, finely chopped	seasoning
2 tablespoons flour	

Sauté onion in butter until tender. Add the flour and cook together for a moment. Add hake, season, and add the milk gradually, stirring all the time. When sauce thickens, remove from fire. Let mixture cool, correct seasoning and add the 3 well-beaten egg yolks. Fold in the well-beaten egg whites. Pour the mix into a well-greased soufflé dish, dot with butter and bake 20 minutes in a 425°F. preheated oven. Serves 4.

CHEESE SOUFFLE
(Suflé de Queso)

1/4 cup butter	1 teaspoon salt
1/4 cup flour	1/8 teaspoon paprika
1 cup milk	pinch of nutmeg
1 cup grated Gruyère cheese	4 eggs, separated

Melt butter, stir in flour and cook for a minute. Add milk, stirring constantly until mixture thickens. Add cheese and seasoning. Stir until cheese is completely blended. Remove from fire and slowly add well-beaten egg yolks. Cool. Fold in stiffly beaten egg whites. Pour in a soufflé dish. Place dish in a pan of hot water and bake 1 hour at 350°F. This soufflé will not fall. Serves 3 to 4.

SAUCES

Sauces play a leading role in Spanish cooking. Many of the best dishes owe their appearance, aroma and taste to the skillful blending of flavors in the sauce that accompanies them. In most cases, as has already been mentioned, the dish and its sauce are prepared together to form an inseparable combination; however, there are typically Spanish sauces that are prepared apart and used as the occasion demands. Of these the best known is mayonnaise or *mahonesa*, named after the city of Mahon in the island of Minorca, where the French found it, picked it up and popularized it.

Ali-oli (literally "garlic-oil"), an invariable accompaniment to many dishes, particularly fish and seafood, on the Mediterranean coast, is probably one of the oldest culinary preparations still in existence. When the Romans came to Spain in the second century B.C., they brought with them olive oil, and the garlic which they prized not only for its flavor, but also for its medicinal value. They also brought this sauce, a combination of the two, in the same form as it exists today. But they had not invented it; they found it in Egypt where it was already old and, in typical Roman fashion, adopted it. It became popular in Spain and even spread beyond its borders—among other places it crossed the Pyrenees to France where it is now called *aïoli* or *beurre de provence* ("Butter of Provence").

MAYONNAISE NO. 1
(Salsa Mahonesa)

2 raw egg yolks   1 cup oil
pinch of salt and pepper
1 tablespoon wine vinegar or
   lemon juice

Put egg yolks with salt and pepper into a deep bowl. Beat

hard until they thicken, then add vinegar or lemon juice drop
by drop until the yolks are diluted.

When it is smooth and without any lumps, add oil very
slowly, beating all the time. Correct seasoning.

The oil thickens the sauce. If it becomes too thick, add a few
more drops of vinegar or lemon, or both, and some more oil
until sufficient quantity of mayonnaise is obtained. Two egg
yolks can make up to 2 cups of mayonnaise, using 2 cups of
oil. If more mayonnaise is needed, more yolks must be added
or the sauce will curdle.

MAYONNAISE FOR FISH

Add 1 teaspoon garlic, well crushed, blending it well with the
sauce.

Pepirrana

No set amount of ingredients are given for this sauce, which
is more or less like a salad.

green peppers	cucumbers
onions	olive oil
mint leaves	vinegar
tomatoes	salt

Chop all the ingredients very fine. Make a dressing with the
oil and vinegar and add to the vegetables. Let it rest 15
minutes. When ready to serve add salt to taste. Serve it with
meat, potatoes or fried fish.

MAYONNAISE NO. 2
(*Mahonesa*)

2 egg yolks	1 cup olive oil
1/2 teaspoon salt	2 tablespoons lemon juice
1 teaspoon vinegar	dash of white pepper

Beat the egg yolks with rotary beater or a wooden spoon; add
salt and pepper and half of the vinegar. Add olive oil drop by

drop at first, beating continually, until a little more than 1/4 cup of oil has been added. Still beating, add the rest of the vinegar and lemon juice in drops and the rest of the oil in a thin stream.

When you make mayonnaise take your time; do not rush it and you will avoid curdling. If it should curdle, wash the beater, and in another bowl beat 1 egg yolk. Add it very slowly to the curdled mayonnaise to form a new emulsion.

MAYONNAISE FOR LOBSTER
(Mahonesa para Langosta)

To the basic mayonnaise add 1 garlic clove crushed, 2 tablespoons Worcestershire sauce, and 1 tablespoon of brandy. Add a little more salt if needed.

MAGIC MAYONNAISE
(Mahonesa Mágica)

1 cup lemon juice or vinegar	1 egg yolk
1/4 cup olive oil	1 teaspoon salt
2/3 cup milk	1 teaspoon mustard

Place all these ingredients in a glass jar with a well fitted lid. Shake 2 minutes. Use as a salad dressing or in any dish that requires a thin mayonnaise.

ALI-OLI

3 cloves garlic	1 cup olive oil
1 tablespoon vinegar or lemon juice	salt and pepper to taste

In a mortar put the garlic and mash it well with the pestle until you have a very smooth paste. Add lemon juice, or vinegar, drop by drop, and the oil in a very thin stream, mixing all the time in the same direction. Season with salt and pepper. You should have a perfect emulsion. If you want to simplify the making of this sauce, add one egg yolk. Use *ali-oli* with fish, seafood, meat, etc., or anywhere you would use a commercial garlic spread.

Note: If the sauce curdles during the preparation or gets too thick, add a few drops of cold water, mixing well until you get the desired consistency.

ALI-OLI (2)

4 cloves garlic	1 cup olive oil
1 egg yolk	juice of 1 lemon
pinch of salt	1/2 tablespoon cold water

Place garlic cloves in a mortar and mash well with the pestle until you have a very smooth paste. Add the egg yolk, pinch of salt and the oil, drop by drop, until the sauce binds. Add also, drop by drop the lemon juice and continue working the sauce wtih the pestle. Add the water. Correct seasoning.

If the sauce curdles, add another egg yolk and mix well until wholly incorporated.

DIANA SAUCE
(Salsa Diana)

1-1/2 cups prepared mayonnaise	3 tablespoons vegetable puree
1/4 teaspoon tarragon	

Boil spinach, watercress and parsley together for 3 minutes. Strain and make a puree. Pass through a sieve with 2 tablespoons mayonnaise. Blend well into the rest of the mayonnaise. Serve with meat or fish.

SEASIGHT SAUCE
(Salsa Miramar)

1 cup mayonnaise	1/4 cup sherry
1 teaspoon tomato sauce	1 tablespoon dry mustard

Mix well all these ingredients.

This sauce is excellent for fish or other seafood.

GREEN SAUCE WITH ALMONDS
(Salsa Verde con Almendras)

To 1 cup prepared mayonnaise add 3 tablespoons spinach puree, and 1/4 cup ground, blanched, toasted almonds. Use with fried fish, steaks, or boiled potatoes.

CUCUMBER SAUCE FOR SALMON
(Salsa de Pepinos para Salmón)

1 small firm cucumber	1 cup whipping cream
2 tablespoons vinegar	salt and pepper to taste

To assure the success of this recipe all the ingredients must be cold. Grate the cucumber. Beat the cream until firm. Add the vinegar and cucumber when ready to serve.

SAUCE FOR ALL DARK MEATS
(Salsa para Todas las Carnes Obscuras)

1-1/3 cups dry white wine	1 sprig thyme
2 tablespoons chopped mushrooms	1/4 teaspoon tarragon
4 leeks, finely chopped	1/4 small bay leaf
	1-3/4 cups meat juice

The meat juice may be a commercial extract, diluted, or you may obtain it by pressing the juice from raw slices of beef. Mix the wine with the five next ingredients and reduce over low fire to half its volume. Strain. Add meat juice and reduce again to half of its volume. Strain and add to the following sauce, blending well:

4 oz. butter	salt and pepper to taste
1 tablespoon chopped parsley	juice of 1 lemon

In a heavy pan melt the butter. Add lemon juice, salt and pepper stirring well all the time with a wooden spoon. Add parsley when ready to serve.

102

SAUCE FOR GRILLED SEAFOOD OR FISH
(Salsa para Mariscos o Pescados a la Parrilla)

1/4 lb. softened butter	1 tablespoon warm water
1 tablespoon vinegar	1/2 teaspoon salt
3 egg yolks	1/4 teaspoon white pepper

Add salt and pepper to butter and mix well. Mix yolks with water and cook for 2 minutes over very low fire. Add the butter little by little, beating all the time. Don't let it boil. Add vinegar and serve.

ANDALUSIAN SAUCE
(Salsa Andaluza)

3 egg yolks	1 tablespoon lemon juice
1/2 cup oil	salt and pepper to taste
1/2 tomato puree	
2 pimientos, mashed, and sieved	

Beat the egg yolks and add the oil drop by drop, mixing in the same direction all the time. Add tomato puree and pimientos that have been passed through a sieve. Add salt, pepper and lemon juice. Serve with cold meat or fish.

OCEAN SAUCE
(Salsa del Mar)

4 anchovies	1-1/2 cups oil
3 hard-boiled egg yolks	1/2 cup vinegar
2 raw egg yolks	salt and pepper to taste
1 teaspoon mustard	

Mash the hard-boiled egg yolks with anchovies into a very smooth paste. Add mustard and raw egg yolks, mixing well. Little by little incorporate the oil with the paste, alternating with drops of vinegar until oil and vinegar are used. Season to taste with salt and pepper.

SAUCE FOR BOILED OR BAKED HAM
(Salsa para Jamón)

2 tablespoons tomato sauce
1 tablespoon vinegar
1 tablespoon Worcestershire
   sauce

1/4 cup sweet sherry
2 tablespoons butter
1 teaspoon dry mustard

Dissolve mustard in the vinegar and sherry. Add the rest of
the ingredients. Simmer to blend the flavors, about 5 minutes.
Serve hot with the ham.

AVOCADO SAUCE FOR EGGS

1 large avocado
1/2 cup cream
1 teaspoon lemon juice

1 teaspoon cornstarch
1 tablespoon water
salt and white pepper to taste

Dissolve cornstarch in water, blend it with the cream and
cook over low fire, stirring vigorously to avoid lumps, about 5
minutes. Add salt and pepper and remove from fire. Peel the
avocado and mash it with a fork, adding the lemon juice. Pass
it through a sieve and blend into the cream. Serve immediately.

MUSHROOM SAUCE FOR STEAKS

1 lb. mushrooms, diced
2 tablespoons butter
1 tablespoon sherry

1 teaspoon flour
3 tablespoons cream
salt and pepper to taste

Melt butter, add flour and cook until golden. Add mushrooms,
cover and simmer 15 minutes, stirring occasionally. Add the
sherry and cream and remove from fire.

SAUCE CATALAN STYLE, FOR PORK OR VEAL
(Salsa Catalana, para Cerdo o Ternera)

2 tablespoons butter
1 onion, minced
2 mint leaves
1 glass sweet wine
4 tablespoons broth

2 lemons, the pulp
1 tablespoon chopped
    parsley
1 tablespoon mustard
1/2 teaspoon tarragon

Over low fire sauté onion in the butter until tender and golden in color. Add broth and tarragon and simmer for 2 or 3 minutes. Add parsley, lemon and mint and continue simmering 5 more minutes. Pass through a fine sieve. When ready to serve add mustard and wine.

SAUCE FOR CHICKEN OR OTHER BIRDS
(Salsa para Pollos o Pájaros)

2 tablespoons chicken fat
2 leeks, chopped
2-1/2 oz. butter
1 teaspoon parsley, chopped
1 tablespoon vinegar

2 cups chicken broth
2 oz. flour
1/4 teaspoon cayenne
    pepper
salt and pepper to taste

Sauté leeks in chicken fat. Add broth and vinegar; simmer to reduce it to half of its volume. Strain. Melt butter, add flour and cook for 2 minutes. Add flour mix to broth, stirring all the time. Strain; add cayenne, salt and pepper. When ready to serve, add the parsley.

ROMESCO SAUCE

A very fine Catalan sauce, served cold with shellfish.

4 big tomatoes
2 cloves garlic
6 dried red peppers
10 toasted almonds

1 pint olive oil
1 pint wine vinegar
salt and white pepper

Bake tomatoes and garlic cloves for 1 hour in a 375°F. oven.

Roast the peppers in another baking dish, taking care not to
burn them. Pound the peppers in a mortar with the almonds
(or whirl in a blender); add the garlic and then the tomatoes.
When it forms a thin paste, add white pepper to give it a
sharp taste. Stir in drop by drop, half of the olive oil; then alternate with the vinegar. Add salt to taste. Let it stand for 6
hours, then strain, beat well and serve.

COSTA BRAVA WALNUT-ANCHOVIES SAUCE

You can dress the most humble cuts of meat with this sauce.
Good on hamburgers, steaks, or grilled fish.

1 pressed garlic clove	1/2 tablespoon vinegar
3 boned anchovies	1/3 cup olive oil
5 large walnuts, shelled, peeled	

Crush together the garlic, anchovies, and vinegar. When you
have a paste add the oil, drop by drop, mixing well. (For this
operation use mortar and pestle.) You should have a very
smooth sauce. Spread over just grilled meat and keep it on the
fire 1 more minute. This recipe makes enough sauce for 2 lbs.
of steak or meat of any kind prepared in the same manner.

SAUCE CARDINAL
(Salsa Cardenal)

1 teaspoon tomato paste	1/3 cup chervil, chopped
1 cup mayonnaise	1/3 cup chives or green
2 anchovy fillets	onions, chopped
1 teaspoon capers	
1/3 cup fresh tarragon, chopped	

Mash in a mortar and sieve, or whirl through a blender, all
the above ingredients. Used with seafood or fish.

SAUCE MOSQUETERA
(Salsa Mosquetera)

1 cup mayonnaise	1 teaspoon chopped chives
1 tablespoon shallots, finely chopped	1/4 teaspoon cayenne pepper
1/4 cup dry white wine	1 tablespoon lemon juice

Blend well all the above ingredients. Used with cold seafood and fish.

SPANISH SAUCE
(Salsa Española)

1/2 cup fresh chervil, chopped	2 tablespoons chopped pickles
1/2 cup parsley, chopped	3 shallots, chopped
1 cup white bread crumbs, soaked in water	juice of 1 lemon
6 anchovies	2 tablespoons capers
	1 cup olive oil

Pound chervil and parsley in a mortar. Add squeezed bread crumbs, anchovies, pickles, shallots, lemon juice, and continue pounding until you have a paste. Add the oil in short streams to bind the sauce. Season to taste with salt and pepper and pass through a fine sieve. Used with grilled or baked fish.

FISH AND OTHER SEAFOOD

Fish is a cornerstone of the Spanish cuisine. Of the fifteen regions of the country, eleven are coastal, and there is no place farther inland than 250 miles from the sea. Many and varied are the kinds of fish available to the cook, and many and varied also are the ways in which the cooks prepare it.

A sharp distinction is made between fish *(pescado)* and other seafood *(mariscos)*. Following the Spanish practice, this chapter only takes up the preparation of true fish, that is, animals with gills and fins; another chapter is devoted to other seafood.

As far as the Spanish are concerned there are three kinds of fish, depending on the color of the flesh: red, blue or white. Any recipe applicable to any fish of one of these types can be used for any other of the same class.

A great deal of codish *(bacalao)* is used in Spain. Most of it is dried and salted, and Spanish recipes normally call for this type of cod, which requires previous preparation of soaking and desalting. If fresh or frozen cod is used in such recipes, this process is omitted.

FRIED HAKE
(Merluza Frita)

This recipe is written for hake *(merluza)*, but it is good for other white fish as well.

1-1/2 lbs. hake fillets	2 eggs
1 cup of milk	1 cup of flour
salt	oil or shortening

Never wash hake; it becomes tasteless and soggy, and does not fry very well. It is a clean fish, anyway, and does not need washing.

When you buy a fish for frying, it is better always to buy it from the center part. You can then fry it in slices with bones and skin. But the most agreeable and delicate way to eat it is to cut it into what the Spanish call *filetes*, that is to say, without either bones or skin.

Ask the man to prepare them for you. But if for some reason that is not possible, here is roughly how to proceed: buy the fish in one piece.

With scissors, cut the fins off and open the fish under the belly. With a sharp knife, separate the central bone from the sides, leaning the blade against the bone and pushing slowly inside; it is done easily, especially if the fish is fresh. Open the fish like a book and cut lengthwise in the middle where the central bone was and on each side where the meat gets thinner. The *filetes* are cut from the two center pieces. To remove the skin, pull one corner of it off with your fingers and pull the rest off carefully with the aid of a sharp knife. Repeat the same operation for the other piece, then slice each one in nice regular slices about 1/2 inch thick. Flatten each *filete* a little with the flat of the hand.

Salt them, place them flat in a hollow dish, cover them with the milk, letting them steep for 1/2 hour or more.

When it is time to fry the fish, heat plenty of oil or shortening in a deep frying pan, until smoking hot. Meanwhile break the eggs, separate the whites from the yolks, beat the whites with a fork, not stiff but just foamy.

Mix with the yolks again, dip each piece of fish in flour, then in the beaten eggs, and immediately throw them into the hot oil. They will first drop to the bottom of the pan, then come up golden and crusty.

Remove them, and drain off excess oil. Place them very hot, on a plate lined with paper towel. Serve decorated with parsley and pieces of lemon. Serves 6.

FROZEN FISH IN SPAIN

Spain has the best fleet of freezer ships in Europe; 125 modern fishing boats equipped with the most advanced quick freezing systems working on the Mediterranean, the northern coast of Spain, the African coast and other seas. The fish arrives at the market fresher than fresh fish, still retaining all the qualities of just-caught fish.

Spain has also an excellent network of warehouses, with freezer lockers, extending from the production point to all the main cities and even to small inland villages, where fresh fish was once completely unknown.

FESTIVE FROZEN HAKE TAIL
(Cola de Merluza Festiva)

1 frozen hake tail of about 2-1/2 lbs.
2 qts. water
1/2 cup white wine
1 bay leaf
6 peppercorns

1 cup mayonnaise, mixed with
1 teaspoon garlic juice
1 tablespoon lemon juice
salt and pepper to taste

In a long container place water, wine, bay leaf, peppercorns and salt and pepper to taste. Place the fish on a grill or lid inside the pan, so it just touches the water surface. Cover the pan, bring the water to a boil, reduce the fire and simmer for 40 minutes. Remove fish from water, let it cool a bit, and remove all the skin and small bones. If you wish to debone the fish completely, make a long slit the length of the fish along one side. Lift the flesh carefully with fingers and pull out the bone—it separates easily as you pull it out. Shape fish with your hand, pressing it to its original shape. Cool in the refrigerator. Cover completely with the mayonnaise. Decorate with strips of red pimientos and sliced black olives. Garnish the platter with greens and serve with your favorite potato salad. Serves 8.

PICKLED HAKE
(Merluza en Escabeche)

2 lbs. frozen hake
1/2 cup flour

salt and pepper to taste
oil to fry

Season hake, dip in flour and fry in oil until golden. Let it cool. Prepare pickling brine in the following manner:

1 cup of oil, in which the
  fish was fried
1 cup dry white wine
1/2 cup vinegar

1/2 cup water
salt to taste
6 peppercorns
1 bay leaf

Place all these ingredients in a pan. Add the fish, cover and bring it to a boil. Remove immediately from the fire and let it cool. The brine should completely cover the fish. Leave hake in brine for 24 hours. Wonderful for cold plates or to add to mixed salads. Serves 6.

Any other fish can be pickled in the same manner.

HAKE WITH HAM AND EGGS
(Merluza con Jamón y Huevos)

2 lbs. hake
1 tablespoon oil
1 tablespoon butter
6 slices of ham
1 cup white dry wine

1 oz. grated bread
1 cup fish stock
3 eggs, beaten
salt and pepper to taste

Clean the fish, split and take out the bones. Melt the butter with the oil in a frying pan and fry the slices of ham. Remove the ham. Pour the fat left in the pan into a Pyrex or other oven dish. Put the fish in the dish and pour the wine over it. Sprinkle with bread crumbs, pour in the stock, season and bake in a 400°F. oven for 20 minutes. Cover the fish with the slices of ham and pour in the well-beaten eggs. Bake until eggs are set. Serve immediately. Serves 6.

111

BAKED FISH AMANDINE
(Pescado al Horno con Almendras)

1-1/2 lb. fillets of sole, or flounder
4 tablespoons olive oil
1-1/2 teaspoons salt

1/4 cup blanched slivered almonds
3 tablespoons dry sherry

Oil well the bottom and sides of a baking dish with half of the oil. Place the fish in pan and pour the rest of the oil over it. Add the salt and sherry. Sprinkle almonds over the fish. Bake at 350° about 25 minutes. The fish should flake easily and the almonds should be delicately browned. Serves 4.

BAKED STUFFED FISH
(Pescado Relleno al Horno)

1 fish (3 lbs.)
6 slices of bread, diced
1 onion, chopped
2 tablespoons melted butter
pinch of white pepper

1/2 cup water or stock
1 teaspoon salt
1 teaspoon celery salt
pinch of sage
1/2 cup tomato juice

Fillet the fish. Mix bread, onion, seasoning, butter and stock. Place 1 layer of fillets on a greased baking dish, spread stuffing over fillets. Place second layer of fillets, skin side up. Pour tomato juice over all and bake in a 375° oven for 40 minutes.

To serve, garnish with chopped parsley and lemon wedges. Serves 6.

BAKED BREAM
(Besugo al Horno)

1 large bream (about 3 lbs.)
4 tablespoons olive oil
1 tablespoon bread crumbs
1 sprig of parsley
1 clove garlic, minced
juice of 1 large lemon
4 tablespoons cooked or
   canned peas

1/2 lb. mussels or clams
1/2 lb. mushrooms
   (optional)
1 hard-boiled egg
salt and white pepper to taste
1/4 cup dry white wine

Remove scales from fish, wash and clean thoroughly. Pat dry with a towel. Squeeze half the lemon juice inside the fish and sprinkle with salt. Place fish in a well greased pan, sprinkle with salt, remaining lemon juice, bread crumbs, parsley, and minced garlic. Bake in a 375°F. oven 25 minutes, basting occasionally with its own juice. Add wine and bake 15 more minutes. In the last 5 minutes add the peas and mushrooms to the pan.

To serve: Place fish on serving platter. Place around it steamed mussels or clams in the half shell. Fill the empty halves of the shells with the peas. Garnish with slices of hard-boiled egg. Serve with the following sauce:

Sauce: To fish juice add 4 tablespoons water and 1 teaspoon cornstarch, dissolved in 2 tablespoons cold water. Let it boil 2 or 3 minutes, stirring constantly to dissolve lumps. Season to taste and strain. Serves 6.

BAKED BREAM WITH POTATOES
(Besugo Asado con Patatas)

1 to 2 lbs. bream or bluefish
4 medium potatoes
1 large onion, sliced
1 teaspoon salt
4 tablespoons oil

3 lemon slices, 1/3 inch
   thick, cut in half
3/4 cup white wine
1/4 cup water

Wash fish and remove black membrane from cavity. Do not

remove the head. Slice potatoes thinly, mix with onion and put into greased oval casserole. Sprinkle with 1/2 teaspoon salt and the oil. Mix wine and water and add to the pan. Rub fish with the remaining salt and place on top of the potatoes. Make a few slanting incisions and wedge into each a slice of lemon. Bake in a 375°F. oven for 30 minutes. Baste occasionally, if sauce dries out add more wine. Serves 2 to 4.

BREAM AU GRATIN
(Besugo al Gratin)

1 to 2 lbs. bream or any blue fish	2 cloves garlic
	1 sprig parsley
2 onions	1 tablespoon butter
1 lb. potatoes	3/4 cup white wine
2 oz. grated bread crumbs	3 tablespoons oil
salt and pepper	

Clean fish. Peel and slice onions and potatoes. Line a greased oven dish with the onions and potatoes and sprinkle with oil. Chop the garlic and the parsley, mix with the breadcrumbs, roll the fish in the mixture, season with salt and pepper and put in the oven dish. Dot with butter. Pour the white wine over it, sprinkle with the bread crumbs and bake in a 375°F. oven for 25 minutes. Serves 4.

FILLETS OF FLOUNDER IN WHITE WINE
(Filetes de Lenguado en Vino Blanco)

1-1/2 lbs. fillets of flounder	1/4 lb. sliced mushrooms
1 cup dry white wine	2 egg yolks
salt and pepper to taste	1/2 cup cream
2 tablespoons butter	1 tablespoon chopped
1 finely chopped shallot	parsley

Spread the fillets in a shallow baking dish. Season with salt and pepper, dot with butter. Add wine, shallots and mushrooms. Bake in moderate oven (350°) 20 minutes. Drain liquid from baking pan and simmer it down to about 1 cup. Mix the egg yolks with the cream and stir carefully into the reduced fish stock. Add parsley, pour the sauce over flounder and glaze it briefly under a hot broiler. Serves 4 to 6.

RED MULLETS
(Salmonetes)

In spite of their name, *salmonetes* have nothing in common with salmon, except the color. In England they are known as red mullets. Anyway, any small red fish can be used as a substitute.

RED MULLETS MALAGUENA STYLE
(Salmonetes a la Malagueña)

6 medium-size mullets	2 cloves garlic, minced
1 tablespoon butter	2 tablespoons bread crumbs
5 tablespoons olive oil	1 tablespoon finely chopped
1 cup chopped onion	parsley
1/2 cup dry white wine	1 teaspoon lemon juice
4 large ripe tomatoes	salt and pepper to taste

Clean the fish carefully, or ask the fishman to do it for you. Do not wash them, just dry them inside and out with a dry towel. Make a few slits in the skin. Place the fish in a well-buttered casserole and set it aside.

Sauce: Heat 3 tablespoons of the oil in a frying pan and fry the chopped onion, stirring to keep it from burning. When brown, add the white wine and simmer slowly until the wine is reduced to half of its volume. Add garlic, salt and pepper and the tomatoes. Bring the mixture to a boil, reduce the heat, and simmer for 10 more minutes, crushing the tomatoes with a wooden spoon to reduce them to a paste. Pour the sauce over the fish. Sprinkle with bread crumbs and the rest of the oil. Bake at 350° for 20 or 25 minutes. Just before serving add the lemon juice and sprinkle with the parsley. Serve with parsley potatoes. Serves 6.

FRIED RED MULLETS
(Salmonetes Fritos)

6 red mullets (12 if very
  small)
2 tablespoons flour
oil for frying

2 oz. chopped parsley
1 lemon, sliced
salt and paprika to taste

Clean the fish. With a knife scrape off the scales, beginning at
the tail and proceeding toward the head. Wash quickly under
running water and dry with a towel. Season with salt and
paprika and dip in flour. Fry in deep oil until golden in color.
Drain over paper towels. To serve, garnish with slices of
lemon. Take 4 tablespoons of oil from the pan, put into a
separate pan and fry the parsley. Pour over the fish. Serves 6.

TUNAFISH MARMITE-KUA
(Atún Marmite-Kua)

1/4 cup oil
2 small onions
2 cloves garlic, minced
1 large slice of tuna (about
  1 lb.)
2 large potatoes, cubed

1 teaspoon paprika
4 pimientos, cut in strips
1/2 cup croutons
salt to taste
water

Pour the oil in an earthenware casserole, place over low fire
and when the oil is hot, add the onion and fry slowly until
golden in color. Add the fish and enough water to cover it
and the potatoes. Cook slowly 20 minutes. Add salt to taste,
paprika and pimientos. Add the croutons when ready to serve.
Serves 3.

TUNAFISH SAN SEBASTIAN STYLE
(Atún a la San Sebastian)

1 lb. tuna
1 onion
2 tablespoons flour
1 glass dry white wine
white pepper to taste

pinch of nutmeg
1 clove, crushed
oil
salt to taste

Cut tuna into 1-inch cubes. Dip in flour and fry. Drain all but

4 tablespoons oil from pan, add onion and cook until golden and tender. Put fish back in the pan; add pepper, nutmeg, clove and salt. Add wine and cover. Let it cook slowly about 15 minutes. Serves 3.

TUNAFISH PAMPLONICA
(Atún Pamplonica)

1 lb. tunafish tail
1 hard-boiled egg, chopped
2 small onions, chopped
2 small pickled cucumbers, chopped
1 tablespoon oil
1 tablespoon parsley, chopped, plus 1 sprig

1 cup mayonnaise
2 tablespoons vinegar
6 peppercorns
salt to taste

Cut fish into 1-inch slices. Place in pan with vinegar, salt, peppercorns, parsley sprig and enough water to cover the fish. Put pan on the fire, and heat it very slowly, until it boils. Simmer 5 minutes. Remove from fire and let it cool. Remove fish from the stock, being very careful not to break the slices. Place on a platter. Remove the skin and drain off any excess juice. Mix well the egg, chopped onion, pickles and parsley. Put some of the mix on every slice of fish. Serve with mayonnaise. Serves 3.

CODFISH "PIL-PIL" STYLE
(Bacalao al Pil-Pil)

2-1/2 lbs. dried codfish
5 cloves garlic
1 small cup fish stock

8 tablespoons oil
1 onion, chopped
1/2 teaspoon pepper

The secret of this dish is never to stir it. The sauce must be made by shaking the pan.

Soak codfish overnight; change the water early in the morning. When ready to prepare the fish, remove the scales, without breaking the skin. It is the skin that gives the sauce the right flavor and consistency. Cut the fish into pieces and squeeze the water out of it.

Crush the garlic, fry in the oil until dark, throw away the garlic and pour off half the oil into a saucepan. Heat and sauté the onion until tender and golden. Add the fish, skin side down, season with pepper and add the stock. Simmer for 10 minutes, shaking the saucepan often to form the sauce. When the sauce begins to thicken, add the oil left in the frying pan very slowly, still shaking the saucepan. Simmer for 15 minutes until the sauce is smooth and thick. Serve with rice or boiled potatoes. Serves 4 to 5.

CODFISH BASQUE STYLE
(Bacalao a la Vasca)

1 lb. dried codfish	flour
1/2 cup olive oil	2 tablespoons tomato sauce
6 cloves garlic, mashed	1/2 cup stock or water

Soak codfish as indicated above. Drain, skin, and cut into 2-inch cubes. Dry pieces with a towel. In a frying pan heat the oil and fry the garlic until dark bown, being very careful not to burn it. Remove garlic. Dust the fish with flour and fry in the oil. Place fish in a casserole, add the fried garlic, the tomato sauce and water or stock. Simmer 20 minutes. Serves 3.

CODFISH IN GREEN SAUCE
(Bacalao en Salsa Verde)

2 lbs. codfish	2 cloves garlic, crushed
4 tablespoons oil	1 cup fish stock
1 tablespoon vinegar	3 tablespoons chopped
1/2 teaspoon pepper	parsley
1 onion, chopped	

Soak the codfish overnight, as above, and cut into 12 pieces. Heat the oil and fry the garlic and when very brown remove from pan and discard. Add the onion and fry it lightly, add the fish, skin side up, and the parsley, the stock and the vinegar. Simmer slowly for 1 hour, shaking the pan once in a while to prevent sticking. Serves 3.

118

ZARZUELA (FISH STEW)
(Zarzuela de Pescados)

3 tablespoons olive oil
3 tablespoons butter
1 lb. halibut, cut in chunks
1/2 lb. shelled shrimps
3 or 4 rock lobster tails, cut
  in thirds
1/2 lb. mussels in shells
  (optional)
1 lb. clams
1/4 cup brandy (optional)
1/4 cup dry white wine

1 medium onion, chopped
  fine
2 cloves garlic, crushed
3 tomatoes, peeled and
  chopped or
1 lb. tomatoes, canned
salt to taste
1 tablespoon minced parsley
1 tablespoon lemon juice
croutons

Heat olive oil and butter in a heavy pan until sizzling; add fish, shrimps, and lobster and sauté, turning occasionally, until lobster shell is red and fish lightly browned. Add clams and mussels. Transfer to casserole; heat brandy in a small pan, ignite and pour, flaming, over seafood. To the first pan add minced onion and garlic, cook slowly until tender, add tomato and salt and cook until mushy. Add to the seafood in casserole with the wine. Simmer 5 minutes. Just before serving, sprinkle lemon juice and additional olive oil over seafood to glaze it. Garnish with fried croutons and parsley. Serves 6.

GALICIAN POT
(Caldereta Gallega)

1/2 lb. sea bass
1/2 lb. hake
1/2 lb. brill
1 lb. haddock
1/4 cup oil
1/2 lb. onions, coarsely
  chopped

3 cloves garlic
1 oz. flour
2 parsley sprigs
1/2 bay leaf
salt and pepper to taste
1 tablespoon vinegar

Scale and clean the fish and cut into pieces. Pour oil in a casserole and place the fish on top. Add flour, onion, garlic cloves, parsley and bay leaf. Let it rest for 2 hours. Add enough water to cover the fish. Season and cook over low fire for 20 minutes. Remove the fish to a separate warm platter.

Add the vinegar to the stock and serve it as a first course with fried bread slices or slices of bread toasted in the oven. Serve fish as a second course with any desired garnish. Serves 6.

HAKE SPANISH STYLE
(Merluza a la Española)

2 lbs. hake, center section	1/2 cup white sauce
juice of 1/2 lemon	1/4 cup chopped ham
1/2 cup bread crumbs	1 tablespoon chopped
2 eggs, beaten	parsley
1 lb. clams	

Divide the center section of the hake in long pieces about 2 inches wide. Dip the pieces in lemon juice and season with salt. Dip in beaten eggs and bread crumbs and fry. Boil the clams until shells open. Remove from shells. Dip clams and ham in the white sauce, then in the beaten eggs and bread crumbs, and fry. Put the fried clams back into their shells. Serve around the strips of hake in the same platter. Garnish with parsley and thin slices of lemon. Serves 6.

CALDERETA (FISH STEW)
(Caldereta)

1 lb. red snapper	1/2 lb. mussels or clams
1 lb. flounder	1 tablespoon parsley,
1 large onion	chopped
2 large ripe tomatoes,	2 cloves garlic
chopped and seeded	1 cup water
1/4 cup olive oil	1 cup white dry wine
1/2 lb. shrimps	1 slice of bread

For this dish you can use any combination of seafood, fish or vegetables cooked in the same manner. For a vegetable *caldereta*, omit the wine.

Sauté chopped onion in the olive oil until transparent. Add the rest of the vegetables. Add the wine and the water, the slice of bread and arrange the washed seafood on top nicely. Cover the casserole and bring it to a boil for 10 minutes. Season to taste with salt and pepper. Serves 6.

HAKE IN GREEN SAUCE
(Merluza en Salsa Verde)

A classic way of serving hake in the Basque country. There are at least six or seven different ways to prepare it, always with a base of parsley and garlic but sometimes adding asparagus tips, or green peas, often both. The recipe we give you here is the basic one with nothing more than garlic and parsley. It is simple to prepare and delicious. As in the case of many Basque specialities, it should be cooked in the typical earthenware dish or *cazuela de barro,* with a wide flat bottom and low edges.

4 slices of hake no less than 1-1/2 inches thick	4 teaspoons chopped parsley
1/2 cup flour	4 cloves garlic
1/2 cup olive oil	2 teaspoons salt
	1 cup water

Remove all the extra fins from the fish so that it has a nice round regular shape. Turn each slice around in the flour, leaving only a very slight coat of flour on it. Heat the oil in a frying pan and put the fish in it. Fry slightly on both sides. Remove it while it is still white and put each slice in the earthenware dish, allowing enough room so that they do not overlap. Pour a little of the frying oil over each slice, add salt and put on a rather low fire for 5 minutes to allow the fish to get rid of its moisture.

While it is cooking, put chopped parsley, garlic and the rest of the salt in a mortar and mash it into a fine paste. Then add the water and pour the mixture evenly over the slices of fish, moving the dish with a circular motion so that all the ingredients mix well. Let it cook on a medium fire, half covered, for about half an hour, watching that the pieces of fish do not stick to the bottom. Serve in the same earthenware dish, alone or with boiled potatoes. Serves 4.

FRIED FISH WITH SPANISH SAUCE

2 lb. fish fillets	4 onions
olive oil	2 cloves garlic
flour	6 ripe tomatoes
salt and pepper to taste	2 sweet peppers

Season fish, dust with flour and fry in plenty of olive oil.
Keep it warm. When oil has settled, pour 1/4 cup oil in
another pan. Heat and add the sliced onions, chopped garlic
and the chopped, skinned tomatoes. Cook slowly until
vegetables are soft. Season. Pour over the fish. Serve with
roasted skinned peppers cut into strips. Serves 4 to 6.

HAKE DONOSTIARRA
(Merluza a la Donostiarra)

This recipe is a speciality of one of the most famous
restaurants of Bilbao, El Antiguo, and a genuine and typical
dish of the Basque cuisine.

2 lbs. sliced hake poached 20 minutes in 2 cups seasoned water. Remove from fumé (fish broth), save liquid	1/2 lb. asparagus tips and 1/4 lb. fresh peas. Cook together, drain

Sauce:

1/4 cup oil	2 tablespoons chopped onions
2 cloves garlic	1 bay leaf
2 tablespoons flour	1/4 cup brandy (optional)
2 tablespoons chopped parsley	salt and pepper to taste

Over medium fire place earthenware casserole with the oil.
When oil is hot add onion, garlic, flour, bay leaf and parsley.
Sauté a few minutes, being careful that parsley does not
discolor. Add *fumé* and boil 2 minutes. Reduce fire. Carefully
place in casserole the cooked hake (*merluza*), garnishing
around with peas and asparagus. Cover casserole and heat 5
more minutes. Serve in the same casserole, wrapping around it
a colorful napkin. At this point, if you wish, add brandy and
ignite. Serves 6.

FILLETS OF WHITE FISH
(Bilbao)

4 fish steaks
1 tablespoon olive oil
2 cloves garlic
1 medium onion
1/2 cup flour
1 teaspoon salt
1/8 teaspoon pepper
1 tablespoon anchovy paste

1 tomato, sliced
1/2 cup black olives
3/4 cup red wine
1 tablespoon chopped parsley
1/8 teaspoon powdered tarragon

Thaw fish if frozen. Pour the olive oil in a baking dish. Mince the garlic and onion and sprinkle in the bottom of the dish. Dip the steaks in flour and place them on top of onion mix. Season with salt and pepper. Spread anchovy paste on the steaks. Place tomato slices and black olives on the fish and add the wine. Bake in moderately hot oven 20 minutes, basting frequently. Just before serving, sprinkle with parsley and tarragon.

TROUT WITH ALMONDS AND CREAM

4 small fresh trout (or two large ones)
4 tablespoons flour
1/4 lb. butter

1/2 cup blanched and slivered almonds
1/2 cup cream or milk

Clean, wash and dry trout. Dip them lightly in flour and sauté in very hot butter. Remove trout to a hot plate when they are very brown. In the butter left in the pan (add more if the pan is dry) lightly brown the blanched almonds. Add cream or milk, stir it briskly so it will take the brown color of the butter, let the liquid reduce a little, and pour this sauce over the trout. Serves 4.

FISH STEW LEVANTINE
(Cazuela de Pescado a la Levantina)

The different fish listed here are of course interchangeable: for

123

instance, you can replace the hake with any other sort of fresh codfish, the *langostinos* with shrimps, or the clams with mussels; the main thing is variety. For successful results it is necessary to keep a reasonable proportion of shellfish and crawfish with the regular fish.

7 oz. surmullet	1 big onion
7 oz. squid	3 cloves garlic
7 oz. hake	1 soup spoon tomato paste
7 oz. conger	1/2 teaspoon paprika
6 prawns (*langostinos*) small	1/2 cup water in which
size	you let stand a little
12 nice size clams	saffron
1/2 cup olive oil	flour, salt and pepper

PREPARATION: takes about 45 minutes altogether.

1) After having cleaned and boned the fish, cut it in fairly big pieces. Separate the *langostinos* from their shells. Roll fish and *langostinos* in flour and salt, and fry them fast in the olive oil without letting them cook too long. Place them in a heat resistant dish.

2) In the same oil where you have fried the fish, fry the onion, finely chopped, until it becomes a nice golden color, then add the garlic, equally finely chopped, the tomato paste, the paprika, the water with the saffron, salt and pepper and let boil for 5 minutes.

3) Wash the clams carefully, let them open over a hot fire in a frying pan. When they are open, take off the top shell and put them in their lower shell around the fish. Strain the juice left in the pan and add it to preparation No. 2. Pour the mixture over the fish that you have kept aside in your baking dish and put in the oven (350°) for 15 minutes. Before serving, adorn with a little chopped parsley and a few slices of lemon, and serve in the same dish. Serves 4.

GOLDEN PUFFS OF FRIED SOLE

1-1/2 lbs. fillets of sole or
  flounder
2 eggs, separated

2 tablespoons flour
1 teaspoon salt
1/2 cup olive oil

Cut fish into pieces about 4x3 inches. Beat the egg whites until stiff; set aside. Beat the egg yolks until thick, stir in flour and salt, then fold in the stiffly-beaten whites until well blended. Heat the olive oil in a 10-inch skillet until tiny bubbles form around edge. Dip each piece of fish in the batter and place in the hot olive oil. As soon as they are golden on one side, carefully turn with spatula to cook until golden on the other side. Serve at once with lemon wedges. Serves 6.

SOUFFLE OF CODFISH
(Suflé de Bacalao)

Codfish is a staple in most Spanish homes. It is inexpensive and adaptable to regional cooking. This recipe is a favorite Castilian dish.

2 lbs. dry cod
3 egg whites
1 cup milk
2 tablespoons flour

2 tablespoons butter
2 tablespoons grated bread
  crumbs
1/2 teaspoon pepper

Soak the codfish overnight. Next day remove the bones and skin and flake the meat.

Prepare a white sauce with the butter, flour and milk. Just before the sauce reaches the boiling point add the flaked cod.

Boil for about 10 minutes, stirring constantly. Season with the pepper and let cool. Beat the egg whites until stiff and fold carefully into the cod mixture. Pour into a buttered baking dish (an angel food cake pan will be suitable), sprinkle with bread crumbs and dot with butter. Bake in a hot oven (450°) for 18 minutes. Serve immediately. Serves 6.

Spanish people are perhaps the best seafood eaters in the world. In Madrid alone over 17 million pounds a year are consumed. The most popular because of their excellent quality and low price are the mussels *(mejillones)*, followed by the shrimps *(gambas)*, prawns *(cigalas and carabineros)*, clams *(almejas)*, squid *(calamares)* and oysters *(ostras)*.

Traditionally oysters and clams are eaten raw, with only the addition of a few drops of lemon juice or special sauce, accompanied with a good white wine or sometimes beer. In Spain, as in America, they are considered in season only during the months with an "R." It was once believed that oysters are indigestible when eaten at night. This has been proved false. Oysters have a high glycogen—sugar content that makes them very digestible. Usually what causes the trouble is the quantity of wine that is drunk with them, and other times the form of preparation, especially when they are fried.

Other famous Spanish seafoods are lobsters *(langostas)*, crabs *(cangrejos)*, sea spiders *(centollas)*, and barnacles *(percebes)*. Famous from Roman times, and still considered the best in the world, are the shrimps from Castellon de la Plana on the Mediterranean coast.

MUSSELS A LA MARINERA
(Mejillones a la Marinera)

3 lbs. mussels (or clams)
1 chopped onion
1 cup dry white wine
1/2 teaspoon pepper
3 tablespoons oil

2 cloves garlic, finely chopped
1 tablespoon bread crumbs
2 tablespoons chopped parsley

Scrub the mussels and rinse them thoroughly. Put the oil in a large pan and sauté the onion until golden. Add the garlic and the wine and then the mussels. Cover and cook over high fire until the mussels open, then simmer five minutes longer. Add the bread crumbs and the chopped parsley, shaking the pan. Simmer another five minutes. Serve with slices of fried bread if you wish. This dish does not need salt. The juice of the mussels is very salty. Serves 6.

LOBSTER WITH CHOCOLATE
(Langosta con Chocolate)

1 large lobster (about 2 lbs.)	salt and pepper to taste
1/2 lb. onions	pinch of nutmeg
1 clove garlic	1/2 oz. grated bitter
1-1/2 oz. sherry	chocolate

This recipe may sound a little peculiar but is actually delicious. Kill the lobster by plunging it head first into boiling water for 2 or 3 minutes. Then remove the intestines. Cut into pieces. Fry the chopped onion, garlic and parsley in plenty of hot olive oil. Add the sherry and a little water, and season with salt, pepper and nutmeg. Add the chocolate. Pour the mixture over the lobster, which you have placed in a fireproof dish. Cover with a tight-fitting lid and cook in a slow oven for 30 minutes. If the lobster is very large it might require a longer cooking time. Serves 2.

LOBSTER AND CHICKEN COSTA BRAVA
(Langosta con Pollo a la Costa Brava)

4 tablespoons olive oil	2 leeks, minced
1-1/2 lbs. live lobster	3/4 cup sherry
1 small chicken, cut in pieces	1/2 cup brandy
dash of pepper	1 tablespoon tomato paste
2 carrots, peeled and grated	1/2 cup beef juice*

Cut lobster in four pieces. Dust chicken with salt and pepper Sauté chicken in the olive oil until brown all over. Add lobster; cook until shell becomes bright red. Push aside; add minced carrot and leeks, cook until soft. Add wine, simmer 2 minutes. Add brandy, set aflame. When flame has burned out add tomato paste. Simmer slowly a few more minutes. Remove chicken and lobster to casserole, add beef juice to sauce remaining in pan; simmer 2 minutes. Pour sauce over chicken lobster in casserole. Serves 6.

*This may be a commercial beef extract, properly diluted, or

you may follow the Spanish method and press the juices from
thin slices of beef.

LOBSTER DIABLA
(Langosta Diabla)

1 live 1-1/2 lb. lobster
1/2 cup olive oil
1 clove garlic
3 tablespoons butter
1/2 cup mushrooms
1/4 cup chopped pimiento
1/8 teaspoon tarragon
  leaves

3 tablespoons sliced ripe
  olives
3 tablespoons grated onion
1/2 teaspoon salt
1/8 teaspoon pepper
3 tablespoons sherry

Split lobster, remove gravel sac, and reserve fat and coral.
(The fishman will do this work for you.) Heat olive oil in
large skillet and add garlic. Place lobster in the oil, split side
down. Cover and steam on medium heat for 5 minutes. Turn
lobster, cover, and continue cooking for 10 more minutes. Let
lobster cool. Remove meat from shell and cut into medium-
sized pieces. Reserve shell. Heat butter in skillet and add
mushrooms, pimientos, tarragon, olives, onion, salt, pepper
and lobster meat. Mix thoroughly and cook 5 minutes. Add
sherry and fit into shells. Top with the following sauce and
brown under broiler, about 5 minutes.

Sauce:

2 tablespoons butter
4 tablespoons sliced scallions
1 teaspoon dry mustard
1 teaspoon anchovy paste
1 hard-cooked egg yolk
2 tablespoons olive oil

2 tablespoons sherry
1 tablespoon tarragon
  vinegar
1/4 teaspoon salt
dash of Tabasco sauce

Heat butter and scallions and cook slowly for 5 minutes. Add
ingredients and spoon over stuffed lobster before broiling.
1 lobster serves 2 people.

BROILED LOBSTER
(Langosta a la Parrilla)

Preheat the broiler for about 5 minutes. Split lobster, removing the vein and sac. Arrange cut side up on the broiler pan. Season with salt and pepper and spread with butter. Broil 15 minutes for 1 lb. lobster, up to 20 minutes if the lobster is larger. Serve with a rich mayonnaise sauce.

SEAFOOD PAELLA
(Paella de Mariscos)

3/4 cup olive oil
1/4 lb. Smithfield ham (jamón serrano)
2 cloves garlic, chopped
1 small onion, chopped
2 tablespoons parsley, chopped
1/2 cup cooked peas (Save cooking water)
6 artichoke hearts, cut in halves (Save juice)
juice of 1/2 lemon
1 small can pimientos (Save juice)

1 cup rice
1/2 lb. brill, cut in small pieces
1 lb. shrimps, medium size, peeled and cleaned
1/2 lb. clams, washed and opened in half shells
6 large crawfish (cigalas)
6 small crabs
1 bay leaf
1 envelope saffron (Dry it in a warm place near stove)

Cook crawfish and crabs for 10 minutes in boiling salted water to which you have added the bay leaf. Remove the shellfish and reserve the broth.

Separate the fat from the ham. Cook the fat in the oil for 3 minutes. Add onion and 1 clove of garlic and cook until onion gets golden and transparent. Add ham. Stir well. Add brill and shrimps; sauté slowly until the fish gets nicely pink. Add 1/2 of the peas, the artichoke hearts, 1 tablespoon of parsley and the clams. Continue sautéing all this together for about 5 minutes, being careful not to let it scorch.

Pick any specks from the rice, but do not wash it. (Washing rice makes the paella mushy.) Now mix the juices you have

saved with the broth from the crabs and crawfish. Add
2-1/2 cups of this to the pan and bring it to a boil. Add rice,
sprinkling it evenly over the mixture.

While the rice cooks, make a paste of the remaining garlic,
parsley, saffron, and a little of the broth (use a mortar and
pestle for this operation). Add paste to the pan. Add lemon
juice; correct the seasoning. (Up to now you haven't used any
salt other than that in the broth and the ham.)

Sprinkle the other half of the peas over the rice. Paint crabs
with oil and place them in a closed circle in center of pan. Arrange crawfish around like the spokes of a wheel. In between
place the pimiento strips, following the wheel pattern. Let all
this simmer for another 15 minutes. Remove from fire. Cover
pan with a platter and let it stand 10 or 15 minutes in a warm
place before serving. Serves 6.

STUFFED SHRIMPS
(Gambas Rellenas)

12 uncooked jumbo shrimps	1 tablespoon grated cheese
1-1/2 cups coarse bread crumbs	1/2 cup dry white wine
1 tablespoon chopped parsley	1 teaspoon paprika
	2 anchovy fillets
	1/4 cup melted butter

Clean, shell and split the shrimps. Combine the rest of the
ingredients and stuff each shrimp with the mix. Hold together
with toothpicks. Place in a buttered casserole and bake 15
minutes in a 400° oven. Serves 4.

GYPSY SHRIMP STEW
(Estofado Gitano de Gambas)

2 lbs. large shrimps	1/4 cup olive oil
1/2 lb. peeled chopped tomatoes	1/2 cup dry white wine
1 medium onion, chopped	1/2 teaspoon saffron
1/2 green pepper, chopped	1 clove garlic, mashed
12 clams	3 tablespoons flour
	salt and paprika to taste

Peel the shrimp, remove black vein and wash well under running water. Heat the oil in a frying pan, add flour and cook 2 minutes. Add wine, onion, clams, chopped green pepper, stir well and simmer until clams open. Remove clams. Add tomatoes, shrimps and all seasoning. Simmer 20 minutes and season with salt and paprika. Remove one shell from each clam and return to pan. Serve with white rice (See recipe) Serves 6.

SQUIDS IN THEIR OWN INK
(Calamares en su Tinta)

1 lb. squids	1 tablespoon chopped
1/4 cup olive oil	parsley
1 clove garlic, minced	1 tablespoon flour
1 small onion, chopped	salt and pepper to taste
1/4 cup red wine	

Clean squids thoroughly, removing the outside skin, intestines and eyes. Wash well under running water, cut off head and tentacles. Carefully remove the ink sac and save it. Cut the body into thin rings and chop tentacles. Brown garlic in oil over low flame; add the squids and sauté 3 minutes, turning frequently. Dredge with flour. Add wine, salt, pepper and parsley, dissolve ink sac in a little water, drain and add to the pot. And chopped onion. Cover pan and simmer until tender, from 10 to 30 minutes. Remove squids to a hot platter. If the sauce is too thick, add a little more red wine. Sieve sauce and pour over the squids. Serve with rice. Serves 4.

STEWED SHRIMPS
(Gambas Guisadas)

24 large shrimps	1/4 teaspoon each: saffron,
2 onions, chopped	thyme, nutmeg
1/2 cup green pepper, chopped	1 cup dry white wine
	salt and pepper to taste
3 large tomatoes, cut up	anchovy fillets
1/2 cup olive oil	1 pimiento, canned
1 clove garlic, mashed	3 tablespoons lemon juice

Sauté chopped onion, green pepper, and tomatoes in oil. Add

131

shelled and deveined shrimps and the seasoning. Pour in wine, mashed garlic, salt and white pepper to taste. Simmer until tender, about 20 minutes. Garnish shrimps with anchovy fillets, sliced pimiento and minced parsley. Sprinkle with lemon juice. Serve steamed white rice in a separate casserole. Serves 6.

SHRIMP WITH CREAM
(Gambas a la Crema)

Butter well some individual china casseroles, and into each put 2 or 3 tablespoons of peeled shrimps. Cover the shrimps with half cream and half milk, sprinkle with fine bread crumbs, and dot with butter. Cook for 20 minutes in a 375° oven. They should be golden on the top.

SHRIMP CASSEROLE
(Cacerola de Gambas)

1 pint cooked shrimps	1 small clove garlic
2 pints mussels or clams	1 oz. flour
1/4 lb. mushrooms,	1 oz. butter
sautéed in butter	salt and paprika to taste
1 glass dry white wine	

Clean the mussels or clams and cook in a 1/2 cup water mixed with the wine. As soon as they open remove from the stock and shell. Strain the stock through a cloth. In a separate pan melt butter, add flour and cook 1 minute, without browning it. Add the stock and cook until very smooth. Add sautéed mushrooms and the shrimps. Add the mussels or clams. Pour the mixture into a well buttered casserole. Sprinkle with bread crumbs and parsley, dot with butter and put in a hot oven until golden and bubbling. Serves 4.

STUFFED MUSSELS
(Mejillones Rellenos)

4 lbs. mussels	1/4 teaspoon paprika
1 glass white wine	2 tablespoons olive oil
4 tablespoons chopped parsley	1/2 cup toasted bread crumbs
1 tablespoon green pepper, finely chopped	1/4 cup toasted chopped almonds
1 garlic clove, minced	1 tablespoon butter
2 small onions, chopped	salt and white pepper to taste

Sauté 1 onion and garlic in olive oil until tender but not brown. Add wine and half of the parsley. Add the mussels and steam until open. Remove mussels from shells. (Reserve shells.) Strain and reserve the liquid. Sauté the other onion in butter until soft, adding the green pepper and rest of the parsley. Remove from heat and add the rest of the ingredients. Add the chopped mussels and enough of the liquid to bind them together. Fill shells with the mixture, dot with butter, sprinkle with paprika and bake in hot oven (450°) until lightly browned. Serve as an entree. Serves 6.

MUSSELS IN BATTER
(Fritura de Mejillones)

2 lbs. mussels	milk
2 tablespoons flour	oil
2 eggs, separated	

Put the mussels on a hot plate to open them. Remove from the shells. Prepare a batter by mixing the flour and the egg yolks with a little milk to form the cream. Fold in the beaten egg whites. Dip the mussels into the mixture, one by one, and fry at once in very hot oil. Serves 4.

Any other shellfish can be cooked in the same manner.

CLAMS A LA MARINERA
(Almejas a la Marinera)

These are clams in a thick spicy sauce and another classic of Spanish cooking. They are generally eaten as *tapas* in Spain but they make a very good first dish especially if you serve them with a good dry white wine.

2 lbs. large clams
1/2 cup water
1 tablespoon olive oil
1 onion and 2 garlic cloves,
   both very finely chopped
1/2 cup bread crumbs

1/2 cup white wine
1 tablespoon lemon juice
1 bay leaf
pepper
1 tablespoon chopped
   parsley

1. After having very carefully washed the clams in clear water 2 or 3 different times, put them in a pan with the 1/2 cup of cold water and let them cook on a high fire. As they open, remove them, take off the top shell and put them aside in their lower shell. Strain the water left in the pan and keep it warm on a corner of the stove.

2. Fry the onion and garlic in the olive oil. When these are well browned, but not too dark, add the bread crumbs, stir a little, and add the water of the clams with the wine, the lemon juice, the bay leaf and the pepper. Bring to a boil.

3. To the gravy thus obtained, add the clams that you kept aside and let cook for 15 minutes. Just before serving, remove the bay leaf and add the chopped parsley.

The sauce must be rather thick. If it looks too thin you may add a few more bread crumbs. Serves 4.

STUFFED SQUID
(Calamares Rellenos)

This recipe is a courtesy of the Chef of the Caballo Blanco in Puerto de Santa Maria, a motel renowned for its charm and comfort.

2 pounds small squids	1 egg
1 small onion, chopped	salt and pepper to taste
1 tablespoon minced parsley	
1 cup soft bread crumbs, soaked in milk	

Have your fish dealer clean the squids thoroughly. Cut off tentacles and chop them very fine. Combine with remaining ingredients and fill the cavity of each squid with this stuffing. Sew squid closed, or fasten with toothpick. Sauté in olive oil. Remove from pan. (Save oil for the sauce).

The sauce:

4 tablespoons olive oil	1 teaspoon chopped parsley
4 tablespoons tomato sauce	1/2 teaspoon saffron
1 carrot, slivered	1 onion, finely chopped
1 glass sherry (or white wine)	1 clove garlic, minced

Brown garlic in oil, add onions and brown slightly, add the rest of the ingredients and boil five minutes. Pour over squids and simmer 45 minutes, or until tender. Serve with rice. Serves 6.

BROILED SHRIMP
(Gambas a la Parrilla)

2 lbs. large shrimps with shells	2 tablespoons Worcestershire sauce
1/2 cup olive oil	1/4 cup diced onion
1-1/2 teaspoons salt	1/2 cup wine vinegar
1 large clove garlic, minced	mixed with 1/2 cup water
1/2 cup catsup	

Combine all ingredients except shrimps to make sauce. Cook 15 minutes and strain. Place shrimps in sauce and marinate at least 1 hour before broiling. Place on grill or charcoal broiler and cook 3 minutes on each side. Serves 4.

Paella

Paella is undoubtedly the star of all Spanish cooking, the dish best known outside the country and the one that has done the most to spread the gastronomic fame of Spain. This succulent combination of rice, chicken or seafood etc., exists in many variations and is the subject of numerous recipes. It is a native of Valencia on the Mediterranean coast, where every chef has his own closely guarded secret formula for preparing it, as has every housewife. Nonetheless, in many of the restaurants that are famous for their paella you go to the dining room by first passing through the kitchen, where you can watch these expert cooks making it. And still not learn their secrets!

However, *paella* is basically a simple dish and not at all complicated to make but it is demanding, and requires the proper ingredients, utensils and procedure.

First, as to the ingredients. Don't use prepared rice of any kind. The twenty minutes that it takes to cook natural, raw rice are necessary for the flavor of the other ingredients to combine with the rice to produce one harmonious whole, and to avoid a flat, soggy *paella*. The saffron is a must. You will find that it gives the dish a flavor that makes it sing, and produces an inimitable color. And use olive oil. This is one case where a neutral-flavored oil is not indicated.

Next, the utensils. If you like *paella* and plan to cook it fairly often, you might consider buying a special pan, a *paellera*, for the purpose. This is a shallow iron pan with sloping sides and two ears to handle it. They are now readily available in the United States. If not, use a shallow frying pan with sloping edges rather than upright. And the burner of the stove should produce a flame that covers the whole bottom of whatever pan you use; if this is not possible, use an asbestos flame deflector to spread the flame. Also, you will find that a wooden fork, spoon and spatula work better than metal ones.

Finally, the procedures. The mixture for the *paella* (except, of course, the rice) can be prepared before hand and even kept in the refrigerator overnight, but when you add the rice, the broth should be boiling hot, and if later you add more broth it also should be boiling hot. The standard proportions between rice and broth are; one cup of rice to two of broth. Both should be measured—don't forget that onions, fish, clams etc. all produce broth. In Valencia they test a *paella* for doneness by plunging a wooden spoon in the middle. If the spoon falls they cook it longer; if it stands upright without moving they add more *hot* broth; if it wiggles without falling over they consider it done. A ten-minute resting period after cooking has finished is essential; any excess broth in the bottom of the pan will be absorbed by the rice during this time. If you are fond of a crust on the bottom of the *paella* (as they are in Valencia), put the pan over a very hot fire for four minutes just before serving.

PAELLA VALENCIAN STYLE
(Paella a la Valenciana)

2/3 cup olive oil	1/2 lb. squids
1 small chicken, about 1-1/2 lbs.	12 shrimps
	12 clams
1/2 lb. pork tenderloin	6 artichoke hearts, canned
4 white sausages	1 cup cooked or canned peas
1/2 cup onion, finely chopped	1 teaspoon paprika
	2 cups rice
4 cloves garlic, chopped	2 cups water
4 large tomatoes, peeled and seeded	1/2 teaspoon saffron
	salt and pepper to taste
5 red peppers, peeled and seeded	

Put 1/2 cup olive oil in a big frying pan and heat. Cut chicken, pork tenderloin, and sausages into pieces and fry about 10 minutes. Add the onion and garlic, stirring everything together with a wooden spoon. Cook a couple of minutes longer and add tomatoes and red peppers, cut into small pieces. Stir a little more and add the squids, cleaned and cut into rings, the shrimps, and clams with their shells. Add salt, pepper, paprika and simmer 5 minutes more.

In another frying pan (or in a *paellera*) heat the rest of the oil, and sauté the rice, stirring all the time so it does not burn. When rice is lightly brown add the fried meat and fish. Measure the broth left in the pan and add enough water to complete 4 cups. Add to pan. Add the vegetables, the saffron, which has been well crushed in a mortar, the parsley, finely chopped, and a little more salt if needed. Bring to a boiling point, reduce fire to medium, and continue cooking, uncovered, for 20 minutes. After this time (or when the rice is cooked), remove from heat, cover, and let it stand ten or twenty minutes before serving. Serve in the same pan. Garnish it with strips of pimientos and slices of lemon. Serves 8.

PAELLA (FOR FOUR PEOPLE)
(Paella para Cuatro Personas)

1/4 cup oil	1/2 teaspoon saffron
2 cloves garlic, minced	1/2 cup string beans
1 ripe tomato, peeled, seeded and chopped	1/4 lb. shrimps, peeled
	4 prawns
1 shallot, chopped	1/2 lb. brill
1/2 lb. pork loin, cut into pieces	8 clams
	lobster rings, if desired
1 small chicken (1-1/2 to 2 lbs.) disjointed	1 to 1-1/2 cups rice
	3 cups water
1/2 cup peas	salt to taste

In a frying pan heat the oil and sauté garlic, tomato and shallot. Add pork, chicken, peas, string beans, shrimp, brill, prawns, clams, lobster and the rice. After 5 minutes add boiling water, saffron and salt to taste. Bring all to a boil over high fire and boil 4 minutes. Put pan in a 350° oven for 15 minutes. Then return it to the top of the stove for 2 minutes over high fire. The rice should be dry with loose grains and lightly attached to the pan. Garnish it with lemon slices and pimiento strips.

GREEN RICE
(Arroz. Verde)

2/3 cup oil
2 cups rice
2 eggs
2 cups white cheese, grated
2 cups milk
3 onions

1 clove garlic
1 cup parsley, chopped
2 green peppers
salt to taste
1 tablespoon lemon juice
2 qts. water

Cook rice in boiling water with lemon juice 20 minutes. Drain. Grind the rest of the ingredients, mix with oil, beaten eggs and milk, and then with the rice. Bake 30 minutes in a 350° oven. Serves 8.

RICE RIOJA STYLE
(Arroz a la Riojana)

1 lb. rice
3 oz. red sausage, chopped
1-1/2 pts. stock
2 red canned pimientos
3 tablespoons butter
1 bay leaf

1/2 cup grated Swiss
 cheese
1/2 lb. ham, minced
1 small onion, chopped
1 cup tomato sauce
salt and pepper to taste

Melt butter, add the ham and sausage. Sauté for a few minutes. Remove to a side dish. In the same butter sauté the onion until tender. Add the rice and sauté slightly. Pour in the stock, season, and add the bay leaf. Cook on high fire for five minutes, add the cheese and continue simmering for another 10 or 15 minutes. Remove from fire and spoon it into a ring mold, pressing down with the spoon to give it shape. Turn it out, garnish it with the ham-sausage mix, and pimientos cut into thin strips. Pour the tomato sauce over it and serve. Serves 8.

SPANISH RICE
(Arroz Graneado)

2 tablespoons oil	2 cups water
1 clove garlic	1 teaspoon lemon juice
1 cup rice	salt to taste

Brown whole clove of garlic in oil, add rice and sauté until golden. Add the boiling water, lemon juice and salt to taste. Boil 5 minutes. Reduce fire and simmer 15 minutes longer. The rice should be dry with loose grains. Serves 4.

SPANISH RICE WITH CLAMS
(Arroz Graneado con Almejas)

1 7-1/2 oz. can minced clams, with juice	1 cup rice
	salt to taste
2 cups water	1 teaspoon minced parsley
2 tablespoons oil	1 teaspoon lemon juice
1/4 teaspoon saffron	1 clove garlic, minced

Sauté garlic in oil. Add rice and cook until lightly brown. Add the remaining ingredients; boil for 5 minutes; reduce fire and simmer 15 minutes longer. Remove from fire and let it rest, covered, 15 more minutes. If there is any excess broth in the rice, it will be absorbed during this period. Serves 4.

SPRING RICE
(Arroz a la Primavera)

4 cups stock	1 teaspoon butter
1 lb. rice	1/2 lb. peas
3 tablespoons lard	1/2 cup asparagus tips
1 cup cooked cauliflower	1 shallot, chopped
1 bay leaf	12 artichoke hearts
3 oz. ham	salt and pepper to taste

Melt lard, add shallot and sauté it until tender. Add diced ham and rice and sauté until rice is golden, stirring all the time. Measure 4 cups of the stock, in which the vegetables have been cooked, and add to rice. When stock boils add the rest of the vegetables. Simmer until all the water evaporates. Put in a hot oven (400°) with butter on top, for 5 minutes before serving. Serves 8.

VEAL

Every autumn, as they have done for centuries in the region of Jerez de la Frontera, men, women, children and old folk go around the sunny vineyards to pick the golden bunches of grapes ripened by the bright Andalusian sun. These grapes are carefully placed in large woven baskets which the men carry on their shoulders to the mule-carts that will take them to the *bodegas* for processing. When the pressing is finished the new wine is poured in the top row of stacked-up casks until it reaches the bottom ones. The miracle of this wine, *sherry*, is that it always has the same "nutty" flavor whether it is dry or semi-sweet. The process of ripening takes years. When finally drawn from the ancient casks it is delicious and tastes exactly the same as it did generations ago. Its flavor harmonizes with a variety of food; soups, fish, chicken, ham, and other meats. It is also a marvelous appetizer. This recipe is typical of the way the Spanish cook with sherry.

VEAL IN SHERRY
(*Ternera al Jerez*)

1 lb. veal cutlets, cut thin
1 tablespoon flour
juice of 1/2 lemon
1/2 lb. mushrooms

1 cup sherry
1 can small peas
salt and pepper to taste
2 tablespoons butter

Sauté mushrooms in half of the butter with the lemon juice. Season and flour veal and brown it quickly on both sides, using the other half of the butter. Remove cutlets. Add sherry, mushrooms and peas. Heat thoroughly; serve immediately. Serves 4.

VEAL SCALLOPS A LA MADRILENA
(Escalopas de Ternera a la Madrileña)

8 individual veal scallops	1 egg, well beaten
8 thin slices of ham	1/4 cup olive oil
1/4 teaspoon salt	1/2 cup tomato sauce
dash pepper	1/2 cup dry sherry
1/4 cup flour	

Pound veal slices to make them as thin as possible. Top each with a slice of ham. Roll up, fasten with a toothpick. Dip each in beaten egg, then roll in flour mixed with salt and pepper. Fry in hot oil until golden on all sides. Set aside. Pour off all but 1 tablespoon olive oil, add tomato sauce and sherry; bring to boil, cook until reduced and thickened. Scallops can be cooked in advance, reheated in sauce. Serve with parsley, potatoes and artichoke hearts. Serves 8.

BEEF AL VINO TINTO
(Carne de Buey en Vino Tinto)

3 lbs. lean beef cut into large
  cubes

Marinade:

1 sliced carrot	2 shallots, quartered
1 onion cut into wedges	2 cloves garlic, minced
1 celery stalk with leaves,	1 bay leaf
cut into pieces	salt and pepper
1 cup red wine	pinch of thyme and rosemary
1/2 cup wine vinegar	6 peppercorns
4 parsley sprigs	

Simmer all the marinating ingredients 30 minutes. Cool and then pour over the meat. Marinate from 12 to 24 hours. If the beef is tender 12 hours are enough; if the beef is tough the whole 24 hours are necessary.

Continued on next page

1/4 lb. bacon, diced	1/2 cup pitted green olives
2 cloves garlic, crushed	3 ripe tomatoes, peeled,
4 carrots, sliced	seeded, chopped
1/2 cup pitted black olives	

Remove the meat from the marinade. Fry the bacon and in the bacon drippings sauté the meat until golden all over. Put the meat and the bacon into an earthenware casserole. Strain the marinade and add all the liquid to the casserole. Add crushed garlic, sliced carrot and olives and simmer very slowly 2-1/2 hours or until meat is tender. Ten minutes before serving time add the tomatoes. Simmer 10 more minutes. If necessary more wine can be added.

Serve with buttered noodles. Serves 8.

STUFFED VEAL RUMP END
(Lomo Bajo de Ternera Relleno)

You can make this dish ahead of time, leaving the final step of baking in the oven for the last minute.

1-1/2 lbs. veal rump end	1 onion
1/2 oz. butter	2 cloves garlic
1 carrot, cut in pieces	salt and pepper

Lard the meat lightly, or have your butcher do it. Put all the above ingredients in a roasting pan. Rub the meat with butter, salt and pepper it and put in the roasting pan with the other ingredients. Roast 25 minutes at 425°. After 15 minutes add 1/2 cup water to the pan. When meat is done on one side turn it over. If the water has evaporated, add 1/2 cup water around the meat. Baste the meat once or twice during the cooking period. When it is done remove to a side dish. Let it cool.

To pan in which the meat was cooked, add 3/4 cup water and cook for a few minutes. Strain the juice and add juice from the meat standing on the dish.

Stuffing:

2 onions, chopped very fine   1-1/2 oz. butter
1/2 lb. mushrooms, cut
   very fine

Melt butter in a pan and sauté onions until transparent. Add mushrooms and sauté 2 or 3 minutes, without stirring too much. Season to taste with salt and pepper.

The Sauce:

1 oz. butter	Meat juices (saved from Step
1 tablespoon flour	1)
1-1/2 cups milk	Gruyère cheese, grated
2 egg yolks	

Melt butter, add the flour and cook for 1 minute, stirring well. Little by little add the hot milk, stirring all the time to avoid lumps. Add the meat juice. Simmer 2 more minutes. Remove pan from fire, beat the egg yolks slightly and add to the sauce, blending them well with a wire wisk. Now return to heat just for 1 minute mixing all the time. Remove from the heat and keep it warm.

Cut the now-cold meat into thin slices. Place some mushroom mixture on each piece. Arrange slices together so it looks like a loaf. If any filling is left over, place it on top of the meat. Heat the sauce over hot water. If it is too thick add a little more hot milk. It should have the consistency of a medium cream sauce. Pour some of his sauce on top of the meat only and let it set. Add 1 tablespoon grated Gruyère cheese to the rest of the sauce; pour it over the meat. The sauce, of course, will run all over the platter. Sprinkle more cheese all over the platter. Place in a 350° oven for 15 minutes. Then raise the temperature to 425° for 5 minutes so the cheese browns. In the last 2 minutes place under the broiler. Serves 6.

VEAL CHOPS RIOJA STYLE
(Chuletas de Ternera a la Riojana)

6 veal chops
3 oz. ham, finely chopped
3 oz. bacon
1-1/2 oz. lard or oil
3 eggs
3 pimientos, cut in thin
  strips

2 tablespoons tomato puree
1 glass white dry wine
1/2 cup broth
1 tablespoon chopped
  parsley
salt and pepper to taste

Cut bacon in thin strips and lard the chops. Sauté in the oil (or lard) until golden brown. Add wine and simmer slowly to reduce wine. Add tomato puree, ham and pimientos. Mix well, add broth and simmer slowly 1 more hour. Serves 6.

BASQUE TOURNEDO
(Turnedo al Estilo Vasco)

1-1/2 lb. sirloin
2 tablespoons lard, or
  drippings
2 tablespoons oil
3/4 lb. mushrooms

6 slices of fried bread
1 teaspoon salt
1/2 teaspoon pepper
2 oz. ham

Wipe the meat with a damp cloth. Put in a shallow oven dish with the lard on top, and place in a hot pre-heated oven (400°). Turn to brown on all sides, then reduce heat until done. Fry slices of bread, cut into rounds. Dice and sauté the ham and the mushrooms. Take the meat out of the oven, cut into 6 slices, (1 per person). Put each slice of meat on a slice of fried bread, covering with the ham and mushroom mixture. Pour over it the juice, formed when cutting the meat, and serve with Potato Buñuelos (See Index). Serves 6.

HUNGER-KILLER OF VEAL
(Matahambre de Ternera)

2 lbs. loin of veal
2 cloves garlic
1/2 teaspoon marjoram

salt and pepper to taste
1 bay leaf
1 cup olive oil

Pound the garlic, marjoram, salt and pepper in a mortar. Add the oil drop by drop to make a thick paste. Stir all the time, mayonnaise fashion, until it gets well mixed. Rub the meat all over with this sauce and leave it for 24 hours. After this time put the meat in a deep pan with the bay leaf and water to cover. Put a tight lid on and simmer for 2 or 3 hours. Serve cold. Serves 4.

BREAST OF VEAL SEVILLA STYLE
(Falda de Ternera a la Sevillana)

2 lbs. breast of veal (in one
    piece, without bones)
10 pickles
2 oz. ham
3 eggs
2 oz. olive oil
1 teaspoon flour
salt and pepper to taste
pinch of thyme

1 small onion
1 medium tomato
1 carrot
2 tablespoons dry white wine
1 cup water
1 teaspoon cornstarch
2 tablespoons cold water
1 bay leaf

Remove fat from veal. Pound to even thinness. Sprinkle with salt and pepper and trim with a knife so that you have the meat in a square piece. Cut the trimmings into very small pieces and brown lightly with the ham, also chopped in a small pieces. Beat eggs, add salt and make an omelet, adding the veal and ham mix. Place the omelet on the square piece of meat and on top of it a row of pickles. Roll the meat around the omelet to make a sausage and tie with strong thread. Sprinkle the meat roll with salt and pepper, dust with flour and fry in the oil until golden brown. Remove meat and place in a pan. In the oil left, sauté chopped tomato, onion and carrot with the herbs. Cover with wine and 1 cup water and cook in medium hot oven about 1 hour. Remove meat. Slice thin.

To thicken the meat sauce add the cornstarch dissolved in the 2 tablespoons water. Boil the sauce 5 minutes, then pass through a sieve. Add slivered blanched almonds and chopped olives to the sauce, and serve it over the veal. Serves 6.

ROLLED FLANK STEAK
(Aleta Enrollada)

1-1/2 lbs. flank steak in 1 piece	1 medium onion
1/2 lb. chopped meat	1 carrot
2 eggs	1 small tomato
6 pitted olives	1 bay leaf
2 pickles	1/4 cup cognac
4 cloves garlic	1/4 cup olive oil

Cut the meat open and spread it membrane side down on a table. Salt and pepper it. Spread minced meat over it. Make a plain omelet with the eggs and place over the minced meat. Add the olives and diced pickles. Roll the meat tightly and tie. Put oil in a suacepan. Brown the meat on all sides. Add onion, quartered; the garlic, crushed; bay leaf and tomato, chopped; the carrot cut into slices and the cognac mixed with 1/2 cup of water. Simmer for 40 minutes. Add more water if necessary. When the meat is tender, remove from pan with the carrot. Pass the rest of the sauce through a colander to obtain a very smooth sauce. Serve meat hot or cold, cut into thin slices. To serve hot, reheat meat in its own sauce. Serves 6.

STUFFED FILLETS "MARIE"
(Filetes Rellenos "Marie")

6 tender fillets of veal	1-1/2 oz. flour
1 hard-boiled egg	3/4 cup dry white wine
3 oz. chopped beef	1/4 cup oil
1 tomato	1 onion, finely chopped
1-1/2 oz. olives, chopped	salt and pepper to taste
3 oz. lard	

Make a stuffing with egg, lard, ground beef and olives. Extend the fillets on the table and divide the stuffing among them. Roll, holding the ends with toothpicks. Heat the oil in a

148

frying pan, dust the rolled fillets with flour and fry in the oil until golden all over. Remove fillets to a side dish. Add onion to the drippings in the pan and sauté 2 minutes. Add tomato and cook 2 minutes. Add wine and boil 5 minutes. Return fillets to pan, cover and simmer 20 minutes. Strain the sauce. Serve with rice. Serves 6.

OLD CLOTHES
(Ropa Vieja)

An excellent way to use leftover meat.

2 large onions, sliced
1 pint cooked tomatoes
5 pimientos, sliced
1 lb. leftover roast meat

salt and pepper to taste
1 oz. oil
pinch each of oregano,
    marjoram, parsley

Brown onions in oil. Add tomatoes, pimientos and the meat, cut in thin strips. Add herbs, seasoning. Cook slowly for 30 minutes. Garnish with croutons. Serves 6.

MEAT BALLS IN RED WINE
(Bolas de Carne al Vino Tinto)

1 lb. ground beef
1 clove garlic, minced
1 egg, slightly beaten
1 teaspoon salt
1/4 teaspoon pepper
1/4 cup flour
2 tablespoons olive oil
1 small onion, chopped

1 cup good red wine
1/4 cup water
1 cup tomato sauce
1/4 teaspoon rosemary
pinch of basil
1 slice of bread soaked in
    milk

Combine beef, squeezed bread, egg, salt and pepper. Mix well and shape into balls. Roll in flour. Heat the oil in a frying pan and saute the meatballs until golden. Remove to a side dish. Add onion to pan and cook over low fire until tender, 3 or 4 minutes; return balls to pan. Mix the wine with the water and combine with the tomato sauce and the herbs. Pour over meat balls. Add the minced garlic. Cover and simmer, very slowly, 1 hour. Serve over hot buttered spaghetti or noodles. Enough for 6 servings.

POOR MAN'S STEAK
(Filetes a Lo Pobre)

6 slices boneless beef chuck,
   or any inexpensive meat
   cut into fillets
6 eggs

2 large Spanish onions,
   sliced featherlike
salt and pepper to taste

Pound the meat to make thin fillets. Put 2 tablespoons oil or
drippings into a frying pan and heat until it smokes. Quickly
brown the meat on both sides, and salt and pepper it. Stack
up on a hot dish. Keep aside. In the drippings left in the pan,
very slowly, without burning it, fry the onion. Add more fat if
necessary. Arrange 1 steak into each plate, top with the fried
onions, which you sprinkle at that minute with salt and pepper, and place on top 1 fried egg. Serve with fried potatoes if
desired. Serves 6.

FESTIVE MEAT LOAF
(Albondigon Festivo)

1 lb. ground beef
1/2 lb. ground veal
1/4 lb. ground pork
1 egg
2 slices of bread, soaked in
   milk
2 tablespoons finely chopped
   onion

1 clove garlic, minced
1 slice of green pepper,
   chopped
1 teaspoon salt
1/2 teaspoon paprika
2 tablespoons oil
2 tablespoons flour

Heat the 2 tablespoons olive oil and sauté onion, garlic, and
green pepper until tender. Mix well with the meat. Add
squeezed bread, egg, salt and paprika and knead it well with
your hand. Prepare filling. Dust the table with flour and on
top pat down the meat to make a rectangle. Arrange the
filling in the center. Fold the bottom third of the meat rectangle over the middle third, then fold the top third over all. Heat
1/4 cup oil into a large frying pan. Carefully lift the meat
loaf from table to pan and sauté the bottom part slowly until
you have a golden crust. With the aid of a spatula, turn it
over. Brown the other side. Tilting the pan, remove excess fat

150

and add the tomato sauce, onion, and green pepper. Simmer
very slowly 1 hour, basting over with the tomato sauce and
lifting the loaf once in a while with the spatula so it does not
stick to the bottom of the pan. Serves 10.

Serve hot, sliced, with mashed potatoes, noodles or rice and
the sauce in a sauce boat.

To serve cold: Slice the loaf thin and place the slices on a
platter garnished with greens. Keeps for a long time in the
refrigerator and it is marvelous for sandwiches or snacks.

The Filling:

2 hard-boiled eggs, sliced
3 anchovy fillets
1/2 cup pitted sliced olives
2 pimientos cut into halves

1 tablespoon minced parsley
leaves or anything else you
care to add such as bacon
bits, sausages, etc.

The Sauce:

2 cups prepared tomato
  sauce
1/2 onion, minced

1/2 green pepper, minced
salt to taste

PORK TENDERLOIN WITH WALNUT SAUCE
(*Lomo de Cerdo con Salsa de Nueces*)

2 lbs. pork tenderloin
1 teaspoon salt
2 garlic cloves, mashed

1 tablespoon olive oil
1 cup water

Trim off all the fat from loin and chop it finely. Place it in
heavy pan with olive oil and heat over low fire till all fat
melts. Rub meat very well with salt and garlic and sauté it
slowly till is golden brown on all sides. Add water and simmer
till tender, basting the meat often with its own juice. Remove
from fire, keeping it hot.

Walnut Sauce:

12 walnuts shelled and
   peeled

3/4 cup milk

Mash walnuts in mortar, moistening with a few drops of water. When you have a very fine paste, place in a small pot with milk and boil for 2 minutes. Remove half of the juices from the meat, skim off fat and add it to walnut sauce, simmering five more minutes. Keep it hot without boiling.

To serve: Slice loin very fine. Pour over the other half of juice. Serve with French fried potatoes and the walnut sauce in a sauce boat.

With blender: Pour boiling water over shelled walnuts. Remove brown skin. Place in blender with milk till creamy. Remove to a small pot and boil two minutes. Add skimmed meat juice, boil five more minutes, whipping all the time. Serves 6.

PORK CHOPS A LA MADRILENA
(Chuletas de Cerdo a la Madrileña)

4 pork chops	dash of paprika
4 tablespoons olive oil	1 bay leaf
1 teaspoon parsley	1/4 teaspoon thyme
2 cloves garlic	salt and pepper to taste

The secret of this recipe is the marinating of the chops in the spicy mixture. Chop the garlic and parsley very fine (this is a good time to get the mortar-and-pestle habit of the Spanish cook). Add these to the oil, bay leaf, thyme, paprika, salt and pepper. Place the chops in a deep platter, and pour the mixture over them. Let them soak for about an hour and a half, turning them occasionally.

Grease a baking dish with olive oil, and place the chops in it. Bake in a moderate oven (350°F.)) until the chops are just done, and still juicy. This paste is specially good served with French fried potatoes. Serves 4.

PORK LOIN BASQUE STYLE
(Lomo de Cerdo al Estilo Vasco)

2 lbs. pork loin in 1 piece
1 oz. butter
1 oz. lard

1 cup milk
3 cloves garlic
salt and white pepper to taste

Dry the loin well with a cloth. Season with salt and pepper and rub well with the garlic. Place lard and butter in a heavy pan. Add pork loin and sauté all over until golden brown. Cover with milk and add some more white pepper. Let it simmer very slowly until milk changes color and the sauce gets thick. Correct seasoning. Slice meat finely and serve with the sauce piping hot. Serves 4.

PICKLED PORK LOIN WITH CLAMS
(Lomo de Cerdo Escabechado con Almejas)

2-1/2 lbs. pork loin
2 lbs. fresh clams
2 tablespoons lard
3 tablespoons olive oil
Marinade:
4 cloves garlic, minced
2 bay leaves

1 tablespoon paprika
2 cloves
1 cup white dry wine
1 tablespoon wine vinegar
salt to taste

Make the marinade by mixing all the ingredients in the order given. Place pork loin in the sauce and marinate for at least 4 hours. After this time drain the meat, reserving the marinade. Place oil and lard in a heavy pan and sauté the pork loin until golden brown. Add marinade. Wash clams thoroughly and add to pot. Simmer 15 minutes or until all clams are open. To serve, place loin on a platter. Remove the top shell from each clam, and place clams around the loin. Pour sauce on top. Serves 6.

ROASTED SUCKLING PIG
(Cochinillo Asado)

1 pig, no older than 21 days	2 tablespoons lard
4 cloves garlic, minced	salt and pepper to taste

Slit pig open from tail to head and sprinkle with salt. Spread out inside up, and place in a large baking pan, resting the pig on three sticks. Put in hot oven, 450°, for 20 minutes. As soon as the inside is roasted, turn the skin part up. Spread with some of the garlic and rub with the lard. Prick the skin with a fork to avoid swelling. Roast 2-1/2 hours at 350°. Add 1 cup of water to pan and baste once in a while.

The suckling pig will come out of the oven with swollen ears and a golden upturned snout. Serves 6 to 8.

LAMB

In Spain lamb has a greater importance than in most countries. It is a traditional dish for many holidays and *fiestas*—particularly it is associated with Eastertime, when the new lambs come in. At this time *cordero lechal* or milk-fed lamb, is available and is considered a great (and somewhat expensive) delicacy. This is the meat from between 25 and 35 days old lambs that have been raised almost exclusively on a maternal milk diet. Their total weight averages about 14 or 15 pounds; they are very tender and have a delicate flavor that requires careful, skillful preparation to retain and enhance it. Most of the rest of the production is sold as *cordero pascual,* quite similar to our spring lamb. Spanish flocks are among the largest in Europe, and their lamb enjoys a well-deserved reputation for quality of the meat, both in texture and flavor.

Spanish shepherds are renowned as the best in the world. They know the art of finding the best pastures and fields of aromatic herbs for their sheep. They also know how much to exercise their flocks, where to find the freshest water and how much to water them. This specialized care that they give the flocks results in the exceptionally good flavor and tenderness of Spanish lamb. This know-how of the Spanish shepherds is recognized in the United States, and Canada, where they are hired for extended terms. Of course many of them remain and became citizens; others feel homesick and nostalgic for the familiar hills and valleys of their youth, and after retirement, protected by their social security checks, they come back to Spain.

SHEPHERD'S LAMB (1)
(Cordero del Pastor)

This special way of cooking lamb combines the flavor of larded lamb with garlic wine-vinegar. Its special flavor is more accented when roasted in an earthenware oven, just after the bread had been baked. Lamb cooked in this fashion has a pickled quality, and the shepherds can carry it in their haversack for as long as a week and it does not spoil even in the hottest weather. We have adapted this recipe to modern cooking. It can be eaten hot, with mashed potatoes topped with the wine-vinegar sauce, or cold for cold plates and sandwiches.

1 4-lb. leg of lamb	1 tablespoon flour
1 tablespoon lard	salt and pepper to taste
6 cloves garlic, 2 slivered	
2 cups red wine mixed with	
2 tablespoons vinegar	

Cut off all fat and thick skin from the leg of lamb. Wash it well in clear water and vinegar and dry it with cloth. Make deep cuts with a sharp knife and insert here and there the slivered garlic. Rub well with the lard, and the salt and pepper, and dust it on top with the flour. Place leg of lamb in open roasting pan, and cook for 30 minutes in a very hot preheated oven. At the end of this time pour over the 2 cups of wine and add the rest of the garlic to pan. Reduce heat to medium, and continue baking for 1-1/2 hours more, basting continuously with the wine. If pan gets dry add more wine. Serves 8 to 10.

SHEPHERD'S LAMB (2)
(Cordero al Pastor)

2 lbs. lamb
5 tablespoons oil
1/2 cup water
1 garlic bud, whole and
unpeeled
1 sprig parsley
salt to taste

In an earthenware casserole, in the order given, place all the ingredients. Cook over low fire, about 1 hour or until the meat is tender and juicy. Serve with tossed green salad. Serves 4-5.

SPRING LAMB WITH ASPARAGUS
(Cordero Lechal con Espárragos)

You will welcome for the family dinner this easy-to-prepare lamb dish that constitutes a whole dinner by itself.

2 lbs. spring lamb shoulder
1/4 cup olive oil
1 bay leaf
8 small potatoes
salt and pepper to taste
3 cups water (or 2 cups
water, and 1 cup dry
white wine)
2 cloves garlic
1/4 lb. lean bacon, diced
8 small onions
1 teaspoon flour

Cut the lamb in small pieces. Heat oil in frying pan. Add to it garlic and lamb and cook over high fire until golden brown. Remove lamb to earthenware casserole. To the oil left in the pan add bacon, bay leaf, onions and potatoes and sauté until golden in color. Add the flour and mix well. Add the water and bring it to a boil. Correct seasoning. Pour this mix over lamb and cook for 45 minutes, over low fire, or until meat is tender.

To serve: Place lamb and vegetables in a large platter, garnishing the center with a bundle of green asparagus cooked separately. Serves 4.

LAMB MEDITERRANEAN

Too many people think of lamb in terms of legs, chops and loin only; however, lamb stew cut from breast or shoulder, when properly made, is a delicious dish.

2 lbs. lamb shoulder	1 lb. peas
1 onion	4 small artichokes
1 lb. small potatoes	1 cup stock
3 tablespoons olive oil	salt and pepper to taste
1 bay leaf	1/2 teaspoon cumin seeds
3 oz. ham	

Dice the ham, fry it in saucepan and remove. Slice the lamb and fry in the same oil. Add to the ham. Chop and fry the onion and, before it gets brown, add the peas, potatoes and stock. Add meat and artichokes, removing the coarse outer leaves and tops and cutting in fourths. Season, put in the bay leaf and cumin. Simmer until the lamb is tender (about 1 hour) and serve. For more zest, 1/2 cup of white wine can be added. Serves 6.

ROASTED LEG OF LAMB WITH STRING BEANS
(Pierna de Cordero Asada con Judías Verdes)

1 4-lb. leg of lamb	2 onions, sliced
1/2 lb. sliced bacon	2 lbs. string beans, cut
1 glass sherry or white wine	French style
1 cup beef broth	1 bay leaf
2 cloves garlic	1/2 teaspoon paprika
1/2 lb. ham in slices	salt and pepper to taste

If the leg is not tender marinate it overnight, or for a few hours, in a mix that you make with oil, mashed garlic, salt, paprika and chopped parsley. Wrap the leg in the slices of ham and secure it with tooth picks. Line a roasting pan with the bacon and onion. Place the leg on top and put in a hot oven to sear. When it starts getting brown, add the seasoning, wine and beef broth. Roast in a 325° oven 25 minutes per pound, basting it often with its own juice. Cook the string beans (See Index); drain and sauté a few minutes in the juice left in the pan. Serve very hot. Serves 8 to 10.

LAMB CASSEROLE
(Cazuela de Cordero)

2 lbs. lamb
2 large carrots
1 cup small round potatoes
12 small onions
1 cup cooked string beans
1 teaspoon Worcestershire
  sauce

1 tablespoon butter
1 tablespoon flour
salt and pepper to taste
2 cups meat stock

Parboil carrots and onions for 15 minutes. Cut carrots into strips. Put lamb, cut into 1-inch cubes, in hot oily frying pan and sear well. Remove meat to covered casserole, season with salt and pepper and bake in a 475° oven for 20 minutes. Add butter and flour to the drippings left in pan in which meat was seared, brown well and make a sauce, adding the meat stock. Season to taste with salt and pepper. Pour sauce over lamb, add carrots and potatoes. Continue cooking until potatoes are tender. Add onions, string beans, and Worcesterhire sauce. Serves 6.

ROASTED LAMB SHOULDER
(Paletilla de Cordero Asada)

1 spring lamb shoulder of
  about 1 pound
1/3 cup olive oil
8 new potatoes

1 clove garlic
1 tablespoon olive oil
1/2 cup white wine
salt and pepper

Bone the lamb shoulder. Shape and tie it up with a cord and season with salt and pepper. In an earthenware casserole put the 1/3 cup of oil, heat and add the lamb, sautéing it until golden all over. Add the potatoes and place in a 375° oven for 20 minutes, turning the potatoes and the meat from time to time. In a separate bowl prepare a sauce with the well-mashed garlic clove, the 1 tablespoon olive oil and the wine. At the end of 20 minutes, when lamb and potatoes are done, remove them to another platter and spread the garlic sauce on the lamb. Put it back in the oven a few more minutes. It is served with the potatoes on the side and bathed with its own juice. Separately serve a green salad. Serves 2.

SHERRY-COFFEE LAMB ROAST
(*Asado de Cordero al Café-Jerez*)

Rub a roast of lamb with salt and pepper and mashed garlic. Place in a hot (400°) oven for 30 minutes or until the lamb is well browned. Pour 1 cup strong coffee over lamb. Reduce heat to 325° and continue baking 2 hours. Baste it often. Add 1 cup of sherry with 1/2 teaspoon mustard, and continue baking for 30 minutes. The more you baste during this period the more delicious is the flavor of the meat. Carve the lamb in slices. Serve with the sauce.

LAMB CHILINDRON
(*Cordero Chilindron*)

5 lbs. spring lamb
1 clove garlic
1 cup oil
3/4 lb. ham, cut in strips
1 large onion, finely chopped

6 red peppers, cut into pieces
8 tomatoes, peeled, seeded, cut into pieces
salt and pepper to taste

Cut lamb into pieces. Heat the oil in a frying pan and add the garlic. Fry it until dark in color. Add the meat, sprinkle it with salt and pepper and sauté until golden. Add ham and onion and continue sautéing until meat browns. Add red peppers and the tomatoes. Cook slowly over low fire until meat is tender. This dish must be not too juicy. Serves 6 to 8.

ROASTED LAMB VILLALON STYLE
(*Asado de Cordero a la Villalón*)

4 lbs. lamb in one piece
3 tablespoons lard
3 bay leaves
3 tablespoons oil

3 tablespoons vinegar
2 tablespoons chopped parsley
salt and pepper to taste

Rub the lamb with lard. Place oil in a large frying pan and sauté the meat all over until golden brown. When ready to turn it over add parsley, bay and vinegar mixed with 1/2 cup

water with salt. Place the meat in a roasting pan in a 425°
oven and cook 20 minutes per pound. Serves 8.

SPRINGTIME LAMB STEW
(Cordero de Primavera)

3 lbs. spring lamb stew meat,
  cubed
1 tablespoon olive oil
2 tablespoons butter
3 small onions, chopped
1 tablespoon flour

1-1/2 cups dry white wine
2 tablespoons tomato paste
salt and pepper to taste
1/2 lb. mushrooms, cut in
  thick slices

Sauté lamb in butter and olive oil, remove to a side dish, and
in the same drippings sauté the onions until tender. Sprinkle
with flour and stir well. Add wine and tomato paste, and
when well blended, return lamb to pot. Cook about 45
minutes, then add the mushrooms. Simmer 15 more minutes.
Serve with buttered peas and carrots and grilled small tomatoes. Serves 6.

LAMB CHOPS WITH RICE
(Chuletas de Cordero con Arroz)

2 lbs. small lamb chops
1/4 cup olive oil
2 onions, sliced
2 cloves garlic, minced
1 green pepper, diced
1 cup canned tomatoes

3 cups water
1 cup wine or beer
1/2 teaspoon saffron
1 cup uncooked rice
3 tablespoons butter
salt and pepper to taste

Brown lamb in the oil. Remove meat to a side dish, and in the
same pot sauté onions, garlic and green pepper. Return meat
to pot, add tomatoes, water, saffron and cook 20 minutes.
Season to taste. Melt the butter in a separate pan, and sauté
the rice until golden in color. Add to the lamb pot with the
wine or beer. Cover and cook 20 minutes, or until lamb is
tender and lamb is done. Serves 4 to 6.

LAMB AND VEAL CHOPS A LA AMPURDESA
(Chuletas de Cordero y Ternera a la Ampurdesa)

This delicious Catalan meat dish can be served to your most difficult guests.

1/4 lb. mushrooms
1/2 teaspoon lemon juice
3 thin slices Smithfield ham
3 tablespoons oil or lard
4 veal chops, 1/2 inch thick
4 lamb chops, 1/2 inch thick
1 onion, chopped
1/3 cup sherry

1/3 cup water
1 tablespoon tomato paste
1 teaspoon saffron
12 almonds, toasted and peeled
1 ounce unsweetened baking chocolate
1 clove
salt to taste

Wash the mushrooms carefully in running water. Slice them thick and add a few drops of lemon juice. Place ham at the bottom of a pan and sprinkle the mushrooms over it. Remove and discard the fat and bones from the lamb and veal chops; use only the meaty center of the chops. Heat the fat in a frying pan and sauté the chops fast on both sides. Place them over ham and mushrooms. In the same fat the meat was fried in, sauté the chopped onion slowly. When tender, drain it of the excess fat, and add to the pan sherry, water and tomato paste. Season to taste. Crush very finely the almonds, the chocolate, the saffron and the clove, add 1 tablespoon water to make a paste and add it to the sauce. Let sauce cook 2 minutes; then pour it over the meat. Cover casserole and cook slowly over low heat until the meat is tender and the sauce reduced to half of its initial volume. (30 minutes).

To serve, put the chops on a round platter, place over each a piece of ham and a spoonful of the mushrooms and cover with the sauce. Adorn it with a handful of watercress in the center. Serves 4.

SPANISH MIXED GRILL
(Parrillada de Cordero)

6 lamb chops
6 lamb kidneys
6 Spanish sausages (red sausage)
6 slices lean bacon (Canadian type)
6 small tomatoes

1/4 cup oil
1 clove garlic, mashed
2 tablespoons vinegar
salt and paprika to taste
1 tablespoon parsley, chopped (for garnish)

Season lamb chops with salt and paprika. Clean and wash kidneys and rinse well in water and vinegar. Make a mix with oil, 2 tablespoons vinegar, garlic, salt and paprika and marinate all the ingredients 1 hour. Place meats and tomatoes under a hot grill and cook five minutes on each side. Serve with shoestring potatoes, freshly fried, sprinkle the tomatoes with parsley, and garnish the plates with watercress or any other green available. Serves 6.

COLD LEG OF LAMB IN MILK
(Pierna de Cordero Fría en Leche)

1 leg of lamb (4 lbs.)
enough milk to cover it

salt and paprika to taste
1 stalk celery

Place leg of lamb in a deep casserole. Cover it with milk, about 1 inch above the meat; add celery, salt and paprika. Simmer very slowly, until tender, about 2 hours. It is done when a toothpick goes in easily. Let it cool in the milk overnight. Serve sliced. The leftover milk can be used in sauces. Serves 8 to 10.

LAMB CHOPS CARMEN
(Chuletas de Cordero Carmen)

1 lb. lamb chops
2 tablespoons butter
1 egg, beaten

1 cup fine bread crumbs
salt and paprika to taste

Pound the lamb chops, season with salt and paprika, dip in beaten egg, then in bread crumbs and fry in hot butter until golden and done to your taste.

2 tablespoons butter	1 cup tomato sauce
6 small eggplants	1 tablespoon butter
1/2 onion	Spanish Rice (See Index)
1 hard-boiled egg	
1 tablespoon chopped parsley	

Boil eggplants 15 minutes. Cool. Cut them lengthwise and scoop out the pulp. Make a filling as follows. Melt butter, add chopped onion and cook until tender. Add eggplant pulp, chopped hard-boiled egg and parsley. Stuff the eggplant shells with this mixture. Place 1 lamb chop on top of each eggplant, and arrange them, crown shape, in a large round platter. Fill the middle of the crown with Spanish rice. Heat the tomato sauce with the 1 tablespoon butter and pour it around the rice. Serves 6.

LEG OF LAMB WITH PINEAPPLE
(Pierna de Cordero con Piña)

1 leg of spring lamb	2 glasses sherry
1 small fresh pineapple, sliced thin	1 onion, sliced thin
3 tablespoons butter	salt and paprika
4 carrots, sliced thin	Spanish Rice (See Index)

Bone the leg of lamb with a pointed knife and loosen the skin. Between meat and skin insert pineapple slices. Place leg in a pan with butter, carrots and onion, and sauté all together until golden brown. Add sherry, salt and paprika, and simmer very slowly during 2 hours. Serve with rice and the sauce in a separate sauce boat. Serves 6.

COUNTRY STYLE LAMB
(*Cordero a la Campera*)

1 3 to 4-lb. leg of lamb
1/2 lb. smoked ham
1/4 cup olive oil
2 cloves garlic, mashed
1 onion, chopped

1/4 cup sherry
1 cup tomato sauce
1 cup stock
1 teaspoon rosemary

Bone the leg of lamb. Place ham in the center; roll and tie with string. Rub meat with salt and pepper; brown well in a heavy pan in the oil. Add onion and garlic and sauté until tender. Add tomato sauce, sherry and rosemary. Cover pan and simmer over low fire until meat is tender. Add the stock as needed during the cooking time, about 1-1/2 hours. Serves 8.

LAMB STEW
(*Estofado de Cordero*)

2 lbs. lean stewing lamb,
   cubed
1/4 cup olive oil
1 clove garlic, minced
1/2 cup dry white wine

1 tablespoon vinegar
3 anchovy fillets, chopped
salt and paprika to taste
2 tablespoons flour
1 onion, chopped

Sprinkle lamb with salt and paprika and dust with flour. In oil, over medium fire, brown it all over. Remove the meat from pan and keep it warm. In the same oil, sauté onion and garlic until tender, add anchovy fillets and mix well. Return meat to the pan, cover and simmer 10 minutes. Add wine and vinegar and simmer 30 more minutes. Serve with mashed potatoes and a tossed green salad. Serves 4.

LAMB WITH ALMOND SAUCE
(*Pepitoria de Cordero*)

2-1/4 lbs. lamb shoulder
1/4 cup oil
2 cloves garlic, minced
1 medium onion, chopped
2 cups toasted, peeled almonds
1 qt. broth or stock
1 tablespoon flour

1 bouquet garni
1 teaspoon saffron
1 cup white dry wine
salt and white pepper to taste
pinch of cinnamon
2 egg yolks
2 tablespoons water

Cut lamb evenly into 18 pieces. Season with salt and paprika. In a frying pan heat the oil and sauté meat, turning it over, without browning it. When done remove to a deep casserole, add wine, bouquet garni, cover and simmer until the wine is reduced to one fourth of its volume. In the oil that remains in the pan, sauté 1 garlic clove and onion until transparent and tender; they should not take color. Add flour, mix well and cook it for a minute; add the broth or stock, stirring well to dissolve all the lumps. Add this sauce to the lamb casserole. In a mortar place 1 clove garlic and the saffron with 1/2 teaspooon salt, and mash well with the pestle. Add 1/4 cup water and make a paste. (All these ingredients can be whirled at once in a blender to make the paste.) Add this paste to the lamb. Correct seasoning, add a pinch of cinnamon and simmer 45 minutes or until meat is tender. When ready to serve, remove meat to a large platter. Blend the egg yolks in 2 tablespoons water and add to sauce, stirring well so sauce does not curdle. Pour sauce over meat. Serve with rice or on toast. Serves 4 to 6.

SAUTEED LAMB WITH POTATOES
(*Cordero Salteado con Patatas*)

For this dish a very tender lamb should be used.

2 lbs. leg of lamb, cubed in large pieces
1/4 cup oil
1 lb. new potatoes
3 tablespoons vinegar

3 cloves garlic
1 tablespoon chopped parsley
salt and pepper to taste

In a heavy covered pan heat the oil. Sauté one garlic well. Season meat with salt and pepper and add to pot. When meat starts to color add the potatoes, cut in fourths, and continue sautéing together until potatoes color. Cover the pan and simmer very slowly until meat is tender, about 25 minutes. Add the other 2 garlic cloves, minced finely, the parsley and vinegar. Correct seasoning and serve immediately. Serves 5 to 6.

FOWL

CHICKEN STUFFED WITH NUTS
(Pollo Relleno con Nueces)

1 2-lb. chicken
1 bay leaf
1 carrot, chopped

1 onion, chopped
1 cup sherry
salt and pepper to taste

Stuffing:

1/2 lb. lean pork
1/2 lb. veal
2 egg yolks

1/2 lb. piñones nuts
1/3 cup seedless raisins
1/2 cup chopped walnuts

Clean the chicken and singe well over an alcohol flame. Salt and pepper and rub inside and out with a little oil. Chop all the stuffing ingredients and make a paste of the yolks. Add to stuffing. Stuff chicken and sew. Place bird breast side up in a roasting pan and cook in preheated oven (425°) for 10 minutes. In the meantime, sauté in olive oil the onion, carrot and bay leaf. Add onion mix to roasting pan and continue cooking for another 15 or 20 minutes, or until the chicken gets done. Remove chicken. To drippings left in pan, add sherry and simmer for 10 minutes. When ready to serve, strain sauce and pour over chicken. Serves 4.

CHICKEN IN WINE
(Pollo al Vino)

2 2-1/2 lb. chickens,
   disjointed
4 tablespoons olive oil
2 onions, chopped
1 cup dry white wine
1 tablespoon tomato paste
1 tablespoon flour
salt and pepper to taste
3 tablespoons chopped olives

1 cup beef stock
4 anchovy fillets, crushed
1/2 cup wine vinegar
4 cloves garlic, mashed
1/4 teaspoon saffron
1 tablespoon capers
   (optional)
3 tablespoons chopped
   parsley

Sprinkle the chicken with salt and pepper and dust with flour. Rub flour well into the skin. Heat the oil in a heavy skillet and sauté the onions until tender. Add the chicken and brown well all over. Add the wine, and cook 5 minutes over high fire. Dissolve the tomato paste in the broth and add to the pan. Simmer for 45 minutes, or until chicken is tender.

In a small pot, bring the vinegar to a boil, add the olives, garlic, anchovies, parsley, saffron, capers, and simmer for 3 or 4 minutes. To serve: Pour sauce over chicken. Serves 8.

CHICKEN IN RED WINE
(Pollo al Vino Tinto)

1 2-1/2 lb. chicken
4 tablespoons butter
3 chopped shallots
1/2 cup mushroom caps

12 small onions
1 glass red wine
1/4 lb. salt pork
1 teaspoon chopped parsley

Soak salt pork in water for 30 minutes. Change the water and simmer 30 minutes. Cool, dice and fry in half of the butter until light golden in color. Quarter chicken and add to the pot. When completely brown, add shallots, mushrooms and onions and simmer 10 minutes. Add wine, cover the pot and simmer until the chicken is tender. Remove chicken, add two more tablespoons butter. When sauce has thickened pour over chicken. Sprinkle parsley on top. Serves 4.

STEWED CAPON
(Estofado de Capón)

1 8-lb. capon	1 cup cream
1 carrot	1/4 teaspoon saffron
1/4 lb. sweet butter	3 egg yolks
1 large onion	1 glass sherry
1 bay leaf	pinch of nutmeg
1 stalk celery	1/2 cup Gruyère cheese,
3 tablespoons flour	grated

Boil the chicken in 2 quarts of stock made with the giblets
and the neck of the chicken. Add carrot, bay leaf, onion,
celery and salt. Simmer about 1 hour. Cool and slice. Strain
broth and continue simmering until reduced to half of its
volume. Melt butter, add flour and mix well. Add chicken
broth, saffron, and cook 10 minutes. Blend the egg yolks with
the cream; remove pot from fire and add the yolks. Season to
taste. Return sauce to fire, and always stirring it, cook for
about 1 minute. Add sherry. To serve, place chicken on a bed
of cooked vegetables (string beans, asparagus or broccoli) on
an oven dish, put chicken on top, cover with the sauce,
sprinkle with the cheese and put in a hot oven until golden
brown. Serves 8.

CHICKEN WITH RICE CASSEROLE
(Pollo con Arroz al Horno)

1 large chicken, disjointed	1/4 cup olive oil
1 clove garlic, minced	1/4 cup tomato paste
1 medium size onion,	salt to taste
chopped	2 cups rice
1 small green pepper,	2 cups chicken broth
chopped	1-1/2 cups water

In a heavy casserole heat the oil and sauté garlic, onion and
green pepper until tender. Add chicken and cook until brown
all over. Add tomato paste and salt to taste. Cover and simmer, very slowly, 20 minutes, turning chicken pieces over
once in a while. Remove chicken from pan. Add the rice to
the pan and sauté in the remaining fat. Add broth and water,

correct seasoning and bring it to a boil. When the liquid is almost absorbed, stir the rice with a fork to loosen it up. Place chicken pieces on top, cover the pot and put in a 375° oven for about 30 minutes. Garnish with pimiento strips and green peas. Serves 5.

STUFFED CHICKEN NECKS
(Cuellos de Pollo Rellenos)

Any leftover meats can be used in this dish, considered one of the tastiest budget stretchers.

2 chicken necks	3 tablespoons chopped ham
1/4 cup chicken, minced	1/2 cup white wine
3 oz. sausages, chopped	1 carrot
1 clove garlic, minced	2 hard-boiled egg yolks,
2 tablespoons onion, finely chopped	pressed through a sieve
1 tablespoon parsley, chopped	

Clean necks, remove inside meat and bones. Sew one end. Mix all the ingredients but the wine, yolks and carrot, and stuff the necks with the mix. Sew the other end. Place oil in a pan and sauté the necks until golden in color. Add 1/2 cup of stock and the wine and carrot and simmer 25 minutes or until tender. To serve: Cut into slices and put on a platter. Serve with any boiled buttered vegetables and the sauce.
Sauce: Add egg yolks to the broth in the pan and mix well. Serves 4.

DUCK WITH GREEN APPLES AND WINE
(Pato con Manzanas Verdes y Vino)

1 duck, 4-1/2 lbs.	1 cup red wine
1 lb. sour green apples	salt and pepper to taste
1 cup orange juice	1 teaspoon cornstarch

Basting sauce:

1 cup orange juice	1 cup good brandy
1 cup juice from the apple marinade	

Peel and dice the apples, add 1 cup of orange juice and wine and marinate over night. Clean the duck, sprinkle inside and out with salt and pepper, drain excess juice from the apples and stuff the duck. Place duck in a covered roaster on rack and roast 2 hours. Remove duck from oven and discard all drippings. Return duck to oven and roast until golden brown, basting with the basting sauce. When duck is brown, add 1 teaspoon cornstarch to pan to make the sauce. Strain and serve in a separate sauce boat. The apple stuffing is served with the duck. Serves 4.

DUCK WITH TURNIPS
(Pato con Nabos)

1 duck	3/4 cup dry white wine
3 oz. bacon	1 cup stock
3 sliced carrots	pinch of ginger
1 doz. shallots, whole	1 teaspoon salt
1 lb. turnips, washed	1/4 teaspoon white pepper
3 tablespoons lard	

Clean the duck, wrap in bacon slices and put in a pan with 1 tablespoon lard. Brown lightly and then cook slowly for 1 hour. Then add shallots, carrots, seasoning, ginger, wine and the stock. In the other 2 tablespoons lard fry the turnips until golden in color. Put in a pot with salted boiling water and cook for 5 minutes. Drain and add to the duck. Serve duck surrounded with the turnips and other vegetables. Serves 4.

DUCK WITH OLIVES
(Pato con Aceitunas)

Spread a duck with softened butter, salt and pepper it, roast in hot oven 20 minutes per pound in a 475° oven. Add 1/2 cup water and 1/2 cup sweet sherry to the fat in the pan and baste the duck often with it. Fifteen minutes before the duck is done, add 1 cup small pitted olives. Serve the duck and the olives together. Skim most the fat from the pan juices and serve the juice in a sauceboat. Serves 4.

CHICKEN IN ALMOND SAUCE (1)
(Pollo en Pepitoria)

1 chicken, cut in pieces
1/4 cup olive oil
1 clove garlic and 1 small
  onion, finely chopped
1 tablespoon flour
1 cup water

1/2 cup white wine
1 bay leaf
1/2 teaspoon saffron
1/2 cup chopped, blanched
  almonds
salt and pepper to taste

Using a heavy pot, brown chicken in olive oil. Add garlic, onion, flour and mix well. Add water and wine and seasonings, except almonds. When the chicken is almost done add the almonds and boil a few minutes longer. Garnish with small pieces of boiled ham, peas and pimientos. Serves 4.

CHICKEN IN ALMOND SAUCE (2)
(Pollo en Pepitoria)

1 small frying chicken, cut
  up; or 2 whole chicken
  breasts
2 tablespoons flour blended
  with 1 teaspoon salt
3 tablespoons Spanish olive
  oil
1/4 cup blanched, slivered
  almonds

1 small onion, chopped
1 clove garlic, minced
1/8 teaspoon saffron
2 tablespoons minced
  parsley
3/4 cup dry sherry
2 hard-cooked eggs, slivered

Dust cut-up chicken, or breasts cut in 4 pieces, with the flour and salt. Meantime, lightly brown the almonds in the olive oil; remove and set aside for garnish. Add the floured chicken to the oil; cook over high heat until well-browned. Lower heat, add the onion, garlic and parsley to the pan, and cook, covered, until onion is soft. Dissolve the saffron in sherry; add to the chicken. Cover once more and simmer until chicken is tender, about 40 minutes. Serve garnished with the almonds and the hard-cooked eggs. Serve 4.

PEPITORIA OF CHICKEN FROM THE CANARIES
(Pepitoria a la Canaria)

1 chicken
1 large onion, finely
  chopped
3 to 4 tablespoons olive oil
  (or lard)
1/2 cup stock
1 glass white wine
salt to taste

8 peppercorns
2 oz. peeled almonds
3 cloves garlic
1 sprig parsley
1/2 glass sherry
1 slice smoked ham
2 hard-boiled egg yolks

Cut chicken and sauté in olive oil until golden. Take chicken out and in the same fat fry the onion. Put the chicken into a saucepan, cover with stock and water, and add the onion with the fat in which it was fried. Simmer 30 minutes, then add wine and peppercorns. Fry the peeled almonds and garlic, mash them together in a mortar with the parsley and add the egg yolks, mixing all into a very smooth paste. Add sherry, stir well and pour the whole mixture over the chicken. Simmer another 20 minutes. Cut ham in strips, add to pepitoria. Garnish with red pimientos. Serve with French fried potatoes if you wish. Serves 4.

SPANISH CASSEROLE CHICKEN
(Pollo en Cacerola)

3 lbs. frying chicken, cut
  into pieces
1 cup flour seasoned with
  1 teaspoon salt,
  1/4 teaspoon pepper,
  1/2 teaspoon paprika
1/4 cup olive oil
1/4 cup chopped onions
3 tablespoons green pepper
1 clove garlic, minced

1/2 cup chopped carrots
1/2 cup chopped celery
  (optional)
1 cup tomato juice
1/2 cup red wine
3/4 cup sautéed
  mushrooms
1/3 cup sliced stuffed
  olives

Dredge chicken with seasoned flour. Heat olive oil in skillet, brown chicken in the oil. Place the pieces in a casserole. Now, in the same oil sauté onion, green pepper and garlic. Add carrots, celery, tomato juice and wine. Pour this mixture over chicken in the casserole. Cover, and bake in oven 325°F (moderate) about 1 hour, or until tender. Five minutes before the chicken is done, add mushrooms and sliced stuffed olives. Thicken drippings with a little flour and if needed add a little more tomato juice, correcting seasoning at this point.

BREAST OF TURKEY IN ASPIC
(Pechuga de Pavo En Gelatina)

1 lb. turkey breast, sliced	1 pint turkey stock
4 tablespoons gelatin	1-1/2 oz. sherry
1 egg white	1 to 2 truffles (small tin)
3 oz. ham	seasoning

Dissolve the gelatin in a cup of hot stock. Add the rest of the stock and sherry. Add egg white. Put back in fire, boil 2 minutes stirring constantly. Pass through a muslin cloth without pressing. Pour 1/3 of the gelatin into a mold. When it sets, arrange over it the sliced truffles and ham. Cover with slices of turkey, season to taste with salt and pepper and add the rest of the gelatin. Chill or let set overnight.

To serve, dip the mold into hot water for a second and turn out on a dish. Serve on greens with mayonnaise. Serves 6.

OLD-FASHIONED TURKEY CROQUETTES
(Croquetas de Pavo a la Antigua)

2 cups turkey meat, finely chopped	2 beaten eggs
1 leek	2 tablespoons lard
1 carrot	2 tablespoons flour
sprig of parsley	salt and pepper to taste
1 onion, chopped	pinch of nutmeg
3 oz. grated bread crumbs	oil for frying

Remove meat off the bones. Make a stock with turkey bones, leek, carrot and parsley, and enough water to yield 2 cups of stock. Fry onion in a little lard. When golden, remove. In the same fat, sauté turkey meat. Sprinkle flour on turkey and sauté three more minutes. Season. Add turkey stock, a little at a time, stirring constantly until the consistency of white sauce is reached. Cool on a shallow dish. Taking a tablespoon of the mixture, roll into croquettes, dip in bread crumbs, then in beaten eggs and once again in bread crumbs. Fry in deep oil till golden in color.

CHICKEN PAELLA
(Paella De Pollo)

1 small chicken, cut in
  8 pieces
1/4 lb. lean pork, cut in
  small dice
1/4 lb. lean veal, cut in
  small dice
3 tablespoons Spanish olive
  oil
1 clove garlic, minced
2 tomatoes, peeled and
  chopped

1/2 lb. green beans
  (1 package frozen) or
1 package frozen peas or
1 package frozen
  artichoke hearts
1-1/2 cups rice
2-1/2 cups well-seasoned
  broth
1/4 teaspoon saffron
1/4 lb. shelled shrimps
1 can (7 oz.) minced clams

Sauté chicken, pork and veal in olive oil in large heavy skillet; when well-browned, add garlic and tomato. Cook 1 minute. Add beans (or peas or artichokes) rice, broth and saffron and bring to a boil. Boil 4 minutes uncovered. Separately sauté shrimp in a little olive oil; add shrimp and clams to rice, place skillet in moderate oven (375°), or transfer to large shallow casserole, and bake 20 minutes or until most of liquid is absorbed and rice is fluffy and tender. Serves 6.

MOCK PHEASANTS
(Faisanes Falsos)

This is another recipe of the domestic repertory, of lovely presentation, easy preparation, and a gourmet's delight.

6 small whole chicken breasts	1/4 cup olive oil
4 chicken livers	1 cup milk
1 large onion, chopped	1 teaspoon flour
	salt and pepper to taste

Wash chicken breasts well and dry thoroughly with towel. Season with salt and pepper and sauté in oil till golden in color. Remove from pan. Add onion and sauté until transparent and soft. Return chicken breasts to pot and add the livers. Simmer 1 hour. When done, remove chicken breasts to platter and keep hot.

The sauce: To sauce in pan (including livers) add the flour and milk, stirring well. Run it through a sieve or electric blender. Reheat and pour over the breasts. Serves 6.

CHICKEN BREASTS ROMAN STYLE
(Pechuga De Pollo a la Romana)

4 chicken breasts	salt and pepper to taste
1 small onion	1 cup bechamel sauce
bunch of parsley	beaten eggs
2 tablespoons white wine	fine bread crumbs and flour
1 bay leaf	oil for frying

Cook the breasts with onion, parsley, wine, bay leaf and water as needed. Remove skin and bones. Make a thick bechamel sauce and cover each breast in it. Put aside until the sauce cools and hardens. Then dip in turn in flour, beaten egg and fine bread crumbs. Just before serving fry in deep hot oil.

Continued on next page

Bechamel Sauce:

1-1/2 cups chicken stock
1/4 cup butter
1/4 cup flour

1 cup scalded milk
salt and pepper to taste

Melt butter, add flour, and gradually hot stock and milk. Season to taste. Equal parts of stock and milk may be used.

Spinach Garnish: Make a purée of cooked, drained spinach. Add bechamel sauce to purée, then a beaten egg, salt and pepper to taste and a little butter. Arrange the spinach purée around the chicken breasts, decorating with sliced hard-boiled egg. Serves 4.

CHICKEN LIVERS IN SHERRY
(Higados de Pollo al Jerez)

12 chicken livers
2 tablespoons butter
2 tablespoons chopped onion
1 teaspoon flour
1/2 cup chicken stock or
  bouillon

1/2 teaspoon Worcestershire sauce
2 tablespoons sherry
salt and pepper to taste

Cut livers in two, season with salt and pepper. Roll in flour. Melt butter in saucepan and sauté the onion, add livers. Stir and sauté them until they are brown. Stir in flour and when well mixed add stock slowly. Add Worcestershire sauce and correct seasoning if needed. Cook 2 minutes longer, adding the sherry at this time. Serve on toast or rice. Serves 4.

GIBLETS WITH MACARONI
(Menudillos con Macarrones)

2 oz. Spanish ham
   (Serrano)*
1 tablespoon tomato paste
1 cup water
2 tablespoons butter
3 tablespoons olive oil
1 lb. macaroni

1 onion
1 lb. chicken giblets
1 cup white wine
1/3 cup grated Parmesan
   cheese
salt and pepper

First boil the macaroni in salted water; drain and set aside. Chop the onion, giblets and ham; fry in the oil until almost done. Add the tomato paste, a cup of water and the wine. Simmer for ten minutes.

Butter a casserole. Add a layer of macaroni, then a layer of the giblet mixture, continuing in this manner until the casserole is filled. Be sure to finish with a layer of giblets.

Top the dish with a few pats of butter, sprinkle with the cheese and bake in a hot oven 15 minutes. Serves 5.

*Note: If Spanish Serrano ham is not available, use Smithfield.

GAME

On the 12 of October the official hunting season opens in Spain and the Spanish *mercados* will be once again filled with all kinds of game. Also the weekend hunters will come back home bringing with them the well-earned prizes of their expedition, which they will proudly hand to their wives for the preparation of a gourmet feast.

Here follow a few suggestions for cooking game *a la española*:

STUFFED PIGEONS
(Pichones Rellenos)

3 pigeons (1/2 per person)
3 oz. ham
3 oz. bacon, sliced
1/2 lb. lean pork
2 onions
3 slices bread soaked in milk
1 cup milk

1 glass white wine
1 cup stock
1 oz. parsley
2 tablespoons lard
1 teaspoon salt
1/2 teaspoon pepper

Stuffing: Mince pork, ham, and pigeon livers; mix well with the bread and seasoning. Clean and stuff the pigeons. Wrap bacon slices around them and brown in a large pan. Add the white wine, stock, sliced onions and chopped parsley. Simmer a few minutes and transfer to oven dish. Put in the oven (medium temperature) for 45 minutes. Pass the sauce through a sieve, reheat, pour over the pigeons and serve. Serves 6.

PARTRIDGE IN CHAMPAGNE
(Perdices En Champana)

3 partridges (1/2 per person)
3 oz. bacon
2 onions
1 glass champagne

1 cup water
1 cup stock
1 tablespoon olive oil
1 teaspoon salt
1/2 teaspoon pepper

Clean and dress partridges. Brown them whole in the oil. Add the giblets, sliced bacon and chopped onion and fry together for about 3 minutes. Add the seasoning, champagne and water. Simmer for 2 hours. When tender, remove from pan, quarter, take out the backbone and ribs. Place the breasts and legs in a Pyrex dish.

Pound the bones, skin and giblets in a mortar (or pass them through a blender) and add to the sauce with a small quantity of stock. Boil the sauce for 3 or 4 minutes, sieve and pour over the partridges. Put in the oven for 15 minutes and serve.

Note: For this dish you can buy a small bottle of champagne that holds less than 2 cups.

STEWED RABBIT OR WILD DUCK
(Conejo o Pato-Silvestre Estofado)

1 rabbit
1 cup olive oil
1 carrot, sliced in rounds
2 bay leaves
1 teaspoon oregano
salt and pepper to taste

1 tablespoon chopped parsley
2 cloves garlic, minced
1 tablespoon flour
1/2 bottle red wine
1 large onion, sliced fine

Cut rabbit or duck in serving pieces. Brown in the olive oil, add onion, carrot, bay leaf, oregano, parsley and garlic and season with salt and pepper. When all looks golden in color add flour and also brown it a little. Add the wine. Let it boil for 2 minutes. Cover the pan and simmer slowly until tender.

Serve with croutons. Serves 4 to 6.

PIGEON GLORIA
(Pichones Gloria)

4 pigeons	1 large glass white wine
16 small onions	1/2 cup broth
1/2 lb. bacon, diced	flour
2 tablespoons olive oil	

The pigeons should be whole. Remove intestines, clean well and put the livers back. Heat the oil in a frying pan, add bacon, and when golden remove to a side dish. Add the pigeons to the pot and cook until golden all over. Remove from the pan to the bacon dish. Clean the onions, add to the drippings left in the pan, and sauté until golden. Sprinkle with the flour, add the broth and the wine. When it starts to boil, add the pigeons to the pot. Add the bacon. Cover the casserole and put in a 350° oven until birds are tender.

To serve, carve the birds and arrange on a platter. Garnish with the onions and fried bread sticks. Skim fat from the sauce, sieve and serve in a separate sauce boat. Serves 4.

OLD-FASHIONED PICKLED PARTRIDGE
(Perdices en Escabeche a la Antigua)

4 partridges	1 cup white wine
1/2 cup olive oil	1/2 cup vinegar
2 cloves garlic	6 peppercorns
2 bay leaves	salt and pepper to taste

Clean and wash the birds, wipe dry with a cloth and sew, so they keep their shape. Heat oil in a pot and sauté the birds until well brown. Place the birds in a casserole. In the drippings left in the pan fry garlic and bay leaves, add the vinegar, wine, peppercorns, salt and pepper and add that mixture to the birds in the casserole. Cover the casserole and simmer until the birds are tender. Place the partridges in a deep platter pouring the sauce over them. Serves 8.

RABBIT VALENCIAN STYLE
(Conejo a la Valenciana)

1 rabbit
1 green pepper, chopped
3 cloves garlic, minced
2 tablespoons flour
1 tablespoon parsley,
  chopped

salt and pepper to taste
1 cup olive oil
1 cup broth

Clean and wash the rabbit and cut into serving pieces. Dip in flour and fry in oil. Place the fried pieces in a casserole. To the oil remaining in the pan add green peppers, garlic and parsley. Sprinkle with salt and black pepper. Add broth and simmer 10 minutes. Pour this mix over the rabbit and continue cooking until meat is tender. Serves 4.

VEGETABLES

ARTICHOKES
(Alcachofas)

Artichokes are rich in iron, mineral salts and iodine and a fondness for them is an acquired taste. There are many ways to prepare artichokes; they can be baked, fried, stuffed, stewed etc., but they are most popular in salads. Many recipes have been developed in the different regions of Spain, dating, some of them, from the time of the Moorish occupation.

Preparation: Wash artichokes, trim the stems at the base, snipping off leaf tips. Boil in abundant salted water until tender.

Test for tenderness: Pull one of the leaves. If it separates easily from the artichoke, they are done. They can be served cold with vinaigrette sauce, lemon sauce or mayonnaise, or hot with lemon butter.

Sauce Vinaigrette:

6 tablespoons olive oil	1/2 teaspoon paprika
3 tablespoons wine vinegar	1 teaspoon onion juice
1 teaspoon lemon juice	1/2 teaspoon salt

Combine all these ingredients. For lemon sauce substitute lemon juice for wine vinegar.

Lemon Butter Sauce: Melt 1/4 cup butter over low fire. Beat in, drop by drop, 1 tablespoon lemon juice.

To eat: Pull each leaf separately, dip the large end in the sauce, biting off the soft part of it. When all the outside leaves are eaten you will reach the cap, which is more tender.

Separate from the heart and dip in the sauce, eating all the tender part. Now you have left the heart, the best part of the artichoke. The heart has inside a spiny choke that should be separated and discarded. In the very tender, small artichokes the whole heart can be eaten as it has practically no choke.

MOORISH ARTICHOKE-LAMB STEW
(Estofado Moro de Alcachofas y Cordero)

1-1/2 lb. lamb shoulder, cut in pieces	2 cloves garlic, minced
1/4 cup olive oil	1 carrot, sliced thin
1 tablespoon vinegar	6 small artichokes, quartered
1 tablespoon flour	1/4 teaspoon cumin seeds
1 large onion, chopped	1 cup white dry wine
	salt and red pepper to taste

Rub lamb with vinegar. Rinse under clear water to remove any odor and dry with a towel. Season with salt and pepper, dredge with flour. Place oil in deep heavy pot. When it starts to smoke, add the lamb and sauté all over until golden. Remove the meat to a side dish. Add garlic to the pot and cook until transparent. Return meat to pot adding all the rest of the ingredients. Simmer about 1-1/2 hours or until meat is tender. Correct seasoning before serving. Serves 6.

STUFFED ARTICHOKES
(Alcachofas Rellenas)

8 large artichokes	2 cloves garlic
3 oz. mushrooms, chopped fine	1 egg
1 large tomato, underripe	1/2 cup oil
1 onion	1 cup consommé

Peel tomato, remove seeds and chop fine. Mix with mushrooms, garlic, egg and parsley. Clean artichokes, cut them lengthwise, and dip for a few minutes in water with a few drops of lemon juice. Drain and dry well. With a pointed knife extract the inside pulp and stuff the cavity with mushroom mix. Put the artichoke halves back together and secure with toothpicks. In a casserole, spread the chopped onion and arrange on top the artichokes. Sprinkle with pepper and salt and add consommé. Cover the casserole and simmer 45 minutes. Let them rest in casserole 15 more minutes. To serve place the artichokes in a platter, without removing the toothpicks. Pour their juice over them. Serves 8.

ARTICHOKES IN WINE SAUCE
(Alcachofas con Vino)

12 artichokes	sprig of parsley
1 onion, chopped	2 oz. bacon, diced
1 clove garlic, minced	3 tablespoons stock
1 cup white wine	salt and pepper to taste
1/4 cup olive oil (or butter)	

Boil and drain the artichokes. Pull off the leaves and the choke, leaving only the hearts. Melt butter, add onion, and when tender add garlic and bacon. Add the white wine and the artichoke hearts. Add the stock. Season. Cover and simmer until tender, about 20 minutes. Serves 12.

ARTICHOKE HEARTS IN CHEESE SAUCE
(Corazones de Alcachofas Gratinados)

12 artichoke hearts (you can use the canned type)	1/2 cup milk
1/2 cup chicken broth	1/2 cup grated Swiss cheese
2 tablespoons butter	1 tablespoon sherry
2 tablespoons flour	salt and pepper to taste

Preheat the oven to 375°F. Drain artichokes and arrange in an oven dish. Melt butter in saucepan and blend in flour. Gradually add milk and broth. Cook until thick, stirring constantly. Remove from heat and add half of the cheese and stir until cheese melts. Add sherry, pour over artichokes and sprinkle with the remaining cheese. Bake 20 minutes until cheese is melted and lightly browned. Serves 6.

POTATO CROQUETTES
(Croquetas de Patatas)

1-1/2 cups mashed
    potatoes
1 tablespoon butter
1 tablespoon parsley,
    chopped

1/2 teaspoon salt
1/4 teaspoon white pepper
1 tablespoon onion juice
2 eggs
oil for frying

Mix potatoes and butter. Add 1 egg and the rest of the ingredients, except bread crumbs, and make a smooth paste. Make into croquettes. Dip into the well-beaten egg, roll in breadcrumbs and fry in deep hot oil. Serves 4.

POTATO CASSEROLE
(Cacerola de Patatas)

1 lb. potatoes
2 tablespoons butter
3 oz. ham, chopped
2 eggs

1 oz. dry bread crumbs
salt and pepper to taste
1 cup white sauce
1 tablespoon cream

Peel and slice the potatoes, boil 2 minutes and drain. Sauté ham in butter and add to the prepared white sauce. Beat the eggs, put them in the sauce and add the cream. Season with salt and pepper. Grease a casserole, sprinkle with bread crumbs, put in potatoes in alternate layers with sauce. Cover and bake 30 minutes at 350° oven. Serves 4 to 6.

POTATO TARTS
(Pastel de Patatas)

This is an excellent dish to take on picnics. It tastes better when served cold.

4 large potatoes
2 tablespoons flour
2 tablespoons butter
salt to taste
pinch of nutmeg
6 slices bacon, boiled in
   water

4 oz. milk
2 egg yolks
1/2 clove garlic, mashed
grated Gruyère cheese

Cook the potatoes in their skins. When cooled, peel and pass them through a sieve. Mix with the flour, butter and salt, until you have a smooth paste. Roll out a quarter of an inch thick and spread in a 9-inch greased pie dish. Cut bacon in small pieces and place in the tart. Mix milk with the egg yolks and pour into tart. Season with nutmeg and garlic juice. Sprinkle the top with cheese. Put into a 350° oven for 20 minutes. Serves 8.

ONION CASSEROLE
(Cebollas al Horno)

6 large mild onions
4 tablespoons butter
1/2 cup soft bread crumbs

1/4 cup grated cheese
1/2 teaspoon paprika
salt and pepper to taste

Skin and slice onions. Sauté in butter until transparent. Season with salt and pepper and place in shallow baking dish. Sprinkle bread crumbs, cheese and paprika on top. Bake at 350° until crumbs are brown. Serves 6.

STUFFED ONIONS
(Cebollas Rellenas)

4 to 8 large onions
2 oz. Parmesan cheese, grated
1-1/2 oz. Edam cheese, grated
2 eggs

2 tablespoons brandy
1/4 cup olive oil
2 tablespoons butter
2 tablespoons fine bread crumbs
salt and pepper to taste

Cut 1/3 off from the top of each onion, and remove the inside layers to make a cup. Boil "cups" 5 minutes and drain. Chop the inside part of the onions very finely and sauté in the oil until tender. Add cheese, eggs, brandy, grated bread crumbs and season to taste. Stuff onion cups with this mixture. Place them in a well-buttered casserole and dot each one with butter. Bake 30 minutes in a 350° oven. Serves 4 to 8.

FENNEL AU GRATIN
(Hinojo al Gratin)

3 lbs. fennel
3 oz. boiled ham, cut into strips

1/4 cup butter
1/2 cup broth
salt and pepper to taste

Remove coarse leaves. Wash fennel and cut in pieces. Use as much of the stalk as is tender. Place butter in casserole, melt, and add the fennel. Sauté slowly 30 minutes. Add broth and simmer another 15 minutes. Add ham and more broth if necessary. Simmer 10 more minutes. In the meanwhile, make the sauce:

1-1/2 oz. butter
1-1/2 oz. flour
2 cups milk
pinch of nutmeg
1 egg

5 oz. Gruyère cheese
grated bread crumbs
salt to taste
butter

Make a bechamel sauce with the butter, flour and milk. Add the nutmeg. Remove from fire and add half of the cheese and the egg. In a well buttered casserole place the fennel, sprinkle with the other part of the cheese (reserve 1 teaspoon) and cover with the bechamel sauce. Sprinkle with about 1/4 cup bread crumbs mixed with the 1 teaspoon cheese you have reserved. Dot with butter and bake 15 minutes in a 425° oven. Serves 8.

FENNEL WITH HAM AND EGGS
(Hinojo con Jamón y Huevos)

2 lbs. fennel
4 eggs
3-1/2 oz. red sausage

5 tablespoons oil
7 oz. boiled ham
salt to taste

Clean fennel and cook in boiling water 30 to 45 minutes, until tender. Drain. In a frying pan heat the oil, add ham cut into strips, chopped sausage, and sauté 10 minutes. Add the chopped fennel. Beat the eggs and add to pan stirring well. Remove immediately to a warm platter. Serves 6.

CONTINENTAL RED PEPPERS
(Pimientos Continentales)

6 red sweet peppers
1/2 lb. pickled tunafish
1 oz. butter
2 oz. pitless olives
lettuces

1 tablespoon chopped
  parsley
1/4 cup vinegar
salt to taste

Rub the peppers with oil. Roast them under the grill 20 minutes, turning them around every 5 minutes. Cool. Carefully remove the skin, cut them in halves and remove the seeds. In a mortar, or in a blender, make a paste with fish and butter. Open each half of the pepper and fill with the tunafish. Roll like a cigar. Place the rolls in a round platter, forming a circle. In the center place the lettuce hearts and olives. Sprinkle peppers with chopped parsley. Make a dressing with oil, vinegar, salt to taste and pour over vegetables. Serves 6.

SPINACH ROMAN STYLE
(Espinacas a la Romana)

3 lbs. spinach
3 oz. butter
2 tablespoons pine nuts

2 tablespoons raisins, soaked
  in hot water
salt and pepper to taste

Clean and wash the spinach, add a pinch of salt and cook, without water, 10 minutes. Drain. Place in a pan, heat and add the butter, stirring to melt it. Cover and simmer 10 more minutes. Add salt and pepper to taste, the pine nuts and well-drained raisins. Serve on buttered toast. Serves 6.

POTATO PUFFS
(Buñuelos de Patatas)

6 large cooked potatoes
2 eggs
2 tablespoons butter

1/2 teaspoon salt
1/4 teaspoon pepper
abundant oil for frying

Mash the potatoes, season and mix with butter and the 2 beaten eggs. With a teaspoon drop a small quantity of the mixture into the hot oil. Fry them quickly; drain on paper towels and serve. Serves 6.

STRING BEANS ANDALUCIAN STYLE
(Judías Verdes a la Andaluza)

1 lb. string beans
2 tablespoons olive oil
1 medium onion, chopped
  fine
2 cloves garlic, minced

1 tablespoon flour
1 cup tomato sauce
1 tablespoon butter
salt and pepper to taste

Cut string beans French style. Cook until tender but firm (10 minutes). Place the onion and garlic in a pan with the olive oil and sauté until transparent. Add flour and cook until slightly colored. Season with salt and pepper. Add the string beans and mix well.

The sauce: To 1 cup of prepared tomato sauce add 1 teaspoon butter and warm well until butter dissolves. Pour sauce in a sauce boat.

Serve with the string beans with cooked potatoes, bathed with lemon butter, and sprinkled with chopped parsley. Serves 6.

STRING BEANS MADRID STYLE
(Judías Verdes a la Madrileña)

3 lbs. string beans
2 cloves garlic
1 teaspoon paprika

1/4 cup olive oil
salt and pepper to taste

Cut string beans lengthwise, then across, (French style) and boil 10 to 15 minutes, uncovered so they retain their green color. When tender but firm remove from water and put in a colander to drain. Heat the oil in a frying pan and sauté the garlic until dark brown. Remove pan from fire and let it cool a bit and add paprika. Add the string beans, return pan to fire, and sauté in the oil until well coated and hot. Pour into a large platter and serve immediately. Serves 6 to 8.

STRING BEANS WITH CHEESE
(Judías Verdes con Queso)

1 lb. cooked green beans, cut
   French style
1 tablespoon oil
1 tablespoon butter

1/4 cup milk
salt and cayenne to taste
1/2 cup grated cheese (save
   1 tablespoon)

Arrange beans in a well-buttered casserole. Season with salt and cayenne and add cheese and the rest of the butter. Beat milk with the oil and pour it over the beans. Sprinkle with remaining grated cheese. Bake 15 minutes in a 400° oven. Serves 4.

LETTUCE CASSEROLE
(Lechugas Al Horno)

8 lettuce hearts
1 large onion, chopped
6 tablespoons Parmesan
cheese

1 teaspoon meat extract
2 cups hot water
3 tablespoons butter, melted
salt to taste

Wash lettuce carefully under clear running water. Tie up each heart with white string. Place in a casserole and add butter and salt. Let it rest 15 minutes. Dissolve meat extract in hot water and add to casserole. Simmer 20 minutes. Remove excess liquid and sprinkle with cheese. Put in a hot oven (375°) for 5 to 10 minutes or until the cheese melts. Serve from the same casserole with buttered, toasted bread sticks. Serves 6.

STUFFED LETTUCE
(Lechuga Pellena)

1 lettuce head
1 lb. cooked prawns,
chopped

1 cup mayonnaise

Remove the outside coarse leaves of lettuce and discard. Wash remainder well under running water. Carefully remove the heart, without disturbing the rest, and fill the center with the prawns mixed well with the mayonnaise. Place also some of the filling between the leaves of the lettuce. Cool very well in the refrigerator. Cut in wedges. Serves 4.

STRING BEAN SALAD
(Ensalada de Judías Verdes)

1 lb. cut green beans, cooked
1 cup small lima beans,
cooked
1 small green pepper,
chopped
1 small jar pimiento

salt and pepper to taste
1/3 cup celery, chopped
1 medium onion, chopped
1/4 cup grated raw carrots
1/2 cup olive oil
1/4 cup wine vinegar

In a bowl mix oil, vinegar, salt and pepper. Add, in the order given, the well-drained string beans and lima beans and the rest of the ingredients. Refrigerate. When ready to serve, toss the salad from bottom up with 2 large forks, until it gets well mixed with the dressing. Serves 6. Very good with grilled meats.

STUFFED CABBAGE
(Repollo Relleno)

1 nice white cabbage	1 cup white wine, dry
1/4 lb. ground pork	2 onions, finely chopped
1/4 lb. ground veal	2 carrots, sliced
3 oz. bacon	1 cup milk
1 clove garlic	3 tablespoons butter
1 teaspoon chopped parsley	2 cups beef stock
1 egg	

Boil the cabbage in salted water about 20 minutes. Mix pork, veal and chopped bacon with 1 onion, parsley and garlic. Mix with the beaten egg and the milk. Discard the outside coarse leaves of the cabbage. Loosen the remaining leaves and put the stuffing between them. Tie the cabbage with a white string to prevent it from opening. Melt the butter in a pan, add the other onion and carrot and sauté until onion is tender. Add the stock and white wine. Put the cabbage in a deep pan, pour the onion mix over, cover the pot and simmer about 45 minutes. To serve cut cabbage in wedges. Serves 4 to 5.

BROCCOLI MULETEER STYLE
(Brocoli al Ajo Arriero)

1 lb. broccoli	2 tablespoons vinegar
2 cloves garlic	1/4 cup beef broth
1/4 cup olive oil	salt and white pepper to taste
2 sweet red peppers	

Clean and cook broccoli 10 minutes. Drain well. Heat oil in frying pan and sauté garlic until dark. Remove garlic, add red peppers cut in strips, to oil and vinegar and mix well. Mash the garlic in a mortar and add to the sauce. Add the beef broth and reduce for 10 minutes. Add broccoli to sauce and mix well. Arrange broccoli in a platter and pour over the sauce. Serves 4.

SPANISH EGGPLANT
(Berenjenas a la Española)

1 medium eggplant, pared
   and cut in small cubes
3 tablespoons olive oil
1/2 cup chopped onion
1 lb. tomatoes, sliced
1 tablespoon parsley,
   chopped

1 teaspoon sugar
1 teaspoon chili powder
1 teaspoon salt
1/8 teaspoon pepper
1 cup buttered coarse bread
   crumbs
1/2 cup grated cheese

Sauté eggplant lightly in olive oil, using a large frying pan.
Then place in a 2-quart earthenware casserole. Sauté onion in
the same pan, add tomatoes, salt, pepper, parsley, sugar, chili
powder and bring to a boil. Pour this mixture over eggplant,
top with crumbs and cheese. Bake 45 minutes at 350°, or until eggplant is tender. Serves 4.

VEGETABLE CASSEROLE WITH HAM
(Pisto Mixto)

2 eggplants
1 lb. tomatoes
2 red pimientos
salt and pepper to taste
olive oil

2 oz. ham
1 medium onion, chopped
   fine
1/2 cup broth

Peel the eggplants, cut in thin slices and soak in salted water
for 1 hour. Fry the eggplant in abundant olive oil, set aside.
Grill the red pimientos, peel off the scorched skin, cut in
small pieces, set aside.

Take 2 tablespoons olive oil from frying pan. Sauté onion until tender. Add the tomatoes, peeled and sliced. When thick
remove from pan. Place eggplant and pimientos in an oven
dish, cover with the tomato sauce, chopped ham and broth
and bake in a medium oven 30 minutes. Serve with rice.
Serves 4 to 6.

VEGETABLE CASSEROLE FROM LA MANCHA
(Pisto Manchego)

2 onions	6 tablespoons oil
3 green pimientos	1 teaspoon salt
2 lbs. ripe tomatoes	4 small zucchini
1 lb. potatoes	3 eggs
3 small eggplants	1/2 teaspoon pepper

Peel all the vegetables except potatoes. Chop the onions and slice the rest. Fry onion in 4 tablespoons oil, and when golden and soft add the rest of the vegetables and continue frying until soft. Peel the potatoes and cut into small squares, and fry separately in the 2 tablespoons oil you have left. Add to the other vegetables and cook together for 10 minutes. Beat the eggs, mix with the vegetables and scramble. Serve on slices of fried bread. Serves 6.

EGGPLANT
(Berenjena)

Eggplant, a vegetable native to Southern Asia, has been cultivated in Europe since ancient times. Its fleshy fruit contains viamins B and C and minerals such as iron and magnesium. It is believed that the eggplant was introduced into Spain by the Moors, since the many methods of preparation still in use were introduced by them.

EGGPLANT FLOWERS
(Flores de Berenjenas)

2 small white eggplants per
   person
1 onion, chopped fine
1 clove garlic, mashed
1 carrot, chopped fine
1 celery stalk, or sprig of
   parsley

a few leaves of sweet basil
pinch of sugar
salt and red pepper to taste
1 cup white wine
1 cup beef stock
1/4 cup olive oil
oil for frying

Wash eggplants, dry, and leaving them whole by the stalk, cut
them into 4 or 6 sections to make a large flower. Fry in abundant oil, 1 or 2 at a time, over moderate fire. When golden
and tender enough to be pierced easily with a fork, remove
from oil and drain. Sprinkle with salt and serve with the
sauce.

Sauce: In a pan pour 1/4 cup oil and when hot sauté slowly
the onion and carrot until tender. Add the rest of the vegetables and herbs, season to taste, add the stock and the
wine and simmer very slowly until carrot is very soft. Pass the
sauce through a sieve, and serve it in a separate sauce bowl.
Serves 4.

EGGPLANT A LA TURCA
(Berenjenas a la Turca)

1 large eggplant
3 or 4 onions
1 teaspoon salt

6 large tomatoes
1/2 teaspoon peppercorns
1/2 cup olive oil

Peel the eggplant and slice it thinly. Salt the slices, pile them
together, and let them stand under pressure for 1 hour to
drain off the liquid. Peel and slice the tomatoes and the
onions. In the bottom of a shallow baking dish, arrange a layer
of sliced onions, a layer of eggplant over the onions, then a
layer of tomatoes over the eggplant. Sprinkle in a few peppercorns and a little salt. Repeat until you have used all the
vegetables, finishing off with a layer of tomatoes. Decorate
each one with a round of onion. Fill corners and empty spaces

with tomatoes. Pour in the olive oil. Bake in a 250° oven 3 hours. Baste the juice over the top several times. Serve chilled. Serves 6.

EGGPLANT WITH RICE AND TUNA
(Berenjena con Arroz y Atún)

1/4 cup olive oil
1 small onion, chopped
1/2 green pepper, chopped
1 cup rice
1 cup water
2 4-oz. cans tomato sauce
1 teaspoon salt

pepper to taste
1 cup solid-pack tuna
1 eggplant
1 egg, well beaten
1 tablespoon water
cracker crumbs
oil for frying

Sauté onion and green pepper in the olive oil until slightly brown. Add rice and sauté until completely coated by oil. Add water, tomato sauce, salt and pepper. Cover tightly and simmer 20 minutes. Add tuna and heat thoroughly.

Meanwhile prepare the eggplant as follows: Wash and peel the eggplant and cut into 1/8 inch slices. Sprinkle with salt and pepper. Mix the egg with the 1 tablespoon water. Dip eggplant slices in egg mixture, then in cracker crumbs. Fry in oil over medium heat turning to brown both sides. Drain on absorbent paper. Arrange the eggplant on a platter and spoon some of the rice mix on each slice of eggplant. Serves 4.

EGGPLANT WITH ANCHOVY SAUCE
(Berenjenas Con Salsa de Anchoas)

4 eggplants
1/2 lb. ripe tomatoes, chopped fine
4 anchovy fillets, minced
1 clove garlic, minced
1 teaspoon sweet basil

salt and pepper to taste
1/4 cup olive oil
1 onion, finely chopped
2 tablespoons Parmesan cheese

Peel eggplant and cut in 1/4-inch slices. Salt slices, pile them together and let them stand under pressure for 1/2 hour to drain off the bitter liquid. Meantime, over low fire prepare the sauce. In 1/4 cup oil sauté garlic and onion, add the anchovy fillets, tomatoes and seasoning, and simmer until creamy. Rinse the eggplant under running water, just cover them with water and boil slowly about 10 minutes. Drain and add to the sauce and simmer 10 more minutes. Serve sprinkled with Parmesan cheese. Serves 4.

EGGPLANT CASSEROLE
(Berenjena al Horno)

1 medium eggplant	1/2 teaspoon sugar
1 beaten egg	salt to taste
1-1/2 cups canned tomatoes	1 cup dry bread crumbs
2 tablespoons olive oil	1/2 cup buttered bread crumbs
1 onion, chopped	1/2 cup grated cheese

Peel and cut eggplants into chunks. Cool in boiling water for 8 minutes. Drain and add egg, tomatoes, onion sautéed in the oil, and dry crumbs.

Place in buttered baking dish and top with buttered crumbs and cheese. Bake 30 minutes at 350° oven.

ZUCCHINI PUFFS
(Buñuelos de Calabacin)

1-1/2 lbs. zucchinis, peeled	1 tablespoon oil
1 onion, finely chopped	flour as needed
2 eggs, beaten	salt and pepper to taste
1 cup milk	oil for frying

Cut off and discard zucchini ends. Wash zucchinis well and chop very finely. Mix with onion. Place in a bowl and add beaten eggs, milk, oil, pepper and enough flour to make a thick batter. Spoon mix into deep hot oil. Reduce fire so the puffs get done inside. When golden brown remove from fire and drain on paper towels. Serve with the tomato sauce.

Continued on next page

Sauce:

2 lbs. tomatoes	1 celery stalk, chopped
1 onion, chopped	2 tablespoons butter
1 carrot, sliced thin	salt and pepper to taste

Wash the tomatoes and cut into pieces. Put in a pan and add onion, carrot, and celery. Add salt and pepper and simmer 30 minutes. Pass through a sieve (or whirl in a blender). Return to fire, add butter, correct seasoning. Reduce the sauce until creamy. Serves 6.

STUFFED ZUCCHINI
(Calabacines Rellenos)

6 zucchinis	3 hard-boiled eggs
1 onion	salt and paprika to taste
1/2 shallot	1 cup stock
1/4 cup butter	1/2 lb. mushrooms,
3 oz. ham	chopped

Peel the zucchinis. Cut off one end and scoop out the pulp. Chop onion and saute in half of the butter until tender. Add mushrooms, chopped hard-boiled eggs and fill the zucchinis with this mixture. Seal the open end with beaten egg and bread crumbs. Place in a buttered casserole, sprinkle with chopped shallot and add the stock. Dot with butter and bake in a 350° oven 30 to 35 minutes. Serve with rice. Serves 6.

LAMB WITH CABBAGE
(Cordero con Repollo)

1 lb. stew lamb	1 tablespoon flour
1 head cabbage	salt and pepper to taste
1 tablespoon butter	2 cups water

Place half of the lamb in the bottom of a heavy pan. Sprinkle with salt and pepper and pour over the olive oil. Cover with wedges of cabbage. Add another layer of meat, seasoning and cabbage. Add water and simmer for 2-1/2 hours. Serve with whole boiled potatoes and a beet-and-onion salad dressed with oil and vinegar. Serves 4 to 6.

CATALAN CABBAGE
(Repollo a la Catalana)

1 cup cooked meat
2 oz. ham
3 green peppers
12 black olives
1/4 cup mushrooms, sliced
2 cloves garlic
1 bay leaf

pinch of marjoram, mace,
   nutmeg, pepper
1 egg
2 small cabbages
bacon slices
1 cup stock
salt to taste

Chop the meat with the ham and 1 of the peppers from which all seeds have been removed, the black olives and garlic. Season with salt to taste. (If the olives are salted add very little salt to the mixture). Add the mace, nutmeg and herbs. Stir in the egg.

Boil the cabbages for 5 minutes in seasoned water. Drain, and when they are cold open out the leaves, putting the stuffing in between until it is all used up. Fold the leaves back again as nearly as possible to its original shape. Tie them carefully with a string. Place the cabbages in a deep earthenware pot, slice the remaining peppers and place them with the sliced mushrooms around the cabbages. Put thick slices of bacon on top and pour in 1 cup stock. Cover tightly and cook in a 325° oven about 3 hours. Serves 4 to 6.

STEWED POTATOES
(Patatas Guisadas)

1 lb. potatoes
1/2 cup wine
1 clove garlic
1 teaspoon chopped parsley
2 onions, chopped

1 bay leaf
salt and pepper to taste
1/2 teaspoon saffron
2 oz. olive oil

Peel and cut the potatoes in two or three pieces and parboil in water. Drain off the water and add the rest of the ingredients. Put on the lid and cook over low heat until the onions and potatoes are soft. Serves 4.

STEWED PEAS
(Guisantes Guisados)

1-1/2 lbs. shelled peas
1 onion
1 glass sherry
1 tablespoon flour

pinch nutmeg
salt and pepper to taste
2 tablespoons olive oil

Boil peas until tender in water to which has been added the nutmeg, salt and pepper. Fry the chopped onion in the oil until golden and soft. Stir in the flour. Mix well. Add sherry and the strained cooked peas. Put on the lid and simmer gently about 10 more minutes before serving. Serves 4.

SPINACH CASSEROLE WITH CHEESE SAUCE
(Budin de Espinacas Con Salsa de Queso)

3 cups finely chopped raw
   spinach
2-1/2 tablespoons bread
   crumbs
3 egg whites

1 egg yolk
1 teaspoon salt
2/3 cup cheese, ground
1/4 cup milk

To the scalded milk add cheese and salt. When well blended add beaten egg yolk, spinach, and crumbs. Fold in stiffly beaten egg whites and pour this mixture in well-buttered casserole. Set casserole in pan of hot water and bake in preheated oven 375° for 45 minutes.

Sauce

2 tablespoons butter
1-1/2 tablespoons sifted
flour
1-1/3 cups Swiss cheese,
ground

3/4 teaspoon salt
2 egg yolks

Make white sauce by blending butter and flour and adding the hot milk, stirring vigorously. Set aside 1/4 cup of this sauce and cool. Add cheese to sauce in the pan, stirring constantly until well blended. Now to the cool sauce add the egg yolks, beat well and add to the rest of the sauce until thoroughly blended. Simmer a little longer. It should be very smooth in texture. Unmold spinach and pour over the sauce. Serves 4.

In Spain, as in the United States, there are many budget stretcher type dishes very tasty and of beautiful appearance that have been developed by the ingenious Spanish housewives. These dishes are often served at the family table but seldom found in restaurants. Here is one example.

CABBAGE ROLLS
(Rollos de Repollo)

12 large cabbage leaves
1 lb. lean ground beef
3 tablespoons olive oil
1 onion, chopped
1 cup cooked rice
1/2 teaspoon thyme

1/2 teaspoon cumin seeds
1 egg
1 tablespoon wine vinegar
1 cup tomato sauce
1/2 cup water
salt and pepper to taste

Cover cabbage leaves with boiling water and let it stand until limp (about 5 minutes).

Brown onion in 1 tablespoon of oil. Add meat and cook until brown. Remove from fire, add rice, seasoning and egg. Place equal portions of meat mixture in the center of each leaf, folding the sides over meat and fastening with toothpick.

To the drippings in the pan add the other 2 tablespoons oil and sauté the cabbage rolls till golden in color. Combine tomato sauce, vinegar and water and pour over rolls. Simmer covered for about 45 minutes. Serves 6.

STUFFED GREEN PEPPERS
(Pimientos Rellenos)

6 large green peppers
1 onion
3 hard-boiled eggs
2 tablespoons grated bread
  crumbs
2 cups tomato sauce

1 raw egg
2 tablespoons butter
4 oz. ham
sprig of parsley
salt and pepper to taste

Stuffing: Chop the onion and parsley and fry in butter with diced ham. Add chopped hard-boiled eggs and bread crumbs. When all is done remove from fire. Cool a little, add the beaten raw egg and season. Carefully cut the top of the peppers at the stalk end and remove the seeds. Fill them with the stuffing, seal off the open end by brushing with a little bit of beaten egg, sprinkling with bread crumbs. Butter an oven dish, put in the stuffed peppers, pour on tomato sauce and bake it in hot oven (425°F.) for about 1 hour. Serves 6.

Although French fried potatoes and mashed potatoes are the most common way of preparing potatoes, in Spain as well as in any other country, there are other excellent recipes for them and one of these is the typical Spanish dish of potatoes in casserole.

POTATOES IN CASSEROLE

3 lbs. potatoes	2 cloves garlic, raw
salt	10 blanched almonds
1/2 large onion	flour
chopped parsley	1 slice of bread
2 eggs	1 cup olive oil
2 cloves garlic, for frying	

Peel and slice the potatoes 1/4 inch thick. Dry them, sprinkle them with salt and dip in beaten egg and then in flour. Fry them one by one in olive oil and place in a casserole. Fry the finely chopped onion, garlic, almonds and bread. Pound the raw garlic, chopped parsley, fried almonds and the bread in a mortar. Mix with a little water and pour the mixture over the potatoes. Add the fried onion and garlic. Cover with lukewarm water and a little salt and cook slowly for 1 to 1-1/2 hours without stirring. Shake occasionally to prevent sticking. Serves 6.

BAKED CAULIFLOWER
(Pastel de Coliflor)

1 cauliflower	1 tablespoon grated bread
2 eggs, separated	1 tablespoon butter
1/2 teaspoon salt	1 cup white sauce

Boil the cauliflower in seasoned water for about 20 to 30 minutes. Drain and separate into sections and set aside to cool. Chop and mash it very fine and add the 2 egg yolks and bread crumbs. Season and fold in the stiffly beaten egg whites. Pour into a buttered baking dish and top with additional bread crumbs. Bake in hot oven for 15 minutes. Serve with white sauce to be spooned over each individual portion. Serves 4 to 6.

SALADS

MUSTS WITH SALADS

Have all salad ingredients, bowls and plates thoroughly chilled.

Trim and rinse greens under cold running water. Shake off excess moisture.

Wet greens make watery salads and the oil does not cling to them.

Allow ample time for chilling.

Greens should be always broken or torn. Cut only, when needed, head lettuce and cabbage.

Add the tomatoes at the last minute. Tomatoes are very juicy and tend to make the dressing watery.

Fruits that discolor, such as apples, peaches, avocados, pears, etc., should be sprinkled with lemon juice.

To be appealing to the eye, salads should always have a fresh look.

THE SPANISH SALAD DRESSING

The Spanish say that it takes four different people to make a good salad dressing: A wise man for the salt, a miser for the vinegar, a spendthrift for the oil, and a crazy man to mix them. The proportions mostly used are: 3 parts of oil, 1 part of vinegar, adding the salt and the pepper to taste.

POTATO CAKE SALAD
(Pastel de Patatas)

1 lb. mashed potatoes
1 tablespoon grated onion
3 tablespoons olive oil
1 tablespoon wine vinegar

1-1/2 cups cooked peas
1 tablespoon onion, chopped
1 tablespoon wine vinegar
2 tablespoons olive oil
salt and pepper to taste

1 cup mayonnaise
a few drops of garlic juice

pitted black olives, sliced
pimientos, cut into thin strips
1 hard-boiled egg, sliced
2 anchovy fillets, cut into
  strips

Mix potatoes with grated onion, olive oil and vinegar and mix well. Mix peas with chopped onion, vinegar and oil and season to taste with salt and pepper.

Spread half of the potato mixture in a round platter. Pour the peas evenly over it and spread on top the other half of the potatoes. Smooth them over and spread with the mayonnaise that you have mixed with the garlic juice. Decorate the top with any design you want, using the slices of egg, pimientos, anchovies and olives. Cool and cut into wedges to serve.

The design mostly used is a clock design. Twelve slices of eggs are placed around to form the clock's face. Make Roman numerals with the anchovy strips and the hand of the clock with the pimiento strips. Use sprigs of parsley to make little flowers. A conversation piece for buffet suppers.

HOT POTATO SALAD
(Ensalada de Patatas Caliente)

2 lbs. hot cubed, cooked
  potatoes
4 slices fried bacon
1/2 cup chopped onion
1/2 cup chopped green
  pepper

1/2 cup olive oil
1/4 cup wine vinegar
3 hard-boiled eggs
1/4 teaspoon white pepper
1/2 cup diced, cooked
  carrots

In 1 tablespoon olive oil, sauté onion and green pepper until soft. Crumble bacon and add to pan. Add vinegar, the rest of the oil, salt and pepper and cook slightly. Add potato, carrots and hard-boiled eggs. Toss slightly and serve hot. Serves 6.

POTATO SALAD
(Ensalada de Patatas)

10 medium potatoes, boiled in jackets, cubed
1 cup diced celery stalks
1/2 cup pickles, chopped
1/4 cup diced green peppers
1/4 cup cut green onions

4 hard-boiled eggs
1 cup mayonnaise
1/4 teaspoon paprika
2 tablespoons wine vinegar
1/2 teaspoon black pepper
2 teaspoons salt

Sprinkle the potatoes with salt. Add pepper, celery, pickles, green peppers, onions and the chopped egg whites.
Mash egg yolks with the vinegar and add to the mayonnaise. Sprinkle with paprika. Blend well with the salad. Serves 8 to 10.

CELERY SALAD
(Ensalada de Apio)

Wash celery and separate the ribs. Cut them into 2-inch lengths. Using a sharp knife, make four or five parallel cuts, about 1/3 the length of the celery. Put in cold water to curl. Season with oil and lemon juice sprinkled with salt and white pepper.

VALENCIAN SALAD
(Ensalada Valenciana)

1 orange, peeled and sliced very thin
1 lemon, peeled and sliced very thin
1 small onion, peeled and sliced very thin
1 lb. tomatoes, cut in small sections

1 lettuce, cut into small pieces
3 tablespoons olive oil
1 tablespoon vinegar
salt to taste

Pour oil, vinegar and salt in the bottom of a salad bowl. Mix

fruits and vegetables and place on top of the dressing. Place
the salad bowl in the refrigerator. When ready to serve toss
salad from bottom up so everything gets well coated with the
dressing. Serves 6.

COOKED MIXED SALAD
(Ensaladilla)

1 lb. potatoes, boiled in their
jackets
2 carrots, cooked with the
skins
1 cup cooked peas
2 hard-boiled eggs
1 pimiento

1 tablespoon onion, grated
1 tablespoon vinegar
1 teaspoon salt
1 cup mayonnaise
1 cup pitted olives, black or
green

Dice potatoes and carrots and mix with the peas. Chop the
egg whites and mash yolks with the vinegar. Add onion and
salt and mix with the mayonnaise. Add the egg whites and
mayonnaise to salad and mix well. Garnish with the pimiento
cut into strips and the olives. Serves 6.

THE QUEEN'S SALAD
(Ensalada de la Reina)

2 endives
1 large sour apple, peeled
1/2 cup celery stalks, diced
6 fresh mushrooms, diced

2 grapefruit, the sections
1 tablespoon olive oil
1 tablespoon lemon juice
mayonnaise

Separate endive leaves. Soak and wash in ice cold water.
Shake to remove excess moisture. Dice apple and mix with
the celery and the mushrooms. Season with the oil, lemon
juice and salt. Place the endive leaves in a round platter, make
a circle with the grapefruit sections and fill the center with the
apple mix. Serve with mayonnaise. Serves 6.

SPANISH SALAD
(Ensalada Española)

2 heads of lettuce
1 large beet, boiled
1/2 lb. pickled tunafish
3 oz. anchovies
2 hard-boiled eggs
1/2 lb. black olives

3 boiled potatoes
3 large tomatoes
1 large green pepper
1/2 cup olive oil
4 tablespoons wine vinegar

Wash and break lettuce leaves. Cut beet into thin slices, quarter eggs and dice potatoes. Cut tomatoes in wedges. Put all the ingredients in a salad bowl. Make a dressing with the oil and vinegar. Add salt to taste and add to the salad. Serves 6.

CANARY ISLAND SALAD
(Ensalada Canaria)

4 small bananas, cut
  lengthwise
2 oranges, cut in sections
1 sweet red pepper, cut into
  strips
1/4 cup shredded coconut

Dressing:
1/4 cup olive oil
1 teaspoon grated onion
1/2 teaspoon salt
1 teaspoon minced fresh
  mint
dash of white pepper

Arrange fruit and red pepper in a bowl. Marinate 1 hour in the dressing. Serve on lettuce sprinkled with coconut. Serves 4.

TUNA SALAD
(Ensalada de Atún)

1 can (7 ounces) tuna fish, drained
1 tablespoon olive oil
1 medium onion, thinly sliced

2 tablespoons minced parsley
1 teaspoon lemon juice

Rinse tuna under cold water. Drain well. Add olive oil and remaining ingredients. Toss to blend. Serve with bread sticks fried in olive oil. Serves 3.

SHRIMP SALAD
(Ensalada de Gambas)

1 lb. shelled shrimp, cooked
3 hard-boiled eggs, chopped
2 pickles, chopped
1 tablespoon capers
1 medium onion, sliced

2 tablespoons wine vinegar
1/4 cup olive oil
salt and pepper to taste
2 pimientos, cut in strips

Mix all the ingredients except the oil and pimientos. Toss to blend. Chill well. Before serving add olive oil and toss lightly. Serve over lettuce leaves garnished with the pimiento strips. Serves 4.

RICE SALAD
(Ensalada de Arroz)

2 cups cooked rice
2 green peppers, sliced fine
2 pimientos, sliced fine
4 tomatoes, peeled and
  cubed
2 tablespoons chopped onion
2 tablespoons chopped
  parsley

3/4 cup olive oil
1/4 cup wine vinegar
1-1/2 teaspoons salt
1/4 teaspoon pepper
1 clove garlic, minced

Combine the cooked rice, green peppers, pimientos, tomatoes, onion and parsley in a bowl. Mix lightly with 2 forks. Mix together the oil, vinegar, salt and pepper and the garlic. Pour over the rice mixture. Chill and serve very cold. Serves 6.

COUNTRY SALAD
(Ensalada Campera)

1 cup cooked chick peas
1/2 lb. white cheese,
  shredded
2 onions, thinly sliced

2 hard-boiled eggs, sliced
1/2 cup olive oil
1/4 cup lemon juice
salt and white pepper to taste

Combine chick peas, cheese and onions. In the bottom of a bowl place olive oil, lemon juice, salt and pepper. Add chick peas mixture and toss lightly. Serve on lettuce leaves garnished with the eggs. Serves 6.

MIXED SALAD
(Ensalada Mixta)

3 tomatoes, cut in sections
1/2 cup celery stalks, cut
  into short sticks
1 onion, sliced into rings
2 cooked potatoes, diced
3 hard-boiled eggs, sliced

1 head of lettuce
3 tablespoons olive oil
1/2 cup wine vinegar
1/2 cup cold water
salt to taste

Mix potatoes with celery and onions and 3 tablespoons of dressing. Place lettuce on a platter and around it the tomato sections. Place the potato mixture in the center. Place the egg slices over all. Garnish top with the rest of the dressing. Serves 6.

APPLE SALAD
(Ensalada de Manzanas)

2 green apples
2 cooked potatoes
4 pickles, sliced
1/2 lb. canned herrings,
  chopped
1 tablespoon chopped onion
1 tablespoon chopped
  parsley

1 cup small cooked beets
1 head of lettuce
1/2 cup olive oil
1 teaspoon salt
1/4 teaspoon pepper
2 tablespoons wine vinegar
2 hard-boiled egg yolks

Peel and cut apples and potatoes into thin slices. Mix with pickles, herrings, onion and parsley. Season with 1 tablespoon oil. Mash the egg yolks, add salt and pepper, beat well with the rest of the oil until homogeneous, then add the vinegar. Add half of the dressing to the apple mixture and also 2 chopped beets. Arrange lettuce leaves with the rest of the beets; fill leaves with the apple mixture. Pour over the rest of the dressing. Serves 6.

CUCUMBER SALAD
(Ensalada de Pepinos)

Peel the cucumbers, remove the seeds and slice, not too thin. Sprinkle with salt and let stand in the refrigerator, about 2 hours, to drain the juice. Place on a platter, sprinkle with chopped parsley and season with an oil and vinegar dressing to taste.

The following two recipes are particularly good for outdoor cooking. The onions and potatoes can be easily roasted in the ashes of a charcoal broiler. Though they are quite simple to make, they are very tasty to accompany any kind of grilled or roasted meat.

ROASTED ONION SALAD
(Ensalada de Cebollas Asadas)

Take large white onions and roast in hot ashes. Remove the burned outside layers, slice and dress with an oil and vinegar dressing.

ROASTED POTATO SALAD
(Ensalada de Patatas Asadas)

Roast the potatoes, as you do with the onions. When cool peel off the skin and slice thin. Serve with Alioli Sauce. (See recipe)

GAZPACHO SALAD
(Ensalada Gazpacho)

Gazpacho, as we know it, is a cold soup which is often served as a salad. It is rather moist but refreshing and delicious when served on lettuce leaves.

1 small onion, chopped
1 clove garlic, minced
1 tablespoon olive oil
1 tablespoon wine vinegar
1 tablespoon lemon juice

2 chopped tomatoes
1/2 chopped green pepper
salt and pepper to taste
chopped cucumber for
    garnishing

Put the vegetables into an electric blender, or pass through a sieve. Add the rest of the ingredients except the cucumbers. Chill very well. Serve on lettuce leaves garnished with cucumbers and a touch of paprika. Serves 2.

MUSHROOM SALAD
(Ensalada de Champiñones)

1/2 lb. large mushrooms
2 boiled potatoes
2 whole truffles
5 oz. cheese, sliced
2 hard-boiled eggs

1 bunch watercress
1 tablespoon anchovy paste
1 tablespoon mustard
olive oil, vinegar and salt

Clean and slice mushrooms and truffles into small pieces. Place in a bowl and add cubed potatoes, cheese and sliced hard-boiled eggs. Make a dressing with oil, mustard, and anchovy paste dissolved in a little vinegar. Add watercress and let salad rest 1/2 hour before serving. Sprinkle with salt to taste at the last moment. Very good to accompany breaded cutlets or cold meats. Serves 4.

TOMATO ONION SALAD LEVANTE STYLE
(Ensalada de Tomate y Cebolla a la Levantina)

3 large round tomatoes,
   sliced
2 onions, cut into thin slices
2 tablespoons chopped
   parsley

1/4 cup olive oil
1 tablespoon vinegar
salt and pepper to taste

Alternate sliced tomatoes and onions on a platter. Refrigerate
1 hour. Sprinkle with parsley, season with the oil mixed with
the vinegar, and sprinkle with salt and pepper. Serves 3.

MOORISH SALAD
(Ensalada Mora)

1 cup soft bread crumbs,
   sautéed in oil
1 onion, chopped fine
1/2 cup pitless black olives
1 tablespoon chopped
   parsley

1/4 cup oil
3 tablespoons vinegar
salt and pepper to taste

Fry the bread crumbs and when golden in color drain them
on paper towels. When cool mix well with the rest of the
ingredients. Serves 3.

Spanish regionalism is important in the national life, giving it color and variety, and in cookery providing interesting combinations of ingredients and flavors. Despite the unifying and centralizing influences at work in Spain, as elsewhere, the regions and their cuisine still retain their individuality. Basques in the north, Catalans in the northeast, and Andalusians in the south all eat differently. Valencia in the east grows and eats rice—it is the home of the sumptuous *paella* now known throughout the world. And the Canary Islands off the coast of Africa is one of the few places outside the Americas where corn is eaten—they even use grits.

The differences in cooking and eating habits between regions can be traced to many causes—types of food available, tradiion, historical influence, to name just a few. A definite line separates those areas where the Moorish influence was dominant from those where they never penetrated.

Sometimes the pecularities of one region are profound and go to the very heart of cooking procedures. For instance, the Basque's use of lard sets them apart from the rest of Spain that normally uses oil. At other times the difference between one place and another is no more than a shade—a small nuance in flavor. *Gazpacho,* the popular and well-known cold soup, as made in Seville differs from that made in Almeria in one small detail—in Almeria croutons, fried in oil, are added at the moment of serving. This small change varies the flavor to a noticeable degree.

One region that deserves special mention is Madrid, the capital of Spain. Its cooking is not, as might be supposed, a combination and synthesis of that of the rest of the country. It is highly individual, and characterized by simplicity in ingredients, seasoning and preparation.

These variations in regional habits make traveling in Spain an always interesting adventure in eating, and guarantee Spanish cookery against monotony. In the front of this book is a map showing the different regions of Spain. In the body of this book there are many recipes from different regions. They are grouped by subject matter, but may be easily distinguished as regional by their names. Here are some further examples of regional cooking.

DUCK STUFFED WITH BLACK OLIVES
(Pato Relleno con Aceitunas Negras)
Extremadura

1 duck	the duck's liver
4 bread slices	2 eggs
1/2 cup milk	2 bacon strips
1/2 cup black olives, chopped	1 teaspoon flour
pinch of each: rosemary and thyme	1 glass dry white wine
	3 carrots, sliced
1 tablespoon parsley, chopped	salt and pepper to taste
	1/2 cup oil
	1/2 cup whole black olives

Clean the duck, sprinkle with salt in and out and stuff.

The stuffing: Place the bread in a bowl with the milk. Add olives, parsley, rosemary, thyme, and the chopped duck's liver. Work all the ingredients into a paste; add the eggs and season with salt and pepper. Stuff the duck and sew the incision with thread. Place a bacon strip on each side of the bird and fry slowly in the oil until golden brown. Remove duck from pan. Add flour to the pan, and when lightly brown add the wine. Simmer slowly for 2 or 3 minutes. Put the duck back into the pan with the carrots and whole olives. Simmer 2-1/2 hours or until the duck is tender. Serves 4 to 6.

EGGS IN CASSEROLE
(Huevos al Plato)
Navarra

1 onion, chopped
1 tomato, chopped
1 tablespoon oil
4 eggs
salt and pepper to taste

1 tablespoon parsley,
  chopped
4 slices sausage
grated cheese

In the oil sauté onion until transparent. Add the tomato and cook until tender. Grease an earthenware casserole and place the onion mix in the bottom. Break eggs on top, place 1 slice of sausage next to each egg yolk, sprinkle with parsley and cheese. Put in a moderate 350° oven about 10 minutes or until the whites are set. The egg yolks should be soft. Serves 2.

PARTRIDGE ARAGON SYLE
(Perdices a la Aragonesa)

6 young partridges
1 cup oil
1 handful each, fresh
  oregano, thyme
1 bay leaf

1/3 cup olives
6 cloves garlic
1 cup vinegar
1 cup fresh oil
2 cups water

Clean the birds carefully. In a frying pan heat 1 cup oil and fry the herbs. Add the garlic and the olives. Sauté 2 or 3 minutes and set aside. Put the partridges in the pan and sauté until golden all over. Place into a deep pot, add vinegar, the cup of unused oil and the water, the sautéed herbs and olives with the garlic. Season with salt and pepper, cover the pot and cook until tender.

To serve, strain the sauce, heat it again and pour over the birds. Serve immediately with croutons. Serves 6.

RICE VALENCIAN STYLE
(*Arroz a la Valenciana*)
Official Recipe From the Rice Growers of Valencia

1 tender chicken
1/4 cup oil
1 tomato, sliced
1 clove garlic, minced
1/2 cup green peas

1/2 teaspoon paprika
1/4 teaspoon saffron
12 snails
2 cups rice

Cut the chicken into pieces, salt and pepper it and sauté until golden brown in a *paella* pan. Add tomato, peas, garlic, paprika. Add 2 quarts boiling water and the saffron. Add the cleaned snails, (you may omit them) and cook until the chicken is almost tender. Sauté the rice in a little oil and add to the pan. Cook 10 to 12 minutes. You can put into the oven for the last 5 or 10 minutes to dry. Otherwise let the rice rest near the fire until you are ready to serve. Serves 4.

MILK CROQUETTES WITH CINNAMON
(*Leche Frita con Canela*)
Castilla la Vieja

4 cups milk
1 cinnamon stick
grated rind of 1 lemon
1 cup sugar
1/2 cup flour
2 whole eggs

6 yolks
1 beaten egg
bread crumbs
powdered sugar
oil or shortening for frying

Boil the milk with the cinnamon stick and the lemon rind. Separately beat 2 whole eggs and the yolks and the sugar. Fold in the flour and continue beating until well incorporated. Now slowly add the hot milk and cook over low fire until it acquires the consistency of a thick white sauce. Put in a deep platter and let it cool. Once cold and solid, cut it into squares, roll pieces in bread crumbs, then dip in beaten egg and again in bread crumbs. Fry in abundant hot oil, or shortening. Drain on paper napkin. Roll in powdered sugar, mixed with powdered cinnamon. Serve hot or cold. Serves 6 to 8.

FILLET STEAKS MURCIAN STYLE
(Solomillo a la Murciana)

4 round pieces of beef
    tenderloin, 1-1/2 inch
    thick
2 tablespoons olive oil
4 rounds of fried bread

1 large red pimiento
4 artichokes, quartered,
    cooked
salt and pepper to taste

Dip the fillets in olive oil and grill to your taste. Salt and pepper them. Place on the bread rounds and garnish with the red pimiento, which has been sautéed and cut into strips. Toss the artichokes with a dressing made with oil and vinegar and serve with the meal. Serves 4.

TUMBET MALLORCA STYLE
(Tumbet Mallorquin)

1/2 lb. eggplant
1 large tomato
1 clove garlic, minced
1 lb. potatoes

1 small can tomato paste
1 small onion, finely
    chopped

Slice eggplant into rounds. Put the slices in salted water 10 minutes. Peel potatoes and slice. In deep hot oil fry first the potatoes, then the eggplants. Put 2 tablespoons oil (from the pan you fried the potatoes and eggplants in) in an earthenware casserole, and sauté in it the onion and garlic until tender and lightly brown. Add the chopped tomato, season with salt and pepper and cook slowly 10 minutes. Now dissolve the tomato paste in one can of cold water and add to the casserole. Place in a greased casserole dish, alternating layers of eggplant and potatoes with the sauce. Cook slowly, on top of the stove, 30 minutes or in the oven. The dish is done when the sauce thickens. Serves 4.

HOMEMADE SAUSAGES WITH TRUFFLES
(Salchichas Caseras con Trufas)
Leon

1 lb. lean pork, finely ground	1 cup cognac
1/2 lb. mushrooms	3 oz. bread crumbs
1 small can truffles	1/3 cup chopped parsley
2 oz. ham	1 oz. butter
2 oz. bacon	1 teaspoon salt
	1/2 teaspoon pepper

Mince together twice the mushrooms, the bacon and the ham and mix with the pork. Add the cognac and season well. Wash and rinse well a long piece of intestine. Soak in warm water to keep it flexible. Squeeze the water out of the intestine, dry with a towel and fill it with the pork mixture. While you are filling it stick a piece of truffle once in a while. Secure the ends. You can leave it in a long sausage or you can make short ones. Brush with melted lard and dip in bread crumbs that have been mixed with the parsley. Cook slowly on a hot greased grill for about 20 minutes. Serve very hot with boiled hot potatoes and butter. Serves 4.

CHICKEN TENERIFE STYLE
(Pollo a la Tenerife)
Canary Islands

1 large, tender chicken, cut into pieces	2 tomatoes, sliced
1/2 cup olive oil	1 egg white
2 cloves garlic, minced	2 tablespoons flour
2 cups dry white wine	1 tablespoon vinegar
pinch of cinnamon and clove	salt and pepper to taste
1 dozen small onions	

Season the chicken with salt and pepper. Chop the gizzard and liver. Heat oil in a pot, add the chicken and liver and sauté well until golden brown. Add garlic and wine and the cinnamon and clove. Simmer very slowly until the liquid almost evaporates. Serve garnished with the whole baked onions and the fried slices of tomatoes dipped in a batter you have made with the egg white, flour, vinegar and salt. Serves 4.

ASTURIAN FABADA
(Fabada Asturiana)

What we know today as *fabada* was originally a lamb-and-beans stew called *fava* that was introduced into Spain by the Arabs. The imaginative cooks from different regions of Spain have added to it their personal touch. Good *fabadas* can be made anywhere combining meats and beans and with or without the traditional sausages. After you follow the recipes given here you can add or subtract whatever you want, creating your own formula. As long as the ingredients you use are good and compatible you can be sure they will create excellent flavor. A dish of piping hot *fabada* hits the spot in the cold winter weather and gives quick pickup and energy. We suggest that it is better to serve it as a noontime dinner. A salad and a good light dessert are perfect accompaniment for this type of luncheon.

5 cups white navy beans, or
   La Granja beans
10 cups cold water
1/2 lb. ham
1/2 lb. salt pork (spine
   with bones)
1 can red pimientos

1/2 lb. *chorizo* sausage
1/2 lb. Asturian blood
   sausage
1/2 teaspoon pepper
1/2 teaspoon saffron
salt to taste

Soak the beans overnight. Add water. When the water begins to boil add ham, salt pork, blood sausage, *chorizo*, the pepper and saffron. When the beans are tender, correct seasoning. Fifteen minutes before serving, add the finely sliced pimientos. Serves 6.

ORIGINAL FABADA

1 lb. white navy beans
1/2 lb. salt pork (soaked in
   cold water for 2 hours)
1/4 teaspoon thyme
1 onion, cut in half
4 cloves garlic
1/2 lb. boiled ham

1 bay leaf
1/2 teaspoon saffron
1 tablespoon olive oil
1/2 teaspoon pepper
1 canned pimiento
1/2 onion sausage

Soak the beans overnight in cold water. Drain, place the
beans in kettle with salt pork, thyme, onion, garlic, bay, and
saffron. Cover these ingredients with water, bring to a boil,
skim, and reduce the heat. Add oil and simmer for 1 hour. At
this time add sliced ham and onion sausages, piercing them
with a pin to remove air, and continue simmering until beans
are tender. Add more water if needed. The beans should be
tender but not mushy. Add the salt to taste and the pepper.
Before serving garnish it with sliced pimiento. Serves 4.

Note: The salt is always added at the last minute since there is
normally enough salt in the meats used to season the broth.

CHICKEN CHILINDRON
(Pollo al Chilindrón)

In the kingdom of Aragón, specially in its capital, Zaragoza,
the *pollos al chilindrón* are very popular. There is not a
family reunion, or *alifara* (country celebration) in which this
dish is not served as a main course and many times as the
only course. The *matraco* (citizens of Aragón) looks forward
to these *fiestas* where he can eat to his heart's content, his
favorite dish of course always washed down with a lot of good
red wine.

3 fryers
salt and pepper to taste
1 clove garlic
1 onion, finely chopped
6 red pimientos, peeled and
   seeded

8 medium tomatoes, peeled
   and seeded and cut in
   small pieces
1/2 pound lean ham, diced
   thin
1/4 cup olive oil

Cut chicken and season with salt and pepper. Place oil in deep
pan. When hot, add garlic and chicken and sauté till light

yellow in color. Remove garlic. Add ham and onion and keep stirring till all ingredients are well mixed. Add pimientos and tomatoes. Let it simmer for about an hour. If sauce is too liquid remove the lid to allow free evaporation. Serves 6.

A baby lamb (*cordero lechal*) can be used instead of the chickens.

White rice and a tossed salad are perfect accompaniments for this dish which makes a splendid dish for a buffet supper.

POTATO ROLL SACROMONTE
(Rollo de Patatas Sacromonte)

2-1/4 lbs. potatoes	1 small can tuna fish
1/2 cup milk	1 cup mixed pickles
5-1/2 ozs. butter	3 ozs. olives
salt	salt and pepper
2 tablespoons olive oil	1 cup mayonnaise
2-1/4 lbs. tomatoes	1 red pepper
1 onion	

1) Boil the potatoes in salted water. Then mash them with the milk and butter to obtain a very thick paste. On a towel sprinkled with flour, spread the mashed potatoes the same way you would with pie dough, forming a square of about 1 foot on each side and 1-1/2 thick. Let it cool.

2) In a frying pan, heat the olive oil. Fry the chopped onion slowly in it. Before it gets brown, add the tomatoes, cut into pieces, and the salt and pepper. Let cook slowly until almost all the water of the tomatoes is gone, then strain it. The sauce obtained should be very thick. You may cook it a little longer after having strained it, if it looks too liquid. Let it cool.

Chop the tuna fish, mixed pickles and olives very finely. Mix them in the tomato sauce, when this is cold. Spread the mixture evenly over the mashed potatoes. Roll it then, carefully helping yourself with the towel, the same way you would with a jelly roll, being very careful not to break it. When it is rolled, hold the two corners of the towel that are closer to you and let it roll gently on an oblong dish.

224

Cut the two ends of the roll if they are not even. If you have
done it right, it should look like an almost perfect cylinder.
But do not worry if some of the stuffing comes out, as it will
be covered with the mayonnaise.

3) Cover the roll completely with mayonnaise. Adorn with a
few olives that you will have kept aside and slices of red pepper.

Surround with lettuce leaves or parsley. Keep in the
refrigerator for an hour and serve very cold. Serves 6.

CHICKEN ANDALUCIAN STYLE
(Pollo a la Andaluza)

1 frying chicken (3-1/2 lbs.)	1/2 teaspoon saffron dissolved in 1/4 cup water
2 tablespoons olive oil	1 clove garlic
1 medium onion, chopped fine	12 almonds, blanched and peeled
1/2 cup sherry (light)	2 hard-boiled egg yolks
1 large bay leaf and a couple of sprigs of parsley tied together	salt pepper flour

Cut up chicken into serving pieces. Wash well. Dry. Roll in
flour seasoned with salt and pepper.

Place olive oil in a frying pan and heat to medium. Fry
chicken to a golden brown. Place chicken aside after it is
fried.

To same oil add onions and fry to a golden brown. Replace
chicken into pan. Add wine. When liquid starts to boil add
saffron water, bay leaf and parsley bunch and add sufficient
water to cover chicken. Cover pan and reduce heat to a slow
boil and cook chicken until tender.

While chicken is cooking, allow almonds to stand in boiling
water for a few minutes. Remove and peel. Fry garlic in a
very small amount of oil until golden brown. Place oil, garlic
and almonds into a mortar and mash well. Gradually add egg
yolks and continue to mash until pasty and well blended. Thin
225

out with a little of the sauce the chicken is cooking in and set aside until the chicken is done.

Remove cooked chicken and spice bunch; add almond mixture to the sauce and cook covered, very slowly (about 15 min), and stir occasionally so the mixture does not stick or burn.

Just prior to serving, place chicken in sauce and reheat.

It can be served in the center of a rice crown sprinkled with parsley; or a crown made up of pieces of fine macaroni. Serves 6.

CATALAN MEAT BALLS
(Albóndigas a la Catalana)

This dish is a Spanish version of Italian meatballs. It is eaten in Spain as a main dish but you may have it as a hot cocktail snack. This recipe will give you approximately 3 dozen meatballs in their sauce.

3-1/2 oz. pork fat (lard)
1 carrot, chopped
1 onion, regular size, chopped
2 tablespoons flour
2 tablespoons tomato paste
1/3 cup white wine
1 cup water
1 clove
salt and pepper
1 lb. ground veal

1/2 lb. ground pork
3-1/2 oz. bread, soaked in milk
2 eggs
2 cloves garlic, very finely chopped
2 tablespoons chopped parsley
salt and pepper
1 cup olive oil
2 tablespoons flour

Sauce:

Heat the pork fat in a frying pan. Fry the carrot and onion in it for 3 to 4 minutes, then add 2 tablespoons flour. Let it toast until light brown, then add the tomato paste, water, wine, salt, pepper and clove. Bring to a boil, skim the foam formed on the top, lower the heat, cover and let simmer slowly for at least an hour, stirring once in a while to prevent sticking.

Meatballs:

Mash the bread into a purée with a fork; mix thoroughly with the veal, pork, parsley, garlic, eggs, salt and pepper until perfectly mixed.

Put half of the required flour in a glass. Put a teaspoonful of the meat paste in it and, covering the top of the glass with the palm of your hand, shake until it takes the form of a ball. Deposit the meatballs on a plate previously sprinkled with flour. Repeat this until there is no meat paste left, adding the rest of the flour in the glass when needed.

Heat the oil in a frying pan, fry the meat balls in it until they are well fried. Keep them aside in a pan.

3 Finally, strain the sauce over the fried meatballs and heat the sauce and meatballs on a very low fire for another half an hour. Do not leave the fire too high. If the sauce is too thick, you may add a little more boiling water.

TRIPE A LA MADRILENA
(Callos a la Madrileña)

2 lbs. tripe	6 tablespoons oil
3 tablespoons vinegar	2 leeks
1 lemon	1 glass white wine
2 tablespoons marjoram	1-1/2 teaspoon salt
2 carrots	3 oz. bacon
3 tablespoons rock salt	3 oz. chorizo
1 calf's foot	1 bay leaf
1 onion, sliced	3 tablespoons tomato puree
1 onion, chopped	2 oz. chopped parsley
1 glass sherry	2 cups stock
12 peppercorns	
2 cloves garlic	

Scrub the tripe, wash in several waters.
Rub with lemon and rock salt and soak for 1/2 hour in water with 3 tablespoons of vinegar.
Throw away this water. Boil the tripe, just covered with fresh water, for 15 minutes and drain. Split the trotter lengthwise and put in a saucepan with the tripe, sliced onion, garlic,

chopped carrots, parsley, seasoning, herbs, sherry, wine and stock. Bring to a boil and simmer for 3 hours. Cool. Cut tripe in square pieces, bone the trotter and dice. Put the oil in a saucepan, fry sliced bacon, chorizo and chopped onion, fry for a few minutes then add the tripe, trotter, tomatoes, and peppercorns. Brown all the ingredients very slowly; transfer to an earthware dish, pour in the liquid left from tripes and simmer 2 hours. Serves 6.

RICE MARINERA
(Arroz a la Marinera)

2 cups rice
1 lb. mussels
1 lb. hake (or any other
   similar fish)
3 leeks
2 onions

1/2 lb. tomatoes
3 cloves garlic
salt and pepper to taste
a pinch of cinnamon
4 tablespoons olive oil
1 bay leaf

Boil the hake and the mussels with 1 sliced onion, garlic and leeks. Chop the other onion and peeled tomatoes. Heat olive oil in frying pan, add chopped onion, tomato and rice and sauté until onion looks transparent. Add the fish, cut into small portions, mussels and any other seafood you might want. Add 3 cups of the fish stock. Season with salt and pepper, add bay leaf and cinnamon. Simmer for 20 minutes. Serves 6.

NATURAL ANCHOVIES
(Boquerones Naturales)

2 lbs. boquerones (or smelts,
   etc.)
salt and pepper to taste
olive oil
2 cloves garlic, crushed
pinch of saffron

1/4 teaspoon cumin seeds
water
vinegar
1/2 lemon, sliced thin
4 bay leaves
1/8 teaspoon ginger

Wash and clean boquerones, removing head and intestines. Season with salt and pepper and fry in bunches of five in plenty of very hot olive oil. After all are done, place them in a deep container (not metal) and add crushed garlic, saffron,

228

cumin seeds, ginger, and equal quantities of water and vinegar, enough to cover fish, and some more salt. On top of all place the lemon slices and bay leaves. Soak for at least 12 hours before serving. Serves 6.

PRAWNS AND CLAMS SAUTEED CORUNA STYLE
(Langostinos y Almejas Salteados a la Coruñesa)

8 nice prawns	1 clove garlic, minced
4 dozen clams	1-1/2 oz. sherry
3 tablespoons oil	salt and white pepper to taste
2 tablespoons tomato puree	pinch of thyme
or sauce	1 bay leaf
1 small onion, chopped fine	

Clean prawns, wash clams and place together in a pot with enough water just to cover them. Add salt, thyme and bay leaf. Bring to boil and after 5 minutes remove seafood from pot. Remove half of the shell from each one of the clams and peel off the shell from the prawns' tails without removing the head.

Put the oil in a frying pan. Add onion and when it starts getting colored add the garlic, then the seafood. Season to taste. Sauté all this over hot fire, adding the wine at the same time. After a few minutes add tomato and chopped parsley. Simmer slowly to heat the sauce. Invert on a platter and serve immediately. Serves 8.

HAKE BILBAO STYLE
(Merluza a la Bilbaína)

2 lbs. hake, cut in slices	4 tablespoons oil
2 red pimientos, cut in strips	peppercorns
2 cloves garlic	1 bay leaf
1 medium onion, chopped	1 teaspoon chopped parsley

Place oil in a pan and sauté onion and garlic until golden. Add pimientos and bay leaf, and simmer slowly until vegetables are soft. If the mix dries up too fast add a few tablespoons of water. Season with salt and peppercorns. Simmer two more minutes and pass sauce through a fine sieve.

Place well seasoned fish in a well-oiled casserole and bake about 10 minutes. Cover fish with the sauce and let it cook about 15 minutes, basting often with the sauce and juices.

Serve with boiled parsley potatoes. The sauce should be made with fresh pimientos but the canned type can be used. Serves 6.

GYPSY TART
(Pastel Gitano)

Centuries ago, gypsies wandered from Castille into Southern Spain and the Granada mountains. Soon the mountains were echoing the sweet music of the guitars and the wild foot-stamping and handclapping of the gypsy girls. It was the festive swirling of their skirts that inspired this popular confection found in all their festivities. This *pastel gitano* is a delicate shell of flavored meringue filled with fresh fruits and cherries imitating polka dots and ruffled with a meringue border. It makes a beautiful centerpiece.

Meringue Shell:

4 egg whites, at room temperature
1/4 teaspoon cream of tartar
1/4 teaspoon salt

1 tablespoon vanilla, or coffee, cold and very strong
1 cup sugar

Combine egg whites, cream of tartar and salt. Beat egg whites until soft moist peaks form. Gradually add sugar, a little at a time, beating well after each addition. Add flavoring and continue beating until very stiff. Spread half of meringue around sides and rim of plate making a decorative edging using spatula or pastry tube. Bake 1 hour in a moderate oven (275°F.) or until crisp to the touch. Cool well before filling.

Continued on next page

231

Filling:

2 bananas, sliced
1 cup whole seedless grapes
2 tablespoons lemon juice

2 oranges, sliced
20 pitted cherries or
    maraschino cherries

Combine bananas and grapes with lemon juice. Arrange with orange slices and cherries in meringue shell. Garnish with additional cherries, melon balls or any other fruit you care to use.

Sauce:

1/2 cup sugar
1/4 cup flour
2 cups milk
4 egg yolks

2 tablespoons butter
2 tablespoons vanilla
1/4 teaspoon salt

Combine sugar, flour, milk, egg yolks and butter. Cook over hot water 4 minutes stirring constantly. Cool. Stir in vanilla. Serve with the tart. Serves 8.

FLAN

Popular Spanish *flan* is, in its simplest form, nothing more than a custard cream, the main difference being that it is cooked in a pan previously lined with caramelized sugar syrup.

6 egg yolks
2/3 cup sugar
2 cups milk

1 teaspoon vanilla
4 tablespoons sugar
2 tablespoons water

Beat the six egg yolks and the 2/3 cups sugar thoroughly. Add the milk and the vanilla. Mix well and pass the mixture through a fine strainer. There are tin molds with two handles and a cover, especially designed for making *flan*. In one of these, place the 4 tablespoons of sugar and the 2 of water. Boil the syrup until it becomes well browned. Watch it carefully, it turns rapidly from light brown to burned brown; don't let it get too dark.

232

While the syrup is still hot, take hold of the pan by one of the handles and incline it one way and then the other, so that the syrup lines the bottom and edges evenly, forming a thin solid crust as it cools.

In the pan thus prepared, pour the mixture of eggs, milk, and sugar. Cover and cook by the double boiler method—with the mold set in a big pan filled with water—for 3/4 of an hour to an hour.

Finish by baking uncovered for about 20 minutes in the oven (preheated to 350°F.) but without removing it from the pan of water. When its crown is dark golden, test to see if it is done by sticking a needle in it. When the needle comes out completely dry, remove it from the oven and from the pan of water and let it cool before trying to get it out of the mold.

To remove it from the mold, hold it over the fire a few seconds, then turn it over.

The same procedure applies for the smaller individual molds but of course they require less cooking.

This is a basic recipe, adaptable to many variations. You can flavor it with coffee, orange, lemon, or anything you prefer. Serves 6.

STRAWBERRY CUP
(Copa de Fresas)

3/4 cup egg whites	pinch salt
5 oz. sugar	1 cup fresh strawberries
2/3 cup strawberry juice	16 lady fingers
1 teaspoon plain gelatin	whipped cream, optional

Beat whites until stiff, add salt and sugar. Soak gelatin in juice and let stand 3 minutes. Heat, then let cool and add to the egg whites and sugar. Just before it sets add strawberries. Line dessert glasses with lady fingers and fill with mixture. Top with whipped cream if desired. Chill very well. Serves 4.

DRUNKEN PEACHES
(Melocotones Borrachos)

1 small sponge cake
1 can of peaches
3 eggs
2 tablespoons cornflour
3 tablespoons apricot jam

1 glass brandy
1 cup milk
5 oz. sugar
a few drops of vanilla essence
3 tablespoons water

Place sponge cake in a china dish and sprinkle with the brandy. Lay peaches on top of the cake. In a saucepan mix the milk with the peach syrup, add 3 eggs and 3 oz. of sugar. Blend 2 tablespoons cornflour with a little of the syrup, making a smooth paste. Slowly add to saucepan, stirring all the time till very smooth. Cook over slow fire, bringing to boil for only 1 minute. Remove from fire and flavor with vanilla. Stir well and pour on the sponge cake. In a small saucepan put 3 tablespoons water, apricot jam and 2 oz. sugar. Cook on slow fire one minute and pour over the cream. Place in refrigerator. Serve very cold. Serves 6.

PEARS IN WINE SAUCE
(Compotas de Peras Donostiarra)

Here is an old Northern recipe from San Sebastián that is prepared when fresh pears are plentiful in the market. To acquire all its bouquet and flavor this delightful dessert has to be prepared with fresh pears.

1 tablespoon toasted slivered
   almonds (optional)
6 pears, peeled and cored
1 cup red wine

1/4 cup sugar
1 cinnamon stick
1 piece lemon peel
1/2 cup water

Boil together the water and wine, with the cinnamon, lemon peel and sugar. Place pears in this syrup and simmer about 25 minutes. Arrange pear halves in a circle in platter. Stick several slivers of toasted almonds in each one, pour the syrup over them and chill in refrigerator. Serves 6.

ALMOND DELIGHT
(Delicias de Almendra)

4 oz. ground almonds	2 egg whites
3 oz. sugar	1 glass rum
1 cup milk	3/4 cup of flour, or less

Add unbeaten egg whites to almonds, mix well and add the sugar, rum, milk and enough flour to bind the whole mix into a paste. Roll out to 1/3 of an inch thickness. Cut into any desired shape and bake in hot oven (475°) for 10 minutes.

CHESTNUT PUDDING
(Pastel de Castañas)

This dessert is particularly popular around Christmas time in Spain as it is the season for chestnuts.

1 lb. peeled chestnuts	4 beaten egg whites
3 oz. sugar	1 pint milk
1 oz. butter	1 vanilla stick (or vanilla
4 egg yolks	extract)

Take a round plain pudding mold holding about one quart. Butter it. Peel the chestnuts and boil them until the skin can be easily removed. Cook in a little less than one pint of milk over low fire until the milk is absorbed.

Pass through a strainer.

Boil the sugar in the milk that is left over until it is somewhat reduced. Add the vanilla stick (or extract) and cover it.

Mix the chestnuts with the butter, stirring constantly; add the milk and the egg yolks, one by one.

Let it cool.

Fold in carefully the beaten egg whites and pour into the mold. Cook the latter over warm water until it reaches boiling point. Put it in a 350° oven, covered, until it is cooked.

When cold, unmold it and cover it with whipped cream. Serves 6.

ASTURIAN CHESTNUT DESSERT
(Postre Asturiano de Castañas)

1 lb. chestnuts	a few drops vanilla essence
4 tablespoons sugar	1 teaspoon butter
1/8 teaspoon salt	juice of 2 oranges
1 glass milk	1 banana, sliced

Split and boil the chestnuts for 10 minutes. Shell, take off the skin and boil again in milk, with 1 teaspoon sugar, salt and flavoring until soft. Mash and pass through a sieve.

Make syrup with 1/2 cup of water and the rest of the sugar. Mix with chestnut purée. Add the juice and chill. Serve in a pyramid, trimmed with slices of banana. Serves 4 to 6.

CHESTNUT SOUFFLE
(Suflé de Castañas)

One of the most colorful figures on the streets of Madrid during the winter months is *la castañera*, the chestnut vendor. Chestnut eating is like a winter sport. Everybody eats them or buys them already prepared to be eaten at home.

Here is a chestnut recipe for a typical winter Spanish dessert.

16 roasted chestnuts	1/4 teaspoon salt
6 egg whites	4 tablespoons sugar
2 tablespoons butter	4 egg yolks
2 cups milk	1 teaspoon vanilla

To prepare the chestnuts at home slit them half way around with a sharp knife and place in a hot (475°) oven until they open. Remove the skins.

Put the chestnuts, 1 tablespoon sugar and the vanilla into the milk and simmer slowly until the nuts are tender.

Mash the chestnuts very fine, or put the mixture through a puree maker, or a blender, to obtain a very fine puree.

Add the remaining sugar, the butter and the egg yolks, mixing well.

Heat slowly for a short time to blend the flavors.

Cool completely and add the beaten egg whites. Pour into a buttered soufflé dish and bake at 425°F. for 20 minutes. Serve immediately. Serves 6.

ALMOND CUSTARD UGIJAR STYLE
(Cuajado de Almendras de Ugijar)

1 dozen eggs, separated	1 lb. sugar, (reserve
1 lb. ground almonds	4 tablespoons)

Pastry:

1/4 cup white wine	1-1/2 cups flour
1/4 cup oil	pinch of salt

Mix oil with wine and slowly add the flour and salt. Mix well with a wooden spoon until no longer sticks to the bowl. Roll the pastry on a floured table and line a greased pie pan with it.

Beat the yolks with the sugar, add the almonds. Pour into lined pie pan. Bake 40 minutes in a 300° oven. Beat egg whites with a drop of lemon juice and the reserved sugar. Cover custard with the meringue and let it brown in the oven. Serves 10.

ORANGE BALLS
(Bolitas de Naranja)

1 tablespoon butter
3/4 cup sugar
1-1/2 cup flour
1-1/2 teaspoon baking
  powder

1/4 teaspoon salt
1/2 cup milk
whipping cream, optional

Cream together butter and sugar. Sift together dry ingredients.
Add alternately with milk to the first mixture. Drop by
teaspoons into hot Orange Sauce.

Orange Sauce:

1/2 tablespoon butter
1 cup sugar
1 cup orange juice

1/2 tablespoon grated
  orange rind
2 cups boiling water

Place butter, sugar, juice and rind in a saucepan. Add boiling
water and bring all to a boil again for 10 minutes. Pour into
shallow baking pan. Add dumplings as indicated above. Bake
at 375°F. 20 to 25 minutes. Serve warm with the sauce or
cold topped with the whipped cream. Serves 10.

RICE DESSERT
(Postre de Arroz)

2 qts. milk
2 cups rice, soaked in water
  1 hour
1/2 cup sugar

1 cinnamon stick
1/2 cup blanched almonds
1/4 cup seedless raisins

Cook milk down with the sugar until is reduced to 1-1/2
quarts. Add the rice and simmer 1 hour, with the cinnamon
stick. Stir occasionally. Add almonds and raisins and cook 30
more minutes. Serve hot or cold with or without cream. Serves
10.

WATERMELON BOWL
(*Frutero de Sandia*)

Cut a watermelon in half. Scoop out the pulp from both halves with a round spoon. Prepare a cantaloupe in the same manner. Mix melon balls with any desired fruit, such as grapes, sliced peaches, pineapple etc. Pour 1 glass sweet sherry over the fruit. Heap fruit into one half of the watermelon shell and chill several hours. Serves 8.

QUICK DESSERT
(*Postre Rápido*)

4 egg yolks
4 egg whites
1/2 cup sugar

1/2 lb. pound cake, sliced
grated chocolate

Beat the egg yolks with 3 tablespoons of sugar. Beat the egg whites until stiff with the remaining sugar to make a meringue. In a fruit bowl place 1 layer of egg yolks, 1 layer of sliced cake, 1 layer of meringue. Repeat until the bowl is full taking care that you finish up with the meringue top. Sprinkle the top with the grated chocolate. Serves 6.

SIGH OF A NUN
(*Suspiros de Monja*)

1/2 lb. flour
3 oz. sugar
2 tablespoons butter
1 cup milk

6 eggs
pinch of salt
1 lemon rind
oil for frying

Heat the milk with lemon rind, butter, salt and sugar. When it begins to boil, add the flour, stirring all the time until it becomes a thick paste. Remove from fire and let it cool a little. Add the eggs, one by one, stirring well after each addition. In a skillet heat the oil, reduce fire, and put in little pieces of the paste, the size of a walnut; do not touch as they will fry themselves, will open, turn and puff up. Serve hot and well drained, sprinkled with sugar or hot syrup. Serves 6.

WINE TURRON
(Turrón de Vino)

1 glass white wine
1 lb. sugar in cubes
4 egg whites

2 tablespoons almonds
pinch of salt

Make a heavy syrup with the wine and sugar. Beat the egg whites until stiff. Pour the wine syrup into the whites, little by little beating well at the time. Continue beating until firm and well blended. Serve in small wine glasses topped with the slivered almonds. Serves 4.

STRAWBERRY CREAM
(Crema de Freson)

1 tablespoon plain gelatin
2 tablespoons water
1-1/2 cups crushed
  strawberries

1 tablespoon lemon juice
1/2 cup sugar
pinch of salt
1 cup cream, whipped

Soak gelatin in cold water, about 5 minutes. Place over hot water and stir until dissolved. Add strawberries, salt, juice and sugar and stir until well blended. Chill until almost set. Fold whipped cream into the gelatin mixture. Pour into 6 glasses and chill until firm. Top glasses with whipped cream and whole fresh strawberries. Serves 6.

DEVIL'S CUP
(Copa Diabólica)

2 eggs
4-1/2 oz. sugar
6 candied cherries or
  maraschino

6 ladyfingers
3/4 cup cognac
6 pieces of canned fruit

In a bowl place the egg yolks with half of the sugar. Beat, slowly, near the fire until it increases to double in volume. Add 1 tablespoon cognac. In another bowl make a meringue with the egg whites and the rest of the sugar. Prepare 6 champagne glasses. Place 1 lady finger standing up in each one of them. Wet with the rest of the cognac. Top with yolk mixture. Place on top any canned fruit you wish such as peaches, apricots or pineapple. Top it all with the meringue and garnish with a cherry. Serves 6.

AUNT CARMEN'S BANANAS
(Els Plàtans de la Meva Tía Carme)

This original banana dessert is more than a hundred years old. I found it in a hundred-year-old Catalan cook book in Barcelona.

For 1 serving:

2 small bananas
2 tablespoons sugar
2 tablespoons cognac or
  brandy

2 tablespoons almonds,
  chopped

Open a lid in each banana, remove and save it. Remove banana pieces from inside the banana, being very careful not to damage the peel. Slice the banana pieces, sprinkle them with lemon juice, and place in a bowl with the nuts, sugar and brandy. Let stand for 1 hour. Refill the banana peel with the mixture, sprinkle with additional sugar and spoon the remaining juice over all. Bake 10 minutes in a 475° oven. To serve: Replace lids on bananas and take to the table. This is a hot dessert; bananas should be baked just before serving. Choose bananas that they are not too ripe.

BAKED APPLES WITH HONEY
(Manzanas Asadas con Miel)

6 medium baking apples　　1/2 cup figs, chopped
1 cup honey　　　　　　　1/3 cup almonds, chopped
1 teaspoon butter　　　　1/2 cup sherry

Dig out the core about 3/4 of the way through each apple.
Chop figs and almonds <u>finely</u> and fill apple cavities. Blend
sherry, honey and melted butter and pour over apples. Bake in
low oven (325°) about 1 hour, basting often with the honey
mixture until apples are tender. Cool. Serve with whipped
cream if desired. Serves 6.

APPLE PRINCESS
(Manzanas Princesa)

6 apples, peeled, cored and　　1 tablespoon sugar
　sliced　　　　　　　　　　3 eggs
6 oz. sugar　　　　　　　　2 oz. melted butter
1 glass sherry (sweet)　　　1 cup milk
4 oz. flour

Sprinkle the apples with 2 tablespoons sugar, cover with the
sherry and soak for 1 hour. Mix the rest of the sugar with the
flour, melted butter and eggs and blend until very smooth.
Line an oven dish with caramel syrup (see recipe for Flan,
p. 232), pour in this mixture and bake in a 325° oven, about 8
minutes. Boil the apples in their juice 1 minute. Place the apples on top of the flan, forming a decorative pattern. Return
to oven and bake until the apples have acquired a beautiful
golden brown color. Cool and sprinkle with icing sugar.
Serves 6.

APPLES BAKED IN CIDER
(*Manzanas Asadas en Sidra*)

2 lbs. apples, sliced   1 tablespoon butter
1 cup brown sugar   cider

Sprinkle apples with sugar and place in an oven dish. Add
cider so as to reach a third of the height of the apples. Dot
with butter and cover the dish with foil. Bake 30 minutes in a
325° oven. At the end of this time uncover dish and baste the
apples well with their juice. Continue baking so the top gets
lightly browned. Serve hot or cold. Serves 6.

FRIED MILK
(Leche Frita)

1 pt. milk
4 oz. sugar
1/2 teaspoon vanilla
1 egg
3 tablespoons powdered
  sugar

1/2 cup sifted flour
1 tablespoon butter
2 oz. bread crumbs
2 tablespoons butter
1/2 cup oil

Mix the remaining milk with the sugar. Mix flour with a small quantity of cold milk and blend into a paste. Add the paste to the milk little by little. Boil, stirring constantly, until it thickens. Add 1 tablespoon butter; stir, and add vanilla. Put into a shallow plate and let it cool. When set, cut into squares, dip in egg and bread crumbs, melt the other tablespoon butter, add oil and fry. Serves 4.

COLD LOVE
(Amor Frío)

2 cups milk
4 egg yolks
4 oz. sugar
a pinch of cinnamon

1 teaspoon gelatin
1 cup rum
1 cup cream
2 cups assorted fruit

Slice together pineapple, peaches, a bunch of grapes, melon, and orange (or any other mix you might desire) and soak in rum for 2 hours.

Beat the egg yolks and mix with the sugar. Rinse a pan with cold water, add the milk and scald it. Add the milk to the yolks, stirring constantly; then transfer to the milk pan again. Place pan over hot water and cook 2 or 3 minutes, stirring always, until the mixture is thick. Add cinnamon. Dissolve the gelatin in 2 tablespoons water and add to the mix. Cool. Drain the fruits and mix to the cream. Whip the cream and fold into the fruit mixture. Chill well in the refrigerator before serving. Serves 8.

QUINCE DESSERT
(Dulce de Membrillo)

3 lbs. quinces   3 lbs. sugar

Peel the quinces and boil in cold water for 30 minutes.
Remove the core and mash. Sieve. Weigh the puree, and add
the same weight of sugar. Put the mix in a heavy pot and
cook over moderate fire until quince separates from the bottom and side of the pan (from 15 to 30 minutes) Put into individual or loaf molds and leave to set. When solid, turn out
and wrap in waxed paper or foil. It will keep for months.
Serve with cheese or plain as dessert, or as breakfast con-
fiture.

MOORISH PASTRY
(Pasta Mora)

The art of cooking with honey and nuts was introduced into Spain by the Arabs. In the Granada region, where they were established for seven centuries, the traditional recipes are still used, many of them known today in other parts of the world by different names.

2 cups flour	2 eggs, slightly beaten
1 teaspoon salt	2 tablespoons water
1/2 cup kidney fat or shortening	

Add salt to the flour. Mix well. Add lard and work with your fingertips until crumbly. Beat the eggs with the water and add to the flour mix. Work the whole mix with a wooden spoon until the flour is completely dampened. Knead lightly and make a ball. Let it rest 1 hour, wrapped in a cloth. Divide the pastry into 5 or 6 portions and roll, paper thin, on a floured smooth surface. Cut square to fit the bottom of a square pan. Place a sheet of pastry in the pan and cover it with a layer of the filling. Place the second layer of pastry over the filling; repeat until all the pastry squares are used. Cut into squares or shape like diamonds by cutting diagonally. Pour half of the honey syrup over all and bake in a moderate (350°) oven for 40 minutes. Pour over the rest of the syrup. Serves 6.

The Filling:

3/4 cup chopped walnuts	3/4 cup brown sugar
3/4 cup chopped almonds	1 cup melted butter

Mix all the ingredients together and divide into equal portions to use as filling.

Syrup:

1-3/4 cups honey, the solid type	1 cup water
	2 tablespoons lemon juice

Mix and boil for 10 minutes.

VALENCIAN ORANGE CAKE
(Tarta Valenciana de Naranjas)

1/2 cup hot water
2 cups sugar
1/2 cup butter
1 teaspoon baking soda
1 small package of dates
2 beaten eggs
2 cups flour

1/2 cup milk
1 cup chopped almonds, or walnuts
1 orange, the rind and the juice
pinch of salt

Pour hot water and baking soda over the dates, which have been chopped into very small pieces. Allow to sit.

Cream the butter with 1 cup sugar, add the beaten eggs, milk, flour and almonds or walnuts. After it is well blended add the grated rind of the orange and a pinch of salt. Now add the date mix, and bake in a moderate 350° oven for 1 hour. Use a greased Angel food pan.

Meanwhile pour the orange juice onto the remaining cup of sugar and let it stand while the cake is baking. Stir occasionally, then pour over the hot cake in the pan and let it rest until next day.

BALTASARES OF WALNUTS
(Baltasares de Nueces)

Put 4 whole eggs and 2 yolks in a bowl.
Ground walnuts, equal in weight to eggs and yolks.
Sugar, equal in weight to walnuts.
Flour, equal to half the weight of the sugar.
Softened butter, equal in weight to the flour.
Grated rind of 1 lemon.
2 glasses (small) of cognac.

Beat all the ingredients well until mixed and smooth. With the pastry make pancakes as follows: Put 2 frying pans on the stove and heat them well. Butter them. Put in one of them 1 tablespoon of the batter, extend it on the bottom, brown on one side; then turn over with the help of the other pan. Drop on table and roll up while still warm. Once all the cakes are made, place them on a paper napkin and sprinkle with powdered sugar. Serves 6.

SAINT GEORGE CAKE
(Tarta San Jorge)

1/3 cup butter, softened
1 cup sugar (reserve
   2 tablespoons)
2 eggs, well beaten
1/2 cup milk

1/4 teaspoon salt
1-3/4 cup sifted flour
1/2 teaspoon vanilla
2 teaspoons baking powder

Sift the flour before measuring. Beat the butter with the sugar until soft and creamy. Beat the eggs with the reserved sugar and add to the butter mix. Add the dry ingredients, alternating with the milk. Beat thoroughly. Put in a rectangular pan and bake 35 minutes at 375° temperature. Cool. Split in the middle, fill and coat with the following cream:

1/2 lb. butter, softened
1/4 lb. sugar, powdered
2 egg yolks

1/4 cup piñon nuts
1/4 cup toasted almonds

Mix all of the first 3 ingredients together until you have a smooth cream. Do not cook. Decorate with the nuts.

GYPSY'S ARM
(Brazo Gitano)

7 eggs, separated
8 tablespoons sugar

1 grated lemon rind
7 tablespoons sifted flour

Beat the yolks, add the sugar and beat until it changes color. Add the flour, 1 tablespoon at a time, the lemon rind, and finally fold in the stiffly beaten egg whites. Pour on a large, shallow greased baking tin. Bake 10 to 15 minutes in a 350° oven, or until it takes a slight color. Turn out immediately on a cloth which has been dampened with water and wrung out, and roll up quickly. Fill with *crema pastelera* (baker's cream):

1 tablespoon butter
2 tablespoons flour
2 tablespoons sugar

1 teaspoon vanilla
2 egg yolks
1 cup scalded milk

Melt butter, add flour and mix well. Add the sugar and mix well. Little by little add the milk, stirring as you add it. Add vanilla. Remove from fire and add the yolks, one by one, beating well after each addition. Return mix to fire, and cook 1 or 2 minutes, stirring all the time. Cool.

Unroll the cake, fill with the cream. Roll it back to its shape and sprinkle with powdered sugar.

TRUNK CAKE
(Tarta Tronco)

Follow all the indications for "Gypsy's Arm". Use any chocolate frosting recipe. Frost the cake. With the tines of a fork etch the frosting to imitate the bark of a tree.

ALMOND CAKE
(Bizcocho de Almendras)

5 eggs, separated	5 oz. sugar
4 oz. flour	1 teaspoon baking powder

Beat the egg whites until stiff. Beat the yolks with the sugar. Sift the dry ingredients and add to the yolks. Fold the egg whites into the yolk mixture. Pour into a pan that has been buttered and dusted with flour, and bake in a 350° oven for 25 minutes. Cool. Cut into three layers and cover each with a third of the following filling:

4 oz. sugar	3 oz. ground almonds
6 oz. water	1 small glass brandy
3 egg yolks	

Make a syrup with water and sugar. Beat the yolks and gradually pour the syrup on them, beating all the time. When well blended add the almonds and the brandy. Put in a double boiler and cook, stirring constantly, until it thickens. Use while still warm. Sprinkle the top of the cake with sugar and ground almonds.

WALNUT CAKE
(Bizcocho de Nueces)

3 oz. chopped walnuts
5 oz. brown sugar
1-1/4 teaspoons baking
  powder

6 eggs, separated
2 oz. sifted flour
powdered sugar for dusting

Beat the yolks and the sugar for 10 minutes. Add walnuts and mix well. Fold in the stiffly beaten egg whites. Sift flour and baking powder together and fold into the mix. Pour into a well-greased pan and cook in a pre-heated 325° oven for 55 to 60 minutes. Sprinkle with powdered sugar and decorate with walnut halves.

BRANDY PUFFS AMPURDAN STYLE
(Buñuelos de Ampurdan)

Typical dessert of the Province of Gerona.
During the Holy Week families crowd around the fireplace to eat *buñuelos* which they wash down with wine that is passed around in a *porrón*, a special glass container for wine. This container has a long beak from which the wine is poured into the mouth, and the skillful drinkers can do this without touching their lips.

2-1/2 oz. bread yeast
5 tablespoons brandy
6 eggs

1 lb. flour
1 pint warm water
oil for frying

Dissolve yeast in water. Add the well beaten eggs and the brandy. Slowly add the flour until you form a smooth dough. Cover with a cloth and place in a warm place from 10 to 12 hours.

Heat the oil in a pot; form the *buñuelos* as you do doughnuts, and fry in hot deep oil. Drain well and sprinkle with sugar. Makes about 60.

HALF MOON SWEET ROLLS
(Medias Lunas)

1-1/2 cups flour
3/4 cup butter
1/3 cup sugar

3 egg yolks
1/4 teaspoon cinnamon

Mix all the ingredients together into a smooth dough. Cut into half moons, brush each one with beaten egg and cover with sifted sugar. Bake 12 to 15 minutes in a 425° oven. Makes about 12.

MAGDALENAS
(Magdalenas)

1/2 cup sugar
1/2 cup butter

1/2 cup cornmeal
3 eggs

Beat eggs well. Mix butter and sugar and beat well. Bit by bit mix the eggs into the sugar mixture. Add the flour in the same manner. Put in greased muffin tins and bake in a 400° oven 12 to 15 minutes. Makes about 18.

CASADIELLES PASTRIES
(Pasteles de Casadielles)

This typical Carnival sweet is eaten as a dessert for supper before *antroxo,* a festivity during which boys and girls paint their faces black and go out on Tuesday night to *echar el goxa*—challenge boys from neighboring villages.

The Filling:

3 lbs. ground almonds or
  walnuts
1 stick cinnamon
a small piece of butter,
  walnut size

1-1/2 cups sugar
1 lemon rind
3/4 cup sherry
1 tablespoon water

Put sugar, water, cinnamon, lemon rind, butter and sherry in a

251

saucepan over the fire. Mix well and when it starts to boil, add the ground nuts. Stir constantly until you have a very smooth paste. Let it cool.

The Pastry:

3 lbs. flour
1 egg
1 tablespoon salt
1-1/2 lbs. butter

1/4 cup of anisette
1 egg
1 cup cold water

Roll the butter in flour. Flatten it with a rolling pin to a 1/2-inch thickness. Let it rest in a cool place.

Put the remaining flour on a table. Make a hole in the center. Pour there 1 cup cold water, 1 tablespoon salt, 1 egg and the anisette. Mix well and work into a very smooth dough. Let it rest 10 minutes and then roll as thin as possible.

Place floured butter in the center of the dough. Fold the dough over the butter, sprinkle with flour and flatten with rolling pin. Fold the dough again, 1 third over the center and the other third on top, sprinkle with flour and roll again. Repeat the same operation 3 times. Finally, roll out to 1/4 inch thickness. Cut into 3" by 5" rectangles. Place 1 teaspoon filling on each one of them, fold over and press the edges together, moistening with water so the filling does not fall out when frying. Fry in deep hot oil sprinkling them with sugar while still hot. Makes about 50.

MALLORCA BUNS
(Ensaimadas Mallorquinas)

2 lbs. flour
1-1/2 oz. yeast
5 eggs

1/2 lb. lard (or shortening)
1 cup milk

Make a dough with the yeast, milk and flour. Let it rise. When double in volume add the eggs, one at a time. Add additional flour if necessary. Work it thoroughly. Let rest 20 minutes. Take portions of dough. Roll out. Spread a layer of lard (or shortening) on top. Roll. Give the dough the form of spiral bun. Let rise in a warm place. When double in size bake in a 375° oven for 20 minutes. Makes about 12.

CHURROS (Madrid Doughnuts)
(Churros Madrileños)

1 cup flour
1 tablespoon oil
hot, deep oil

1 cup water
1/2 teaspoon salt

Put water, salt and 1 tablespoon oil in a saucepan. Bring it to a boil. Add the flour all at once, stirring with a spatula until the dough is smooth and thick. When dough is cool put it in a *churrera* (a churro-making gadget) or use a cake decorator with a big holed tip; press dough through funnel, and drop the paste into abundant hot oil. Serve hot sprinkled with sugar. Makes about 18.

TYPICAL CARNIVAL BALLS
(Bolillos)

6 eggs
12 oz. sugar
1 tablespoon lard
1 tablespoon cinnamon
3 oz. brandy

enough flour to make a dough that will not stick to the hands
oil for deep frying

Put the eggs in a bowl and beat well. Add sugar, lard, cinnamon and brandy. Mix well. Add the flour, little by little, until a smooth dough is formed. Make dough into small balls and fry a few at a time in the deep hot oil until golden. Sprinkle with sugar. Makes about 36.

MANCHA COOKIES
(Mantecados Manchegos)

1 lb. lard (shortening or
   butter)
2 lbs. sifted flour

grated rind and juice of
   1 small orange
2/3 cup white wine

Put wine, orange juice and rind in a bowl with the lard, or
shortening. Mix well. Add flour until dough is formed. Work
well on the table. Put to cool overnight. Roll out thin and cut
with cookie molds. Cook for 30 minutes in a 350° oven. Immediately after they are done dust both sides with powdered
sugar. Makes about 50.

ALL SAINTS' DAY SWEETS
(Panellets)

2 cups sugar
1/2 lb. sweet potatoes
3 oz. pine nuts
2 eggs, separated
1/4 cup currant syrup or
   juice
2-1/4 tablespoons flour

1 teaspoon vanilla
1 lb. ground almonds
1-1/2 oz. candied cherries
3 oz. hazelnuts
1-1/2 oz. grated chocolate
1/2 lemon, the rind

Peel the sweet potatoes, cut in pieces, cook in water and pass
through a sieve. Mix with the almonds. Add sugar, 2 egg
yolks and grated lemon rind. Flour a smooth surface and work
the dough. Form a roll and cut into three pieces. Add the
chocolate to one of the pieces. Add the currant syrup or juice
to the other, and keep the last piece unflavored. Make into
balls the size of walnuts. The ones with the currant syrup are
trimmed with the red cherries, the chocolate remain natural,
and the unflavored ones are dipped in egg white and covered
with the nuts, that have been chopped. Place all on cookie
trays, sprinkle with powdered sugar and bake 12 minutes in a
400° oven. Makes about 36.

SUGARCOATED ALMONDS
(Almendras Garrapiñadas)

1 lb. almonds   1 tablespoon water
1 lb. sugar

Put sugar, water and almonds in a pan on the stove, stirring constantly with a wooden spoon until the almonds are coated with the sugar, and colored a light brown.

HARD CANDY FOR CHRISTMAS
(Turron de Alicante)

2-3/4 lbs. honey   4 lbs. almonds, peeled, very
1-1/2 lbs. sugar   dry
2 egg whites   1 lemon, the rind

Put honey in a heavy pot and simmer slowly, about 30 minutes, so the water that the honey contains evaporates. Add sugar, stir well with a wooden spatula. Beat the egg whites until stiff and add to pot. Continue stirring constantly 10 minutes. When it starts to caramelize, add the crushed almonds.

Almond Preparation:
Break almonds coarsely, put on a tray and toast in the oven until slightly colored. When still warm add to the honey mix, add the lemon rind and stir well. Pour the mix over a smooth counter, with a marble or tin top, that you have oiled well, giving it a rectangular shape about 1 inch thick, and let it set. After 2-1/2 hours cut the candy into strips, 1-1/4 inches wide. When completely cold wrap each tablet in waxed paper and store, away from draughts, in a tightly closed container. Makes about 100.

SANTA TERESA EGG YOLK CANDY
(Yemas de Santa Teresa)

12 egg yolks
6 oz. sugar
14 tablespoons water

1 cinnamon stick
1 lemon, the rind
powdered sugar

Into an enameled pot put water, cinnamon, and the whole lemon rind. Simmer until you have a heavy syrup that spins a thread from the spoon. Place the yolks into another enameled pot, strain the syrup, and drop by drop add to the yolks, beating well. Return the mixture to fire and cook, stirring all the time, until the mixture separates from the bottom and sides of the pan. Pour the mixture on a platter and let it cool. When cold make a roll about 1-inch diameter, cut into small pieces, slightly round them, and dust with powdered sugar. Place each one into a paper candy cup. Makes about 24.

GLOSSARY

Aceite—Oil, especially olive oil.

Aceitunas—Olives. Introduced by the Greeks, promoted by the Carthaginians and Romans, taken over by the Arabs, they exist in a whole gamut of types. The olive tree is very hardy and does not easily die—some of these trees are thousands of years old.

Ajo—Garlic, a dish made with garlic.

Ajillo, al—Prepared with a garlic sauce; especially applied to seafood.

Almendra—Almond. The use of almonds in cooking was introduced by the Arabs.

Alcachofa—Artichoke.

Alicante, a la—From Alicante on the southeast coast of Spain.

Alicantino, a—In the Alicante style.

Alifarra—Any fiesta or holiday in Aragon, particularly in the region of Saragossa.

Ali Oli—A sauce, probably the oldest one in existence, made with garlic and olive oil.

Albóndiga—A meat ball.

Albondigón—A meat loaf.

Aleta—Flank steak.

Alfajores—A pastry of Moorish ancestry.

Ampurdán, a la—From a region in Catalonia originally settled by the Greeks and still retaining some traces of their influence.

Ampurdesa, a la—Same as a la Ampurdan.

Anchoas—Anchovies. In any recipe calling for fresh anchovies, any small fish, such as smelts, can be substituted. In other cases, use canned anchovies.

Andaluza, a la—From Andalusia, in the south of Spain, including such cities as Seville, Cordova, Cadiz, Malaga, and Jerez.

Antigua, a la—Old-fashioned. As in English, this can mean almost anything.

Arriero—A muledriver, "muleskinner". Normally anything *de arriero* is a strong, hearty dish.

Arroz—Rice.

Aragonesa, a la—From Aragon, the region around Saragossa.

Aprovechamientos—Leftovers.

Asado—Roasted.

Asturiano, a—From Asturias on the north coast of Spain.

Atún—Tunafish.

Azucarillo—Sugar candy.

Bacalao—Codfish.

Bajo—Low or lower.

Baltasar—One of the *Reyes Magos,* the three Wise Men who come on Twelfth Night to bring presents to the children. Baltasar is the one who comes from Africa and is black.

Barquitas—Little boats.

Berenjena—Eggplant.

Besugo—Sea bream. Any blue fish, for instance sea bass, can be used in recipes calling for this fish.

Bilbaino—From Bilbao, a city on the north coast (Basque).

Bizcocho—A cake similar to pound cake. A yellow sponge cake can be used.

Blanco—White. *Vino blanco*—white wine.

Bocadillo—A sandwich.

Boda—A wedding.

Bola—A ball.

Bolita—A small ball.

Bolillo—"Spindle", hence something in the form of bars.

Bonito—Tunafish.

Boquerones—Small, fresh anchovies. Any available small fish such as smelts can be used.

Borracho—"drunk," hence a dessert to which brandy or other spirits has been added.

Brazo—"Arm," hence anything shaped like an arm, for instance a cylindrical cake.

Budin—A casserole dish. Also a blood sausage.

Buey—"Ox." *Carne de buey* is beef.

Buñelo—A "puff."

Cacerola—A casserole, hence a dish prepared in a casserole.

Café—coffee.

Calabacin—Zucchini squash.

Calabaza—Pumpkin; as in the United States, the pumpkin is often associated with All Souls Day.

Calamar—Squid.

Caldereta—A type of stew, normally made with fish or seafood.

Caliente—Hot.

Callos—Tripe.

Canaria, a la—From the Canary Islands off the coast of Africa.

Campesino—Country Style.

Campero—Country Style.

Carnaval—Carnival, anything around Mardi Gras time. Formerly this season was celebrated. Now it is quite unimportant.

Canela—Cinnamon.

Caontin—Name of a Gypsy dance.

Carmen—A very popular female name.

Carne—Meat. If not otherwise specified, normally beef. *Carne picada* is ground beef.

Casaca—A type of jacket.

Casero—Homemade.

Castaña—Chestnut.

Catalán—From Catalonia in the northeast part of Spain. Its principal city is Barcelona.

Cazuela—A casserole or casserole dish; type of stew.

Cebolla—Onion.

Cerdo—Pork.

Champaña—Champagne. Most Spanish champagne is produced in Catalonia.

Champiñones—Mushrooms.

Chilindrón—Dishes from Aragón (chicken, lamb etc.), prepared with ham, pimientos and tomatoes.

Chufa—A nut-like root found around Valencia used to make *Horchata*.

Chuleta—A chop.

Churro—A fried doughnut.

Clara (de huevo)—An egg white.

Cochinillo—A suckling pig.

Cocido—The national dish of Spain. It exists in many variations, normally made with chickpeas or other leguminous vegetables.

Cocina—Kitchen; stove; cuisine. *De cocina* means something cooked; *tapas de cocina* are cooked appetizers.

Coliflor—Cauliflower.

Compota—Stewed fruit.

Compuesto—Mixed, a combination.

Conejo—Rabbit.

Copa—A wine glass; a cup, as in a "fruit cup."

Corazones de Alcachofa—Artichoke hearts.

Cordero—Lamb. *Cordero lechal* is milk-fed lamb; *cordero pascual* is spring lamb.

Coruñesa, a la—From La Coruña, a Galician (Gallego) city in northwest Spain on the coast.

Costa Brava—"Savage Coast." The northeast coast of Spain extending from the French border to about Barcelona.

Crema—A cream soup.

Crema pastelera. Cream filling for pastry.

Croquetas—Croquettes.

Cuajado—Curdled.

Cuello—A neck.

Delicias—Delights; something tasty and delicious.

Diabla—"devilish", hence something zesty.

Diabólico—Same as *diabla*.

Diana—The name of this Roman goddess is frequently found in Spanish gastronomy.

Donostiarra—From San Sebastian, a Basque city near the French border on the northern coast of Spain.

Dorado—Golden; in cooking, "golden brown."

Duro—Hard, *Huevo duro*—a hard-boiled egg. *Pan duro* —stale bread.

Empanada—A type of meat turnover.

Enrollado—Rolled.

Ensaimada—A type of bun, typical of Majorca.

Ensalada—A salad.

Ensaladilla—Potato salad.

Entremeses—Hors d'oeuvres; cold buffet.

Escabeche, en—Pickled.

Española, a la—Spanish from the Spanish point of view. Not necessarily with tomatoes, onions, garlic etc.

Espárragos—Asparagus.

Espinacas—Spinach.

Estofado—A type of stew.

Fabada—A dish, principally from Asturias, made with broad lima beans called *alubias,* salt pork, etc.

Faisan—Pheasant.

Fallas—*The* big fiesta of Valencia. Processions, parades, beauty queens, fireworks, floats, food, drink; everything!

Fiesta—A holiday; celebration; party. A *fiesta* can be nation-wide, local, public, private, programmed or impromptu.

Flamenco—Typical Gypsy—type singing and dancing, the style best known outside Spain.

Flan—A type of custard.

Flores—Flowers or something shaped like flowers.

Fresas—Strawberries.

Fresones—Large strawberries.

Frio—Cold.

Frito—Fried.

Fritura—A fried dish.

Frontera, a la—Frontier style, often something with Moorish influence.

Gallego—From Galicia in the northwest part of Spain.

Gamba—Shrimp.

Garrapiñado—With a hard coat of sugar.

Gazpacho—A soup normally served cold.

Gelatina—Gelatin.

Gitano—Gypsy.

Graneado—With every grain separate.

Granizado—Made with shaved ice; frappe.

Gratin, al—Au gratin.

Gratinado—With grated cheese; au gratin.

Guisantes—Peas.

Guisado—A dish with the ingredients cooked slowly together; a stew.

Guiso—Same as *guisado*.

Harina—Flour.

Higado—Liver.

Hinojo—Fennel.

Horchata—A refreshing drink made from *chufas* or almonds, served cold.

Horno—An oven. *De horno*—baked in the oven.

Huevos—Eggs.

Jamón—Ham.

Jamón Serrano—A type of ham with a long, slow cure, somewhat similar to Smithfield.

Jerez—An Andalusian city, home of sherry wine; sherry.

Jerezana, a la—From Jerez.

Judías—Beans. *Judías* means Jewish; as in many other cases, the language testifies to one of the many influences that formed Spanish cuisine.

Judías Verdes—String beans.

Langosta—Lobster.

Langostinos—Prawns.

Las Palmas—A seaport in the Canary Islands.

Leche—Milk.

Lechal—Suckling; refers to an animal whose only food has been milk.

Lechuga—Lettuce, normally leaf lettuce. Head lettuce is virtually unknown.

Lenguado—Sole or flounder.

Levantina—From *Levante,* the southeast coast of Spain, including Valencia, Alicante, etc.

Limón—Lemon. *Limón verde*—a lime.

Lomo—Loin.

Lomito—Loin fillets; pork loin cut similar to Canadian bacon.

Madrileña, a la—From Madrid, the capital of Spain.

Magdalenas—Type of buns.

Mahonesa—From Mahon on the Island of Minorca in the Baleares. *Salsa Mahonesa* is the original mayonnaise; the name in English has been passed through French.

Malagueña—From Malaga on the south Mediterranean coast of Spain (Andalusia).

Mallorquina, a la—From Mallorca or Majorca, the largest of the Baleares.

Manchega, a la—From La Mancha in the south center of Spain, the home of Don Quixote, and a big grape-and-wine producing region.

Mantecado—A short cookie; the word means "buttery."

Manzana—Apple.

Marinera, a la—"Sailor style," hence seafood or fish prepared the way fishermen do.

Marisco—Seafood, normally as distinguished from fish.

Medias Lunas—"Half moons," hence crescent shaped rolls.

Mejillones—Mussels. If mussels are not available, clams can be substituted.

Melocotón—Peach.

Membrillo—Quince.

Menudillos—Giblets.

262

Mercedes—Mercedes was a beautiful girl who married Alphonso XII, a true love match, thus becoming queen of Spain. Eleven months afterward she died, and is still mourned in Spain in story and song. A thoroughly romantic figure, many things are named for her.

Merluza—Hake. Cod, whitefish, flounder, haddock, halibut, or any other good sized white fish can be substituted in recipes.

Miel—Honey.

Mollejas—Sweetbreads.

Montado—Mounted; a canape.

Moro—Moorish. Moorish customs and cooking left a deep impression on Spain.

Muñecos—Dolls.

Nabo—Turnip.

Naranja—Orange.

Nata—Cream. *Nata montada*—whipped cream.

Natural—Something served without cooking or other preparation; "as is." *"Una Coco Cola natural"* is a Coca Cola not iced or chilled.

Navideña—Pertaining to *Navidad* (Christmas).

Nido—Nest.

Nueces—Walnuts. The word is not normally applied to nuts in general.

Olla—A pot, hence something prepared in a pot, a type of stew.

Ostra—Oyster, normally eaten raw on the half-shell with lemon juice.

Paella—A special way of preparing rice combined with seafood, chicken, fish etc, native to Valencia.

Paellera—A shallow metal pan with sloping sides for cooking *paella*.

Paletilla—Shoulder of an animal.

Pamplónica—From Pamplona, capital city of the old kingdom of Navarre, home of the famous *fiesta* of San Fermin, familiar to Hemingway readers.

Parrilla—A grill. *A la parrilla*—grilled, normally over live coals.

Pasta—Paste.

Pastel—A pastry.

Pastor—A shepherd. Anything "shepherd style" is normally prepared so as to keep well for some time.

Patata—A potato.

Pato—A duck.

Pavo—A turkey.

Pebre—A sauce with green herbs such as parsley, basil etc., to enliven boiled meat. It is very much used with *cocido*.

Pechuga—The breast of a fowl.

Pepino—A cucumber; sarcastically applied to an unripe melon.

Pepitoria—Various dishes prepared with almonds and egg yolks.

Pepirrana—A dish using toasted flour; also a sauce made with chopped vegetables for fish, eggs, meat etc.

Pera—A pear.

Perdices—Partridges.

Pescado—Fish, not applied to seafood in general.

Pétalos—Petals.

Pierna—Leg.

Pichones—Pigeons or squabs.

Pil Pil—Basque method of preparing codfish in its own sauce by shaking the casserole while cooking.

Pimienta—Black pepper.

Pimiento—A sweet pepper; pimiento.

Pincho—A small brochette.

Piña—Pineapple.

Píperada—A Basque dish such as an omelet made with pepper.

Pisto—A vegetable casserole often made with ham, eggplant, squash, codfish, etc.

Plancha, a la—Grilled, broiled.

Plátano—Banana.

Plato—Plate, dish; a mealtime course.

Pobre, a lo—"Poor man's style"; often applied to a steak with fried onions, topped with a fried egg.

Pollo—Chicken.

Ponche—Punch.

Postre—Dessert.

Pote—A pot, jar etc., hence a stew.

Pradera—Very fertile, green meadow.

Primavera—Springtime; *a la primavera*—with fresh spring vegetables.

Princesa—Princess.

Principe—Prince.

Provenzal—From Provence in France. May or may not have originated there!

Queso—Cheese.

Rapido—Quick; fast.
Reina—Queen.
Relleno—Stuffed; a stuffing.
Repollo—Cabbage.
Reyes—Kings; Twelfth Night (January 6.) The night before, the three Wise Men (*Los Tres Reyes Magos*) come and bring gifts to all good children. Christmas in Spain is a religious holiday, but *Reyes* belong to the children.
Riñones—Kidneys.
Riojana, a la—From the Rioja region, on the Ebro River in north central Spain, one of the important wine-producing areas.
Rollo—A roll; something shaped like a roll.
Romana, a la—Dipped in batter and deep fried. Has very little to do with Rome, Italy.
Ron—Rum.
Roncal—A charming, green valley in the Navarrese Pyrenees area.
Ropa vieja—Old clothes; a sort of hash, splendid for leftovers.
Rosa—A rose; also its color.
Rosado—Pink; rose-color. *Vino rosado*—rosé or pink wine.

Sacromonte—A hill near Granada where the gypsies live in caves dug into the hillside. Some of the caves are quite luxurious, since some of the great singing and dancing artists of Spain are gypsies and maintain their residence there.
Sal—Salt.
Salchicha—Sausage.
Salmonete—Red mullet; a small red fish found in several varieties in the Mediterranean. Smelts or any similar small fish can be substituted.
Salsa—Sauce.
Salteado—Sauteed.
Sandía—Watermelon.
Sangría—A refreshing summer drink made from red wine, sugar, lemon peel, ice, etc.
San Sebastian—A seacoast city near the French border in the north of Spain (Basque). See *Donostiarra*.

Sevillana, a la—From Seville in Andalusia in the south of Spain.

Sidra—Hard cider, normally produced in Asturias in the north of Spain as a bubbling, champagne-like beverage.

Silvestre—Wild; from the woods.

Sopa—Soup.

Suflé—Alternate spelling of soufflé.

Tapas—Spanish appetizers, often eaten in a *tasca* or tavern.

Tarta—Cake.

Tenerife, a la—From Tenerife, a port in the Canary Islands.

Ternera—Veal.

Tinta, en su—"In its own ink"; applies to squid cooked in the black liquid inside the animal.

Tinto—Red, as applied to wine. *Vino tinto*—red wine.

Todos los Santos—All Saints' Day (November 1) this is the Spanish Memorial Day.

Tomate—Tomato.

Torero—A bullfighter, a very popular type of hero in Spain.

Tortilla—An omelet, not a Mexican *tortilla,* which is unknown in Spain.

Tortilla española—Spanish omelet; an omelet made with potatoes, has no tomatoes. It is not the same thing as a French *omelette a l'espagnole,* or what some cookbooks call "Spanish omelet. This omelet is good hot or cold, can be used as an appetizer, and since it keeps well, can be taken on a picnic.

Tostado—Toasted. *Pan tostado* or *una tostada*—toast.

Tronco—Tree trunk; something shaped like a trunk or log.

Trucha—Trout.

Trufa—Truffle.

Turca, a la—"Turkish style". Does not necessarily mean from Turkey, but generally is applied to something from the eastern Mediterranean.

Turnedo—A tournedos; a steak made from the beef fillet.

Turrón—A nougat-like candy made with honey and almonds. Traditional during the Christmas holiday season.

Ugijar—A town in Andalusia famous for its Moorish ruins.

Uva—Grape. *Las doce uvas,* or "the twelve grapes", are swallowed one by one at each stroke of midnight on New Year's Eve.

Valenciana—From Valencia on the eastern Mediterranean coast of Spain.

Variados—Assorted.

Vasca, a la—Basque style.

Vascongada, a la—Same as *a la Vasca*.

Verde—Green.

Villalon, a la—From a city in north central Spain, famous for its cheeses.

Vinagre—Vinegar. Spanish vinegar is always wine vinegar.

Vino—Wine; *vino blanco*—white wine; *vino tinto*—red wine.

Virgen del Mar—"The Virgin of the Sea," the sailors' protector; hence sailor or fisherman style.

Yema—Yolk.

Yemas de Santa Teresa—"*Saint Theresa's Egg Yolks,*" a candy.

Yerbas—Herbs; Spanish cooking uses herbs, but with great discretion.

Zarzuela—A fish stew, typical of Catalonia.

MENUS

CHRISTMAS EVE MENU

Cocktails
Breast of Turkey in Aspic
Almond Soup
Baked Bream
Stuffed Capon
Cauliflower Casserole
Ste. Teresa Egg Yolk Candy
Cakes with Cream filling
Marzipan
Mixed Nuts
Dry Fruits
Almond Horchata
Wines
Coffee
Liqueurs

NEW YEAR'S EVE MENU

Cocktails
Cold Rose Consommé
Baked Oysters with Almond Sauce
Lobster Costa Brava
Veal in Sherry
Soufflé de Castañas
The Traditional 12 Grapes
Champagne
Wines, White Priorato, Rioja Red
Coffee
Cognac
Liqueurs

12TH NIGHT MENU
(REYES)

Sherry
Entremeses Variados
Egg Dolls for Children
Potato Soup with Ham and Egg
Chicken in Almond Sauce
Rice with Milk
Roscon de Reyes
Sugar Coated Almonds
Turron
Soft Drinks, Wines

BIRTHDAY MENU

Champagne Cocktail
Entremeses Variados
Lamb Shepherd Style
Eggplant Flowers
Fruits
Almond Birthday Cake
Wines
Coffee
Liqueurs

FALLAS DE VALENCIA MENU

Chilled Sherry
Fisherman Soup
Paella de Pollo a la Valenciana
Valencian Salad
Valencian Orange Cake
Pastry Balls
Sangria
Vinos

ZARAGOZA "ALIFARA"
(Country Festivity)

Regional Sausages
Pickled Fish
Lamb and Chicken Chilindron
Leche Frita
Ensaimadas
Carinena Red and White wines

SAINT'S DAY MENU

People in Spain celebrate their Saint's Day more than their
birthday, though more often than not both coincide. Babies
are named after the saint whose day they are born on.

Chilled Sherry
Entremeses Variados
Hake Soufflé
Beef in Red Wine
Broccoli
Fruits
Gypsy Arm Cake
Wine
Coffee
Liqueur

WEDDING BANQUET MENU

A Spanish wedding is always a gala affair with many
guests—even in the poorest families it is not at all unusual to
have a hundred or more at the wedding banquet people may
save for years to be able to have a good wedding party. In the
country villages it is still not abnormal for the celebration to
last several days. In the cities, of course, such long-drawn-out
bodas are out of the question, but they are always sumptuous.

Assorted Seafood
Truffled Chicken, Veal, Turkey
Pork Loin baked in Milk

Liver Pâté
Pickled fish
Olives
Almonds
Roasted Chicken in Sherry Sauce and Champiñon
Ensaladilla
Ice Cream
Wedding Cake
Champagne
Wines
Punch
Coffee
Liqueurs

EASTER MENU

Garlic Soup Queen Style
Eggs in Jackets
Golden Puffs of Fried Sole
Lettuce Casserole
Gypsy Tart
Torrijas
Wines

EVERYDAY MENUS

Breakfast
Coffee, Milk, Bread and Butter
Confitures (preserves)

Summer Lunch
Gazpacho Blanco with grapes
Chicken Chilindron
Rice
Green Salad
Watermelon Bowl

Summer Dinner
Gazpacho Andaluz
Sole Platter Style
Strawberries with Orange Juice or Flan

Springtime Lunch

Grilled Shrimp
Springtime Lamb Stew
Salad
Fruits

Winter Lunch

Stuffed Mussels
Cocido Madrileño
Pebre Sauce
Quince Preserve
Wine
Coffee

Winter Dinner

Clam Soup
Potato Omelet
Sliced Boiled Ham
Compota de Frutas

SUNDAY MENU

Breakfast

Coffee, milk, bread, butter, preserves
Hot Chocolate and Churros
Sweet Rolls

Lunch

Cold Sherry
Asparagus with Mahonesa
Shrimps in Garlic Sauce
Baked Pork Loin in Almond sauce
Buttered Green Noodles
Fruits
Cold Love
Wines
Coffee

Artichoke Vinagreta
Hake in Green Sauce
String Bean Salad
Melon

THRIFTY MENUS

Winter Lunch
Mussels Marinera Style
Rolled Flank Steak
Baked Apples with Honey

Winter Lunch
Cod Fish Pil Pil Style
Fabada Asturiana
Bananas With Honey and Orange Juice

Winter Dinner
Consommé Madrilene, hot
Pisto Manchego
Chestnut Pudding

Leftover Menus
Soup from Cocido
Ropa Vieja
Milk Croquettes with Cinnamon

Fish Stew
Stuffed Cabbage
Stewed Pears

INDEX

274

275